We Burned
Our Boats

We Burned Our Boats

"And far across the hills they went
In that new life which is the old"

Karen Jones Gowen

WiDo Publishing
Salt Lake City

WiDō Publishing
Salt Lake City, Utah
www.widopublishing.com

This book is a work of creative nonfiction. It is a product of the author's memory, which is flawed. Several names and personal details have been changed; others have not.

Cover Photo of Lake Atitlán by Karen Gowen
Cover Design by Steven Novak
Book Design by Marny K. Parkin

Print ISBN: 978-1-947966-68-0

And on her lover's arm she leaned
And round her waist she felt it fold,
And far across the hills they went
In that new life which is the old.
Across the hills and far away
Beyond their utmost purple rim
And deep into the dying day,
The happy princess followed him.
—Tennyson

Contents

PART ONE

Guatemala

So we thy people and sheep of thy pasture will give thee thanks forever:
we will shew forth thy praise to all generations.
Psalm 79:13

Our beginning, August 1970

1

As Long as We Die Together

I will sing unto the Lord,
because he hath dealt bountifully with me.
Psalm 13:6

I pulled our two carry-ons while Bruce and his crutches maneuvered through swarming passengers, his cowboy hat inching forward to the front of the plane. His ample back supported the roomy backpack, black and manly, stuffed as full as could be. The backpack was a gift from Key Bank during his mortgage business days, bestowed by an appreciative loan officer after Bruce helped one of her clients. Before this trip, it had never been used, my husband being more of a leather briefcase kind of guy. Not fancy but your typically traditional, conservative businessman.

"I can finally use my backpack," he had announced during one of our packing sessions. He dug it out of the bedroom closet and tossed it on the luggage pile.

Now as we exited the jetway, Bruce complained, "That was a miserable flight crammed into a seat designed for somebody half my size." Physical discomfort tended to make him grumpy.

"It's over now, my love. We made it!"

"Yeah, and RJ better be waiting outside like he said." Still grumpy, thinking he might have to stand and wait with his sore knees.

"I hope Travis is with him," I said. Our son, his wife, and their baby girl had arrived in Guatemala the previous month.

The Guatemala City airport was modern and efficient, yet seemed small for a big city hub. Not regional airport size but compared to major U.S. airports, it was a fraction of the size and rather quiet. What a relief, I breathed. Gigantic, hectic airports can be overwhelming when you're tired.

Bruce and I followed the overhead signs and our fellow passengers to luggage pick-up.

When ours came round the carousel, we jointly managed the awkward negotiations for the four heavy suitcases. I looked around for a cart. A short, thin but muscular older man of indeterminate age approached us with a battered metal cart. He wore a yellow vest, signifying official airport helper. What a nice surprise—luggage assistance at your service! He stacked our suitcases and carry-ons into a magnificent tower. When it was balanced to his satisfaction, he beckoned us to follow him through to customs. Uncertain over where to go or what to do next, we gladly let the silent little man in the yellow vest take possession of us as well as our luggage.

With our helper's proficient assistance, passing through baggage check was easy. He then reloaded our things back on the cart and directed us to the visa line to get our passports stamped for ninety days. We had three months before we had to worry about leaving the country and then reentering to get another ninety-day visa.

That done, the little man joined us with the cart and led the way to the glass exit doors. This entire process took less than an hour, providing a positive first impression of Guatemala, or at least its airport. Outside the doors, people waited behind the orange cones. Many held balloon bouquets, stuffed animals, or decorated signs. Taxi drivers clustered forward to call out offers. Flower vendors weaved among the welcome crowd.

Despite the confusion of sound and activity, we somehow heard RJ from the far right side, beyond the throng. He hollered and waved both arms. "Bruce, Karen! Over here!"

Still acting as our personal valet, the man with the cart followed us to our son-in-law, who stood next to a gleaming, full sized van with tinted windows. The van driver and RJ smiled their welcomes. No Travis.

RJ seemed happy and relaxed. He wore run down sneakers, cargo shorts and a partly buttoned long sleeved shirt over his usual black, sleeveless tee. I hugged him in greeting, getting an unpleasant dose of patchouli cologne.

Bruce gave him a one arm embrace from his crutches. "Glad you were here," he said with a big grin, no longer grumpy.

"Bruce, Karen, good to see you," RJ greeted. "This is Pedro. He's gonna be the van driver for our hotel." In Spanish, he gave Pedro our names and identified us as his in-laws.

"*Bienvenidos a Guatemala!*" Pedro, who looked about thirty, shook hands and smiled in open friendliness. Cleanly shaven and well groomed, he wore a blue dress shirt tucked into belted jeans with a neat crease in front. His white athletic shoes, like his white van, looked brand new.

"Pedro doesn't speak any English," RJ said, "but he wants to learn."

The faithful little man in the yellow vest handed our bags to RJ, who loaded them into the back of the van. Inside, Pedro arranged everything to fit. After agonizing months of decisions and downsizing, I watched with relief as these three managed what remained of our worldly possessions. No lost or missing luggage—thank you, God. Thank you, Guatemala airport people.

Bruce handed RJ the crutches. "Here, pack 'em. They were for the airport and flight. I can walk well enough without them." He was twelve weeks out of double knee surgery.

RJ grinned. "Good job, Bruce."

I asked RJ if he could please tip the man, as I only had dollars. He did, hopefully a generous one. I had yet to learn about quetzales and how they compared to dollars. I did know the exchange rate: seven quetzales to one dollar.

Pedro stood ready to assist Bruce and me into the vehicle with its high step up. RJ sat in front, while I took the bench seat behind the driver. Bruce collapsed into the single aisle seat with extra leg room. Finally, he could stretch out his long legs and get comfortable.

"I thought Travis might come," I commented.

"We couldn't both afford to take the day off," RJ replied. "There's too much to do. But things are coming along great with the hotel. Wait 'til you see it."

I took a white sack with two extra large macadamia nut cookies out of my oversized handbag. "Here, RJ, these are for you." He loved a good homemade cookie.

"Thanks! Are these your cookies?"

"No, I bought them for you in Houston. They were made fresh this morning at an airport café. They're almost as good as mine."

He dug right in, sharing with Pedro, and proclaimed that yes, they were nearly as good as mine but not quite. "You guys hungry?"

"Not me," I responded. "We got a meal on the plane, but can we stop for water? Bruce, you want anything?"

"Let's just get on our way."

I opened the window next to my seat. After the deep winter of Utah and the rainy Houston February, I delighted in the warm air. Bright sunshine bathed the world in a happy glow.

RJ and Pedro chatted together in Spanish. The city landscape passed by as Pedro skillfully navigated traffic. The sidewalks were alive with people, the streets crowded with vehicles. We passed an official-looking, oversized black truck carrying uniformed men with Uzis. They stood at attention in the back, facing out. I had also noticed pairs of armed guards in front of banks and large stores. Unsmiling, they stood legs akimbo, their rifles held in readiness.

"Is there a war going on?" I asked RJ.

He laughed. "No, just normal security."

Well, that's good, I thought. Keeping the bad guys away. I took it all in, stimulated by this new environment, so different than settling into comfortable retirement back in Utah. Sure, we could've stayed where everything was familiar, close to kids and grandkids, but at what price? The soccer games, school plays and band concerts, the birthday parties and holiday dinners are nice for a while, but not every day for the next twenty years. I had done that with my own kids. Decades of it. Besides, the cost of living was up so much that most folks, including us, needed a post-retirement job to survive. For the lucky ones, there might be some travel, time for hobbies, maybe buying new furniture, the sort of thing we saw our friends doing.

Forty plus years of marriage Bruce and I had devoted to raising our large family. Work and kids, kids and work. The nest was finally empty, and it was our time to spend together, away from everything old and familiar. We would carve out a new life in a new land.

My female acquaintances couldn't help leaking their opinions of our decision.

"I could never live so far away from my grandchildren."

"Are you sure it's safe?"

"What will you *do*?"

"Aren't you scared?"

In contrast, their husbands listened with interest as Bruce explained his prospective job in Guatemala, assisting our daughter and son-in-law run their boutique hotel. Invariably, the men said, "I wish it were me, but the wife would never agree to leave Utah."

Bruce was energized with renewed purpose, exactly what he needed after the collapse of the mortgage industry. He could work and help Sally and RJ. His favorite thing, besides work, was helping people. He had helped his clients avoid risky deals and find affordable loans, while other brokers pushed garbage loans to make more money. It was an unpleasant, greedy business in those years before the crash.

The exhilarating clamor of Guatemala City kept unfolding before my eyes. People bustled in and out of shops whose signs I tried to read. Sewing. Used furniture. Repair of phones and computers. Tires for sale. Food markets, either open air or small supermarkets. Cheap hotels, like that one where two women in high heels and short, tight dresses posed in front.

The smell of exhaust reached me, and I shut the window. Feeling too warm, I took off my shoes and jacket. I had dressed for comfort not style. Knit pants and athletic shoes with a long-sleeved t-shirt and my comfortably worn denim jacket.

Pedro pulled into a gas station, and RJ ran in for water bottles. Did we need anything else or to stop again for any reason? Bruce shook his head no, let's keep driving. Three hours on the plane, three more to Panajachel, and we were there.

The city went on and on, until at last we were out of it and driving through trees instead of traffic. Pedro, RJ and I opened our windows to let the fresh sweet air waft through the van.

"This sure doesn't feel like February," I said. "When we left Utah, there was snow on the ground."

RJ laughed. "You're in Guatemala now. No snow! Perfect weather!"

Guatemala! Six months ago, this was only a thought, a crazy idea. It was hard to believe we were actually here.

The countryside was hilly and forested except in level areas cleared for crops. The clearings, about the size of a football field, joined seamlessly one to another. Scrawny pigs and cows grazed alongside goats and chickens like one big happy animal farm. We had entered the highland region, where the Maya still populated the land of their ancestors. After all the ancient wars and battles, the Maya stayed on, as though chosen and protected by

God. They still wore the traditional, colorfully patterned clothing. Some men wore regular Western clothes of jeans and t-shirts, while the women and girls universally dressed in the typical Maya skirts and blouses.

Nearly everyone, including children, carried loads of wood on their backs, their bodies bent to support the burden. The older the person, the more bent over they were. Babies and toddlers snuggled inside cloth tapestries tied over the shoulders of girls and women.

Along the narrow highway we drove, uphill and down, tropical vegetation thick on both sides. Vines hung from tall trees. High among the branches or against the trunks, flowering plants had attached themselves to the bark and flourished in perhaps a symbiotic relationship. Unlike the cleared fields where men ruled over nature, in these hills nature reigned. The dense, thick growth waited only for humans to relax their effort, or better yet, to disappear altogether. Then it could freely cover any sign of the former inhabitants—no more farmland, no more villages or roads—human civilization buried under voracious plants with their giant leaves and creeping vines.

The air, much cooler at this elevation, smelled of burning wood, apparently to cook the dinners and heat the abodes in the mostly hidden villages scattered among the hills. Perhaps it was the pleasant firewood smell or the idea of folks returning home for dinner, but the late afternoon atmosphere seemed one of peaceful comfort, as though all was right in the world. Or at least in this part of it.

After an hour and a half, still in the lush green mountains, we came to a resort area cut into a swath of mowed land. Pedro pulled in as RJ said, "We can take a break here. They have nice clean restrooms and a good restaurant. Anyone want dinner?"

Bruce sat up, straightened his glasses and ran a hand through his hair. Once dark brown and curly, it had thinned and turned gray through the years. It still grew out faster than his random haircuts could keep up with, especially at the back and sides, his curls making it unruly. "Yes! I'm starving," he declared.

Earlier, RJ had whipped off his Oxford shirt and put on sunglasses, kicking back in the black tee, his bare arm hanging out the open window. Now, he put his wire-rimmed glasses and shirt back on, buttoning it up.

I pulled on my socks and athletic shoes and grabbed my jacket. "I'm going to walk around a bit to stretch my legs." Outside the resort, six or seven stalls were lined up to the side with displays of bags and blankets, no doubt locally made. I headed in that direction.

"Don't buy anything," RJ warned. "The prices are jacked up for tourists."

I only had dollars with me anyway, but it didn't hurt to go see what they had.

After a quick pass through the stalls followed by a visit to the nice restroom inside, I joined the others in the lobby of the main building. A waiter led us to a booth in the restaurant, where decorative brass heaters took the chill off the air. I put on my denim jacket and slid in next to Bruce, cuddling up for warmth. RJ waved away the menus and asked the waiter a few questions in Spanish before ordering for the table. With the prospect of dinner coming, Bruce perked up. He and RJ chatted about the hotel, their favorite topic.

"We're on track to open Easter weekend, Bruce. What's that, four months away?"

"Less than three." Bruce held up three fingers and folded each one down to emphasize the point. "You've got the rest of February, all of March, then Easter halfway through April."

"There's still a lot to do, but it's gonna happen. People are excited about it." RJ rambled on about this guy who builds jacked up bikes for thrill rides down the steep roads. Some woman who knows about websites. Thom with the dreadlocks who makes jewelry to sell. "You met Thom, Bruce, back in September when you and I drove the truck down. He's in Australia now but he's coming back. Thom always comes back, and he knows everyone. He'll tell his customers to stay at our hotel."

RJ went on about crown molding and cisterns, curtains and grout, plants for the balconies. I had heard it for twelve years, since 2002, when Sally, our second oldest, invited her new boyfriend to meet the family at Christmas. Both just shy of thirty, they met at nursing school in Los Angeles, when RJ Martín, short for Ricardo Juan—"RJ is more Americanized" he said—attended a class she tutored. Back then, he dressed in black. Despite wrapping himself in this dark aura, he was outgoing and friendly, with a quick smile. He willingly shared information: mother Mexican, dad Guatemalan, but he was born and raised in Southern California.

His eyes were small and black, his face pockmarked from teen acne, his features uneven and not particularly handsome. Yet, he carried himself with confidence, with the air of an attractive, successful man. He was close to six feet, Sally told me, but wore lifts in his shoes to appear taller. "RJ says he doesn't want to look like a short Mexican," she confided, "especially around my tall brothers." I always wondered if RJ knew Sally had told me about the lifts. "It's why he doesn't take off his shoes in the house," she explained.

RJ had a twin sister, a brother, and parents he never saw. He no longer spoke to his mother due to business dealings between them gone bad. He expressed admiration for our family, the strong bond between parents and children, the shared religious faith.

"That's how our kids are going to be, Sally. Raised Mormon. I was raised Catholic, and I don't want anything to do with that. Our boys will go off to church in their white shirts and ties, like your little brothers."

Back then and in the years since, RJ raved about Guatemala and a hotel his family owned. Since he had carpentry skills and a vision, he was the one who kept returning to work on it. It was in the Lake Atitlán region, an area that attracted American expats due to its beauty and climate.

"You can live like kings there on social security. I don't know what your retirement fund is or your plans, but whatever it is, it'll go farther in Guatemala. You can have a maid, plenty of fresh fruits and vegetables, a nice house." He looked around at our two-story home with finished basement. "Nothing as grand as this, of course, but the kind that sells for over half a million in LA."

I couldn't imagine going to Guatemala to visit, let alone to live. Wasn't it a crime ridden country with rampant political corruption and drug lords running the place?

"Not in Panajachel, where my hotel is. It's in the southern highlands, away from the city. It's a tourist location. Very safe, like a small town."

Neither Bruce nor I were much interested in Latin America or the new boyfriend's hotel back then. Yet here we now were in the Guatemala highlands, eating dinner with our son-in-law and a pleasant fellow named Pedro. RJ had ordered a platter of grilled chicken, beef and pork accompanied by rice, tortillas, and a few vegetables—carrots, squash and grilled onions—with a spicy vegetable relish on the side.

While Bruce and RJ discussed the hotel, Pedro ate with restraint and impeccable manners. Barely hungry, I sampled the vegetables and a bit of relish folded into a tortilla. Outside the windows moved the softly dying light of day. So much to think about, to remember and ponder when considering the ins and outs of a life journey. Decisions made or not made, roads taken and not taken.

"I'll get you walking all over town, Bruce," RJ said. "Your new knees will get such a workout. You'll lose weight easily. Everybody does if they stay long enough. Wait 'til you see Travis and Jessica. They've dropped a lot already."

"Well, they're in their twenties," I put in. "I still carry the weight from those last two pregnancies, Travis and Forrest."

RJ laughed. "You'll lose it in Guatemala, Karen, don't worry."

I doubted that, since Forrest was twenty-three. If simply living in Guatemala could disappear forty pounds, then truly it was my dream destination.

Dinner over, with our group refreshed and well fed, we climbed back into the van. "We should get there in a couple hours, around eight," RJ predicted. "Pedro has to drive slower at night."

We continued onward, up the winding, narrow road that twisted through the darkening landscape with its misshapen shadows eerily close. At times we veered toward a steep drop off when another vehicle approached, particularly those highly decorated, refurbished school buses from the States. RJ called them chicken buses. "Because people board with all kinds of stuff—live chickens in a box, rabbits, anything."

The drivers barely slowed down. One would appear suddenly, an apparition emerging from the black night, with only our headlights and the lights outlining the bus for visibility. It was terrifying. I had to stop looking. I laid down on the seat, shut my eyes and prayed for safety. I came to terms with the van plunging off the edge into a deep ravine.

At least Bruce and I will die together, I thought. I stretched an arm out to my lifelong companion. He leaned towards me, his warm hand enfolding my cold one. As long as we are together, then who cares what happens.

2
Panajachel

That our sons may be as plants grown up in their youth;
that our daughters may be as cornerstones,
polished after the similitude of a palace.
Psalm 144:12

It was eight-thirty when RJ pointed out a barely visible expanse of dark emptiness to our right. "There's the lake!"

"That huge black space?" I asked.

"Yep. That's Lake Atitlán."

The famous lake, this area's major tourist attraction. The great unknown. Soon, Lake Atitlán, we will meet and I hope that you, like Pedro, welcome us to Guatemala.

A few minutes later, we pulled up in front of Casa Colonial. Although my fatigue factor felt like midnight, the time was just past eight-thirty, exactly as RJ had predicted.

My first impression of the hotel was high and narrow. The glass front was flush to the sidewalk. Rising like a crown of glory were two white-pillared balconies, one above the other on the second and third floors. Colonial-style exterior lamps three across on each floor sparkled an inviting welcome.

Travis, my tall, broad-shouldered son, emerged from the hotel. After hugs and happy greetings, he took charge of our luggage and carried it up to Room 2 on the second floor. I followed while Bruce stayed behind. Stairs were still hard for him and besides, he wanted to linger in the workplace. I, on the other hand, could hardly wait to see our room and stretch out on a bed.

On the landing, visibility suddenly decreased. Not wanting to trip on the steps, I paused to regain my bearings. Wondering what happened to the light, I looked down to see RJ flipping switches by the door. "Outside lights *off*, Travis," he called. "Gotta save on electricity."

Travis and Jessica with one-year-old Emree had arrived a month ago, right after New Year's. He proudly showed me Room 2. "I got it cleaned up and ready for you, Mom."

Besides the adjoining bathroom and shower, the room also had a sink cabinet with countertop. "In case you want to do some food prep, cut up fruit or whatever." A rod beneath a single shelf held some hangers. A wooden chair and double bed with bedside table completed the decor. "It's small but the space is well utilized," Travis pointed out.

The walls were freshly painted in bright orange and deep blue. A matching striped curtain covered a single window next to the bed. The room smelled of new construction and fresh paint.

"See the crown molding, Mom? RJ made it himself. I installed it and painted the walls. You can see where the crown molding is not quite square in places. That's because in old buildings like this with plaster walls, it's impossible to square the corners exactly. Instead, you have to slightly adjust the pieces. Enough to fit but not too much or they break."

"Huh, no kidding? It looks fine to me. Looks great, actually. I can't even tell."

As Travis listed the many other carpenter-like tasks he had completed, my brain translated: *I worked hard, I'm super knowledgeable, can do lots of useful stuff, and it's a good thing I'm here because I've helped a lot.*

"It's nice, Travis. Everything is so clean and colorful. I like it. You guys are living here, right?"

"We were, but a couple days ago we moved to the Bungalows in Jucanya. It's where RJ and Sally used to stay when they came down. Before the hotel was livable."

"I thought they said you guys would be at the hotel rent free."

"RJ doesn't really want anyone but him living here. Well, and sometimes he lets a friend have a room. He set us up at the Bungalows, but I pay the rent. It's super cheap. Good thing, because our budget is tight. I get Guatemala wages, same as Dago. That's who RJ hired a year ago to help with construction. Dago's a pretty cool guy. You'll meet him tomorrow."

"Maybe Dad and I should check out the Bungalows. We don't have a house yet, although Sally said RJ has followed up on a few possibilities. They're supposed to pay our rent and utilities in exchange for Dad's work. At least that's what RJ originally offered. I'm not sure how Dad will feel about asking his son-in-law for rent money though." I chuckled at that scenario.

"Dad won't do it, that's all. I didn't like it either, which is why I pay my own rent for my own family. Besides, I'm pretty sure you wouldn't like the Bungalows, Mom. They're across the river in Jucanya, with some sleazy characters around, and we've seen cockroaches. Jessica won't stay there by herself. She and Emree come with me every morning to the hotel."

Just then, Bruce stepped in.

"We'll be fine for now in this room, won't we, Bruce?"

He hesitated, a big guy in a tiny space. "I don't plan on spending much time here," he said, taking it in, "but it will do for sleeping and getting ready in the morning. At least until we get our own place. RJ said he has a month long house-sitting gig set up for us."

Travis chuckled. "You won't have much time to sit around and get bored, Dad. RJ will keep you busy."

"Good! I'm ready to go to work. I've had enough of this retirement business."

Travis turned to me. "Jessica is putting Emree to bed, laying down with her in Room 6, right down the hall."

"I'll see them in the morning. I'm ready for bed myself. Thanks for doing such a great job with this room, Travis."

We said our goodnights, then Bruce and I dug around in the luggage for pajamas and toothbrushes. We were asleep well before ten.

During the night I heard loud partying from a street festival that continued until the wee hours. People danced and sang their way through my dreams. Horns honked amidst shouting and laughing. The rich aromas of grilled meat, scorched tortillas and fried dough wafted through my semiconsciousness. It combined into a sensory blanket that wrapped me in a safe cocoon. I found the hubbub strangely comforting. Not even the flashing lights disturbed my peace. I'd wake up, hear the ruckus, and think *We made it*. We are in Guatemala! Then curl back up next to my warm solid husband and slip again into contented slumber.

I awoke calm and rested, unlike the previous months of overwhelming stress buried under dozens of endless to do lists. In the distance, a rooster crowed, the call that proclaims Good Morning! All is well! I heard a few cars passing and children at play, such a contrast to the nighttime commotion. From downstairs came the ringing of a hammer and the buzz of an electric drill; RJ and his crew were at work.

Bruce was up and gone, yesterday's clothes slung over the chair. Lounging in bed, I wrote in my journal and updated my blog. I had the whole day if I wanted, plenty of time to reflect on the past and ponder the future.

For the past three months, the streamlining, packing, and clearing out had hung over me like a heavy weight. Bruce, recovering from double knee surgery, had been unable to assist. Even before the surgery, all he could manage was a light sorting of his two oversized filing cabinets. Despite WiFi and the cloud, Bruce had printed out anything of importance, not content to keep it solely on a computer. He wanted a hard copy to touch and move, to add to a file folder where "it won't get lost." Deciding what to keep and what to shred of this collection paralyzed him. In the end, I finished the job while he was laid up after surgery. I kept birth and marriage certificates, recent tax returns and little else. Afterward, of course, in 2013 you couldn't give away file cabinets, let alone sell them, those dinosaurs that ended up in the landfill along with analog TVs.

These struggles lay behind us. The house and cars, even one of our businesses, were sold, along with the possessions of over forty years of family life. Everything except what we brought with us was sold or given away.

Before that, Sally and RJ had been in an escalating dilemma over the hotel. RJ spent months at a time in Guatemala finishing the project while also pursuing his nursing degree. For ten years, they had kept after this dream, while Sally worked and sent him money. He came back for a month or she went down for a week, but generally they lived apart.

Six months ago, she had called me in frustration, unlike her usual calm temperament. "RJ says he needs outside help to finish things up. He's so close, but that means there's more for people to steal. He can't leave without someone he trusts staying on the site. And when he does finish, he will need a reliable person to stay and run the place. The other day he said, 'You've got all these brothers. Aren't there any who can come to Guatemala?'"

As for the Gowen brother situation, Forrest had recently returned from a church mission and enrolled in college. Travis had graduated from a two-year college and transferred to the U of U. "Travis might," I responded. "Although I don't know how Jessica would feel about it. Everyone else has jobs, careers, mortgages, kids in school."

"We've come so far! With the right help, RJ can finish and open for business."

I didn't know what to tell her. I wished I could help. The whole family knew about their hotel struggles, although I'd never heard

Sally quite so upset about it. A couple of her more established brothers had recently loaned them money to help accelerate the project. Sally and RJ had worked so hard and so long to realize this dream; the family wanted to help however we could.

"It's gonna be worth it," RJ always said. "It's right off the main drag, within walking distance to the lake. It will be such a money maker." Then there were the paddleboards he designed and constructed himself, believing in their limitless marketing potential. "Nobody's got paddleboards on Lake Atitlán. It's a wide open market. If you do see them, they're inflatable and don't work as well as my fiberglass ones."

He had named his paddleboard business Sally-oh. He wanted to branch out with surf clothes also labelled with the Sally-oh brand. "I can see these rich kids from the city coming down to Panajachel on weekends and spring breaks. They're wearing Sally-oh surfer clothes and carrying the Sally-oh paddleboards down to the lake."

According to RJ, the only thing standing in the way of success was the lack of trusted workers. If only he had someone capable and honest who wouldn't steal from him, then he could return to the States and work as a nurse. With two solid incomes, they could quickly pay off the mounting construction debt.

"Such a clear and simple solution," Sally continued, "if only we had the right people. RJ wonders why we Gowens don't have anyone down there in Guatemala. We have such a big family. *Where are our people?*"

The morning after this conversation, I woke up with the answer staring me in the face. Bruce and I would be their people!

RJ always said how cheaply Americans could live in Panajachel. "You can get by on a thousand quetzales a month, easy." That was only one hundred fifty dollars, no doubt an exaggerated claim, but five times that was $750. Where could you survive in the States for $800 a month?

When I told Bruce, the notion of a working retirement in Guatemala appealed to him. "It will be like we're serving a mission together!" he exclaimed. Retired senior couples often served missions for our church at their own expense. We had investigated it, but the monthly cost for a foreign senior mission was out of our reach. If you're financially dependent on your small business, giving it up to serve a pricey full-time mission is impossible.

When we mentioned the idea to Sally and RJ, they were enthusiastic. "We'll pay your rent and utilities in exchange," RJ offered. "Both Sally and I will be working, and the hotel making money, too."

They came to Utah to further discuss logistics. Sally and I refined the website while Bruce and RJ talked business. Bruce had spent his career in sales and small business management, along the way getting his MBA.

When I mentioned the degree to Sally, she turned to RJ in excitement. "Honey, Dad has a master's degree in business administration. I didn't know this! How did I not know this?" To kids, their parents are simply Mom and Dad. The comfortable dad who plods along with pleasant calm, Sally saw with new eyes. He was the business whiz who would resolve this great obstacle keeping her and her husband apart.

My daydreaming ended when Bruce opened the door and popped his head in. "Hey, Karen, Travis is frying eggs. You want any?"

"No, I'm fine, not really in the mood for eggs. I want fruit, I think."

"I didn't see any fruit down there. You got signed into the WiFi okay?" He entered the room. I patted the bed for him to sit next to me.

"Yes, no problem. Mostly I've been writing in my journal, reflecting on everything that's happened the past six months."

"You could write a book about everything that's happened. How'd you sleep? I woke up before six like always." He couldn't relax, I could tell, wanting to get back to breakfast and to work. Eggs for breakfast, a son and a son-in-law for companionship, a job to do—no wonder he was cheerful.

I wondered what to do with myself today. First, unpack then get quetzales, then what? It wouldn't include Bruce, that was obvious. He couldn't wait to get back downstairs.

"RJ said it's not usually noisy like that at night. Yesterday was some holiday or another." Bruce stood and moved toward the open door. "I better go help Travis with breakfast. Take your time getting ready. There's no rush for anything. Journal and blog to your heart's content. The shower is decent, probably not hot enough for you though."

"I'll write for longer, unpack, then go out and change our dollars into quetzales."

"Sounds good, my love. See you downstairs."

When I finally went down close to noon, I passed Bruce and RJ in the lobby, deep in conversation. Bruce sat on a wooden chair while RJ stood and paced as usual. Travis and Dago were engaged in a noisy construction project in the adjoining side room. RJ was right, Travis had lost weight, and he was handsomer than ever. Not as thin as when he came home from his mission to Africa, but that was too thin for his strapping build. At his mission homecoming, a circle of girls had swarmed around him. A year later, he met Jessica in their college orchestra.

Jessica and Emree weren't anywhere around. I decided to head out and look for a money exchange place, except I couldn't find the right exit among the three front glass doors. I kept fiddling at the door in the middle, the long curtain swishing in my way. I turned the handle this way and that, pushed, pulled, slid to no avail.

RJ noticed my struggle and came to help. "It's this one, Karen," he said, opening the door on the far left of the glass wall. "The others are locked. I'll make sure you and Bruce both have keys." He stepped outside with me and pointed to the right. "This way leads to Santander, the main street. Just go a half block then turn left and you're there."

"Wow, that's close. No wonder the street fiesta sounded like it was right outside our window."

"Yeah, like I say, we're basically on the main drag. Really the best location."

Turning left at Santander, I noticed a little money exchange shop. The day's rate posted on the wall was 7.60. In exchange for my $250, the man handed me almost 2000 in quetzales. I walked out with this thick wad of cash stuffed in my wallet. I felt rich and rather like I had robbed a bank. Suddenly anxious and uncertain, I returned the way I came. I saw Jessica in the lobby, and we hugged like long-lost sisters. She had put Emree down for a nap and was free to walk around if I wanted a tour.

"Of course!" I didn't see Bruce or RJ around, but Travis showed up with Dago.

"This is my mom," he said to Dago, who responded with a friendly smile and a greeting: "*Buenos días, Doña* Karen."

Dago was only about ten years older than Travis but looked more like a settled family man, with a little paunch and sloping shoulders. He was married to Rosa, and they had two young girls in school. Working at Casa Colonial was his first real job of importance, beyond a part-time paid ministry at his church and other odd jobs he picked up now and then. He had walked into the hotel upon hearing the owner was looking for an assistant. RJ asked him if he had any construction experience. Dago hesitated then said, no but I can learn. RJ hired him on the spot for his honesty.

On the van ride down, RJ had told us that he instructed Dago what to call us: Doña Karen and Mister Bruce. "So don't correct him, Karen," he warned me. "It's what he needs to call you to show proper respect."

Dago called Jessica "Yessica." Travis, however, was "Mister Travis." I'm not sure why Jessica was not a Doña like me, perhaps due to being so young.

She and I headed to Santander, Jessica leading the way. When Travis and Jessica were dating, she was such a slight, quiet girl next to his more dominant, confident personality. After Emree was born, the lingering pregnancy weight made her even more attractive, giving her a statuesque, regal look. Her Guatemala weight loss didn't seem as evident to me as Travis's, other than she appeared more queenlike than ever.

What a beauty she is, I thought, and she has no idea. Jessica had a wide, engaging smile and intelligent, deep brown eyes. Her chestnut hair was long and thick, naturally curly, although usually straightened or pulled into a ponytail.

The two of us passed my little money exchange shop and continued up Santander Street. Vendors in stalls next to shops and cafés were packed close together in a vibrant blend. Vehicles crowded the street, tourists from around the world hurried past us or milled about in clusters. Besides American English, I heard snippets of German and French, British and Australian accents, and an occasional Asian dialect.

"Where's the fruit stalls?" I asked Jessica. "Sally's always talking about the tropical fruit, cut up fresh for only seventy-five cents."

"They are mostly down by the lake. We can go that way if you want."

"Let's stick to the main road for now. I don't want to get lost."

"Oh, you won't. It's easy to find your way around."

"There's so much to see! People and traffic everywhere, and so many stores crammed together."

"Most of the smaller stalls right next to the street are temporary," Jessica explained, "only for daylight hours. When the sun goes down, they pack everything up and leave the space for food vendors to set up for the evenings."

"Sharing rent. That's clever. Look at those cute little red cars," I exclaimed, "weaving in and out, like enclosed scooters. Are they taxis?"

"Kind of. Everyone calls them tuk tuks. They cost about seven quetzales to take you anywhere in town. It's a bumpy ride and kind of scary the way drivers go so fast. Sometimes you feel like you're going to slide right out the open door onto the street."

"They do look fun though." I could hardly wait to go for a tuk tuk ride.

"Karen, see that street right up ahead? It takes you to the Dispensa and the mercado." Jessica pointed to a fast food place at a fork in the road. "And there's Pollo Campero, RJ's favorite restaurant."

It looked like every typical fast food eatery in America—as artificial as plastic and as garishly colorful.

"They have fried chicken, burgers, fries, ice cream, salads and pizza. It's super popular. On Wednesdays you can get two pizzas for the price of one."

"Bruce and I better avoid Pollo Campero. We need to get healthy."

"Travis and I don't eat as much fast food as we did in Salt Lake, and no sweets like what we used to have."

"What do you do for meals?"

"A lot of eggs, tortillas, pancakes, and pasta. There's a decent kitchen downstairs and one in Room 6. RJ, Travis, and I take turns cooking when we're at the hotel. Since we moved to the

Bungalows, Travis and I eat breakfast at home. We like Pollo Campero, but we have so little money. Living here is not as cheap as RJ said, especially now that we have rent to pay."

"What about fruits and vegetables? Where do we buy those?"

"I'll show you the mercado, where you can find produce and pretty much anything else."

"I'm going to get lost once I venture out beyond this main street," I said, laughing.

"You will learn your way around in no time. It's not as complicated as it seems."

Jessica was right, of course. For all its fame and foreignness, Panajachel was basically a small town like any other, except with perfect weather. It was cooler at night for sleeping, warming up to the mid-seventies when the sun was high in the deep blue sky.

After a few days I navigated easily from the hotel to the Dispensa, the mercado and points in between, including down to the lake.

Lago de Atitlán is the center jewel of the southern highlands. Once you see that lake, you can never forget it. For me, it was love at first sight. Besides the picturesque beauty, something about it goes right to your soul. No photo can capture the brilliance of its spirit. No wonder people come from far away to visit Lake Atitlán and the villages that encircle it.

3
House-Sitting Gig

Therefore my heart is glad, and my glory rejoiceth:
my flesh also shall rest in hope.
Psalm 16:9

Bruce and I continued to follow the pattern of that first morning. He got up early to shower and dress in his usual cotton casual pants with plaid, short sleeve shirt tucked in. Then downstairs to make breakfast and sit at the small round table in the kitchen to study scriptures and check our bank and business accounts. I woke up early too, but stayed in bed until midmorning to write, answer work emails, and do social media marketing.

Pana was a walkable town with plenty to see and do. I walked everywhere, either alone or with Jessica, and wrote for hours. I kept up with my publishing business, worked on my novel, and connected with family back home via Skype and Google chat. Bruce with his new knees was fully engaged with his new job.

We occasionally went out for dinner with Travis, Jessica and Emree before they left for their trek home across the river. RJ rarely came along since he went to the gym in the evenings. Our favorite family dinner was street food on Santander. More often though, someone cooked a simple meal to share at the hotel. Once RJ bought fresh fish from an expat named Turk and I fried it up. Breakfast was eggs downstairs in the kitchen for whoever wanted them. Lunch was every man for himself.

Dago and Travis worked together under RJ's direction. Time pressures of opening weekend had forced RJ to delegate many of his pet projects. As much as he talked about running the hotel, it was in the actual design, planning, and perfecting of its physical appearance where lay his true talents and passions. But one can't keep building a thing for years without at last finishing the job, or otherwise admitting you have no intention of ever getting to the end of it.

RJ liked to bounce operational ideas off Bruce, who then created spreadsheets to match. Bruce also enjoyed meeting people, and RJ knew a lot of people. The two of them often left to go meet someone or check out a good restaurant or a tourist attraction to recommend to prospective guests. These trips around town supported RJ's personal commitment to "get Bruce in shape." On my own afternoon walks, I occasionally came across them, to my delight.

One day on a side street I saw Bruce up ahead on a bench. RJ paced in his typical restless manner, waving his arms in expressive conversation. The guy was never still for a minute. No wonder he could eat so much ice cream, cookies, and Pollo Campero and never get fat. He probably burned calories like an Olympic athlete in his regular routine, besides working out at the gym for hours.

Afraid they'd take off without seeing me, I hurried forward, shouting, "Bruce!"

Bruce watched as I narrowed the distance between us. He seemed tired.

"Hey, Karen," RJ greeted as I approached. "We're on our way to get tamales. It's a Wednesday, and they're still open. Have you had those tamales yet?"

"This is the first time I've heard anything about tamales."

"A lady sells them out of her house but only on Tuesdays, Wednesdays, and Thursdays. If you don't get there before one, she's sold out. Want to come?"

"Sure. All I've had so far today is papaya, and I love tamales. If I knew where to find them, I'd eat tamales every day."

"Let's go, and you can see where it is. Come on, Bruce."

Bruce remained unmoved. I sat next to him, concerned by how hot and worn out he looked. "Do you have water?"

"I already drank it. Yeah, maybe I do need more water."

I handed him my full water bottle. He drank a few sips and gave it back. "That's all you want? Drink as much as you need."

"You ready?" RJ asked, checking his watch.

Bruce took a few more swallows. "That's enough. I only needed to wet my whistle. I guess we better go get the tamales before she closes."

"You don't need to rest a bit longer?" I ignored RJ's restless pacing. Couldn't he see that Bruce needed a rest? That he was dehydrated? His health was more important than stupid tamales.

"I'm fine." Bruce stood to pull on his backpack. Since we landed on Guatemala soil, he never went anywhere without that Key Bank backpack holding the tools of his new job. A Kindle for its calculator, calendar, and Spanish translation app. A yellow pad with an ongoing to do list and pens available for taking quick notes. And of course, a portable set of the basics: screwdriver, pliers, pocketknife or what have you.

"You better start carrying an extra water bottle, Bruce, for these jaunts through town," I said. He nodded and said okay.

RJ led us down a winding side alley with so many twists and turns I gave up the notion of ever finding it on my own. He stopped in front of a faded, chipped door that had once seen a coat of green paint, and gave a knock that sounded like code. Someone opened the metal plate over a narrow opening. RJ leaned forward and spoke in rapid Spanish. He handed cash through the opening, and it slid shut again. A few seconds later, a hand passed out a steaming bag of tamales.

We dug right into the tamales—the joys of street food to eat with both hands where you stand. I tried one without meat—corn masa wrapped around seasoned mashed potatoes—indeed delicious, mildly spicy and sweet. When we finished, we exited the alley and my companions went on their way to someplace RJ described that didn't sound very interesting. No, I told him, I better get back to work but thanks, anyway, and for the tamales.

I continued my solitary walk, feeling rather lonely. Bruce had seemed better after he ate. I would pick up a larger water bottle for him on my way back to the hotel.

The next morning as I sat in bed writing, I thought I heard a rap on the door. Uncertain, I waited. People didn't bother me in the mornings. The knock came again, slightly louder. Wearing flannel pants and sweatshirt, okay for answering the door, I pulled it open.

It was a short, stocky, gray-haired man in his vague mid-sixties. With a friendly smile, he said, "Sorry to bother you, Karen, but I wanted to introduce myself. I'm Paul. I have the apartment where you and Bruce are going to housesit."

I invited him in, glad to finally meet Pauly, as RJ called him, an expat American who lived near the hotel. "Is it Paul or Pauly?" I asked.

He smiled. "That's just what RJ calls me. My actual name is Paul."

"Well, good to meet you, Paul." We stood just inside the room.

"I already talked to Bruce downstairs, but I wanted to meet you particularly. Karen, I'll tell you what I told your husband. It's what I tell every expat." He paused to let this sink in.

I waited expectantly. Was it some insider secret about the town? Something to watch out for? RJ had given us plenty of warnings. Count your change, don't leave anything laying around, lock your door even if you just walk out for a minute.

Paul took a deep breath and his eyes sparkled as if to say, *Are you ready for this?*

I waited.

"Burn your boats," he stated. Another significant pause. "It's what I did when I came to Guatemala. I burned my boats."

This was it? Paul spoke with such sincerity, however, I couldn't take his counsel lightly. "What do you mean by 'burn your boats'?"

"It's an expression from when the early Spaniards came over. No matter what difficulties they encountered in the new land, they didn't want anyone to back out. So, Cortez commanded the crew to burn the boats."

"I feel like Bruce and I burned our boats," I said thoughtfully. "We sold our house in Utah and here we are, ready to make a new home in Pana."

Paul smiled warmly and held eye contact. "When I came to Panajachel, my siblings were upset about it. I had been pretty depressed about things, especially my health, and they thought this was me giving up and going off to die. They were worried about suicide, in fact. They were wrong. I wasn't coming here to die. I was coming to live. I knew if I didn't burn my boats and stay no matter what, I wouldn't have a chance."

No wonder Paul was so earnest about sharing this message with his fellow expats. Burning his boats had saved his life. "Has it been worth it?" I asked.

He leaned in closer, his smile spreading and lighting up his face. "Every second has been worth it! The weather is beautiful and perfect. The people are wonderful. I can relax and enjoy each day."

"I'm glad Bruce and I already burned our boats. Like you, we came to stay."

"I've met a lot of expats in Pana. Some came because of health, like me, needing a healthier, more laid-back lifestyle. For many, it's financial, where they can live within their means and not have to work like most retired people in the States. For others, especially the younger ones, they're looking to escape whatever they don't like back home."

"For us, it's financial, I guess, plus wanting to help our daughter. Bruce had a mortgage business when the housing market collapsed, and he decided to shut down and take early retirement. For a while, we ran a moderately successful cookie business, but it was too physically demanding to be sustainable. We sold it, sold or gave away everything, and moved to Guatemala."

"No matter what happens from now on, if you burn your boats, you will make the best of things and have a wonderful new life," Paul promised.

"That is exactly what we want."

"You won't regret a thing. I'm sure of that." He turned toward the door. "Oh, by the way, I arranged with Bruce for the two of you to come see my place today. I'll give you a key and show you around."

Keys! Our own place for a month! "Thank you so much! It's been ten days and let me tell you, it's getting old living in a hotel room. It will be nice to have more space while we find a house to rent."

"You're doing me a favor," Paul insisted in his courteous way. "I don't feel comfortable leaving my apartment empty for a whole month. It's not easy to find trustworthy house sitters. I could tell you some stories about that!"

Our new friend said goodbye, and I showered, dressed and tidied up the room. Paul's apartment soared through my thoughts as the highlight of the day, a rare outing for Bruce and me. We should go out for lunch.

As I descended the stairs, I scoped out the main floor to see who was around, if Bruce was free to talk. I heard RJ in back speaking Spanish, which meant he was with Dago. Every now and then, he broke into English, meaning Travis was there as well.

Before reaching the last step, I heard Bruce. "Hello, my love. You're down early. It's barely ten o'clock."

He sat behind a makeshift desk in a previously empty corner space, next to the stairs and in front of a dividing wall. "Look at you!" I exclaimed. "You have a desk for your laptop. And there's a phone!" He had the essentials of his typical home office, except with a plastic white lawn chair instead of his preferred swivel chair on wheels. And minus the file cabinets, of course.

"Yep. The desk and counter are made from scraps in Room 9. Travis helped me design and build it." He pointed out the printer on the counter behind him. "We got the printer hooked up. See how I organized the cords under the desk."

I glanced under the table at the collection of cords gathered with zip ties and pulled neatly to the side. A hook held the bundle in place.

"There's even room for my books." Neatly stacked were his brown leather set of the Bible and the Book of Mormon. Next to them leaned the LDS hymnbook in Spanish, a Spanish-English dictionary, and our two publishing "bibles"—a biography of famed editor Maxwell Perkins and Michael Korda's memoir *Another Life*.

Bruce had fashioned plywood and wooden beams to make use of this empty space. His chair was one of the less battered ones scattered around the back areas of the main floor.

"Very impressive!" I exclaimed, glad to see how he had created a place for himself in RJ's domain. I had my privacy in Room 2, and now Bruce had an office.

"I'm pleased with how it came out." He sat back, admiring his new quarters. "Hey, did you see Paul? I told him it was okay to go up, that you were most likely up there writing."

"Yeah, we chatted awhile. He said he wants us to go over today at one."

Bruce looked at his round office clock. It leaned precariously against the staircase wall. "What do you think about hanging my clock on this wall?"

It was ten-twenty. "Perfect spot." I could still hear RJ talking in back. He might come from behind any second to interrupt us and hijack my plans.

"I knew I'd find a place for it." Bruce gazed affectionately at the clock with its green and gold frame and clear, large numbers. The secondhand tick tick ticked away.

"Me too. I'm glad you have it for your new office. Hey, Bruce, let's you and I go out for lunch today before we head over to Paul's."

Bruce straightened a pile of papers on his desk, his oh so familiar nervous habit. He leaned slightly back in the plastic chair that I felt sure would soon give way to a rolling swivel model. He lifted a hand to his face, the long, slender fingers playing over his cheek like piano keys. His other nervous habit. Clearly, he was unwilling to commit unless RJ okayed it.

"How about for once we make a plan on our own?" I blurted in annoyance. I imagined RJ sweeping Bruce away any minute now to go out somewhere for hours.

A few ticks of the second hand later, our son-in-law emerged from behind the wall. Turning to him, I spoke quickly before he could engage Bruce in business. "Bruce and I are talking about him and me going to lunch before we see Paul's place at one."

"Sure thing," he said. "I was about to head out anyway. We'll see you guys later." He exited the hotel, leaving me feeling rather guilty.

"When do you want to go to lunch?" Bruce asked.

I checked his clock. "How about quarter to twelve? Is that too late or are you hungry now?"

"Later is fine. I have things to do here for an hour." He pushed a stack of papers an inch to one side. He seemed as contented at his plywood desk and plastic chair as if it were the finest manager's office in the finest hotel. I left to go pick up a few things at the store and found him an hour later still there, still happily busy but ready to go eat.

We decided on a little Italian place around the corner that I had noticed on one of my walks. Turn right on Santander instead of left, and there it is. Paul's place, Macombo Apartments, was a block away—don't turn on Santander either left or right; instead go straight and the next block down is Macombo. Another block past Macombo was our church, everything wonderfully convenient and accessible.

We entered the restaurant, more like a cozy café, and found a table. This was one of those many businesses in town created from a garage-like opening cut into one long building, sharing walls with other shops or dwellings next door and behind, even above. Everything connected like a rabbit warren, each shop with its wide front opening. Street dogs walked in along with people but quickly got scooted back out. The owners raised the metal doors in the morning and pulled them down at night, securing them with double locks and large padlocks.

A short stocky man in a white apron brought menus. I asked for a Coca-Lite with ice and lime. Bruce ordered a strawberry milk smoothie, a *licuado con leche.*

When the waiter left, I said, "I have no idea what I want. Everything looks so good. The problem with Italian food is that after two or three days, you're hungry again."

Bruce gave a courtesy laugh, having heard my old joke many times.

Our drinks arrived. "Where you from?" the waiter asked in English.

"Utah," Bruce said.

"I lived in California. Los Angeles. I worked in restaurants."

"Italian restaurants?" I asked.

"Italian, Chino, Mexican, many restaurants. Lots of Chinese, but already there is too much Chinese food here. Why I open Italian restaurant."

When Bruce asked what he might suggest, the man pointed to the pizza. "Everybody likes our pizza. Real Italian pizza."

We decided on a small cheese pizza to share, and I got an appetizer order of bruschetta. Bruce ordered pasta with white sauce. The waiter, who was also the owner and the chef, left to fix our food somewhere in back. Enticing aromas soon wafted out.

"I am so excited about Paul's place, Bruce. Aren't you?"

"I'm excited about living like normal people instead of out of our suitcases in a hotel room. We need our own space, and I need to not be at RJ's every beck and call. I hope by the end of the month we can move to a house. In fact, we will. That's all there is to it."

"I hope you're right."

"RJ's been talking to people, getting names and numbers. He's a connector."

"I'd like to get into another house-sitting situation. Where we don't have to pay rent."

"Those are hard to come by according to RJ. He says every expat anywhere near Lake Atitlán wants to house sit and not pay rent. The only reason we got this is because he and Pauly are such good friends."

"Well, lucky for us then." I took a long sip of Coke then squeezed more lime into my glass. "RJ is good to us. I need to quit worrying about him taking advantage of your easygoing nature and monopolizing your time."

"You have nothing to worry about, Karen. Nobody's taking advantage of me."

"You're not as young and fit as you used to be, and it seems like he pushes you too hard."

"I can handle RJ."

"I hope so. You do enjoy the work, I can tell."

"I'm learning the ropes. Gotta be ready to take over once he leaves."

"When is that? Is there a timeline?"

Bruce laughed at that. "RJ doesn't do timelines. He doesn't like getting pinned down. But from what I gather, he's leaving soon after the hotel opens for *Semana Santa*. That's *my* timeline. I came down to run the place, and it's what I intend to do."

"Two months away. Will everything be ready by then?"

"It should. Everyone's working hard to make it happen. Travis is there ten, twelve hours a day, even longer than Dago who leaves by six for his church meetings."

"What church is that?"

"It's a Christian church, Protestant of some kind. He and his wife Rosa are very active. Dago volunteers with the youth and Rosa with the women."

The man brought our food and set it delicately before us. He made sure we were happy before retreating to the kitchen, although he showed up at the counter now and then to stay available. We were his only customers. We finished a little over half our meal before others came in and took two more tables. We were done eating and ready to go.

I asked for the leftovers wrapped to go. *"Para llevar,"* two helpful words I had learned quickly. We paid the ridiculously low bill, left a generous tip, and said goodbye to the owner, waiter, chef. We wished him luck with his excellent restaurant and promised to return soon.

"This place needs to stay in business," I said to Bruce. "He sure knows how to cook Italian."

We arrived at Macombo Apartments a little before one, and I pushed the doorbell outside the building. It was an imposing structure of red brick, wide and high, that looked more like a school or an institution than an apartment building. There were no balconies, and the equidistant front windows were without ornamentation.

No one came to open the door. We waited, rang several more times, waited awhile longer, until finally a young man opened it. In Spanish, I asked him about Paul. He said to wait, he would go check if Paul was there.

A few minutes later, Paul came to the front door and broke into smiles when he saw us. He pointed out his apartment on the left, adjacent to the locked front entrance. "I'm right here. If anyone wants me, they bang on the window. Like this." He hit the glass twice with the flat of his hand. "Since I'm hard of hearing, I don't hear the front bell ring. Come on in, I'll show you around."

We entered a wide hallway leading to an impressive patio garden with flowers, shrubs, and ornamental trees. Wrought iron chairs and benches were artistically placed. The space opened upward to the second floor, where doors around the U-shaped hallway signified the upstairs apartments.

"This is gorgeous!" I exclaimed. "Golly, why don't we just live here?"

"Unfortunately, nothing is available right now," Paul said, "and there's a waiting list besides."

"Oh, too bad! I would love one of those upstairs apartments."

Paul's apartment was the first one to the left. "Some of the units are one and two bedroom. Mine is a studio, the smallest they offer." He opened the door and ushered us in.

His kitchen was small but efficient, with refrigerator and propane stove top, no oven. The counter wrapped around from the sink to a bar with a couple stools. On the other side of the bar was a small table and two chairs. The living area had a sofa and upholstered chairs centered around a coffee table. The bedroom consisted of a double bed, a freestanding wardrobe, and a dresser. Paul's studio apartment felt spacious after two weeks in Room 2.

Every inch was immaculately clean and orderly. Paul had been a cook in the Navy. "I keep my apartment like it's a room on the ship. With a place for everything and everything in its place." He emphasized the need to towel dry the sink and counter after each use. "Tiny ants live in the pipes, and if they get a hint of water or crumbs, they come up through the drain and crawl over everything."

He showed us where he kept the cleaning supplies. "You'll need to sweep the floor daily or the dust builds up and gets everywhere. Same with taking out the garbage every night. Otherwise, it attracts ants and bugs." He gestured to the wall of windows that opened to the street, high enough to prevent pedestrians from seeing inside. "Bugs and flies will find their way to the garbage if it's not emptied regularly. This is a tropical environment, remember, despite the cool nights."

Paul pointed out the two trash cans, one in the kitchen and one in the bathroom and which liners he used for each. He reused plastic bags, folding and storing them flat in a drawer. He cut the plastic off his four to eight roll packages of toilet paper to save for lining the kitchen bin. Snack or cookie wrappings held leftovers in the fridge. I noticed half a sandwich saved in a tiny snack bag. He reused the zipper-type bags of granola for dry goods storage in the cabinet, to seal against the ants. He lived frugally, took excellent care of what little he had and seemed quite pleased with his home. It was hard to think he had once been so depressed his family worried about suicide.

Paul gave us each a set of keys for the apartment and the main door. "My flight is in two days, so I probably won't see you again before I go. Any questions, you can ask RJ. He knows my place. The kid who let you in works here, if you need to ask him for anything. I told him you're staying for the month."

We thanked him and said we'd move in the day he leaves so as not to have it empty overnight.

"I'm glad this worked out for both of us. You're doing me a big favor. I'm never comfortable leaving my home empty. There's a doctor I see regularly in Florida. And of course, my family."

Shortly after we moved to Paul's, I invited everyone over for dinner. I stir fried broccoli with chunks of fresh cheese browned in oil. The smell attracted a swarm of iridescent green flies, coming in through the open door and buzzing around like crazy. I quickly shut the door, and the five of us went after the flies with rolled up magazines. Strangely enough, cooked broccoli seemed to be the only food that attracted those big, ugly flies.

A couple times Jessica made pasta with tomato sauce to share. Once RJ came from Sololá, a nearby town up the hill, with

Chinese food and bags of hamburgers and fries. He called Bruce at the hotel to say he would arrive by six with plenty of dinner for everyone and to wait at Paul's for him. Occasionally after dinner, RJ said, "Who wants dessert?" Then he ran over to the bakery and the ice cream shop and brought back cookies and ice cream to pass around.

Semana Santa, the week leading up to Easter Sunday, was Pana's busiest time of year. It was RJ's target date for opening day. Despite the rush of getting Casa Colonial ready for business, we continued to meet in the evenings for dinner whenever schedules allowed. It was a time of shared excitement and family togetherness that transformed a temporary house-sitting arrangement into a happy home.

I didn't worry about where Bruce and I would live after this. Guatemala had welcomed us, and good things lie ahead. Our next home would come in its own time.

4
I May Be a Gringa
but at Least I'm not a Tourist

For riches certainly make themselves wings;
they fly away as an eagle toward heaven.
Proverbs 23:5

In the mornings, Bruce walked the two blocks to the hotel, and I hunkered down to business tasks. Our publishing company, opened in 2007, required daily processing of manuscripts on their path to publication. That completed, I devoted the remainder of the workday to my own book, a novel close to done.

Around one, after Emree woke up from her nap, Jessica brought her in the stroller to see if I wanted to go for a walk. Emree's stroller, one RJ had picked up somewhere, could also attach to the back of a bike like a cart. I tried steering it once and couldn't handle the job. It was heavy and unwieldy, especially on the cobblestone streets and rough sidewalks. Jessica, a tall, strong girl, made it look easy.

She knocked on the window to get my attention. "Do you want to go to Dispensa with us?" Jessica asked when I came outside.

"Sure. There's always something I can use at the store."

We headed up Santander, turned toward the Dispensa and stopped at our favorite fruit stand. I ordered mango. "You want pineapple, Jessica? I'm buying." She liked it with honey for her and Emree.

"You don't have to buy me fruit," she protested.

"I know, but I want to. It's only five quetzales, don't worry about it. Besides, you save me from myself when you come by. Too much isolation. I owe you." She laughed and ordered the pineapple.

After trying different fruit stands around town and near the lake, Jessica and I had found this one, run by a slightly plump, thirty-something woman named Mercedes. She kept her work area clean and efficient, her product inside a glass shelter away from flies. Normal flies, not the big green, broccoli-loving kind. Mercedes frequently wiped down surfaces. She used fresh, perfect fruit and stuffed the serving bags full. Like most of the local women, she dressed in the traditional skirt, blouse and apron.

Mercedes stood smiling and ready for action the moment we chose our fruit. With sharp knife and deft fingers, she cut and sliced and neatly packed it into plastic bags. The selections were whatever was in season, mostly pineapple, papaya, ripe or green mango, and oranges. You could get honey, lime or other seasoning added. I liked the papaya plain, but for the mango I would request the spicy, salty seasoning, especially good on slightly green mango.

We took a seat on the bench behind the fruit stand and in front of the small grocery store called Charo's. Their prices were too high for regular grocery shopping, although tourists and expats kept them in business buying specialty items unavailable at the Dispensa.

A woman on a bicycle rode up to the front of the store, parked and looked over at us. Her long gray hair was pulled back in a thin ponytail. "I can't wait until the rainy season starts, when all these damn tourists leave," she shouted in our direction. Then she went into Charo's.

Jessica and I exchanged glances and giggled. "Do you know her?" I asked.

"No, do you?"

"No, but I've seen her around town. She's an expat woman from upstate New York," I explained.

"How do you know?"

"I recognize her accent. I had a friend once from upstate New York who sounded exactly like that. Only an expat will know the rainy season and complain about tourists. Not to mention the hair. Everything about her says I may be a gringa but I'm not a tourist."

Jessica laughed and agreed with me.

We sat with our separate thoughts and watched the crowd as we ate our fruit. The tourists, always in a hurry, passed the local folks on both sides of the sidewalk, swarming around them.

Charo's was on a corner of two busy streets with plenty to see. Teens in their school uniforms clustered together laughing and chatting. The girls wore blue and green plaid pleated skirts, white polo shirts, and knee socks to match, either white, blue or green. The boys had tailored tan pants with blue or green polo shirts tucked into the belted, pressed pants. Their youthful, clear faces glowed with vitality. They were neither fat nor thin. The girls held back their shining, thick dark hair with barrettes, headbands or in a ponytail. I thought of the kids in jeans and hoodies walking to and from the junior high near our home in Utah. A disturbing majority slouched along the sidewalk looking weak and unhealthy with sullen expressions. The girls were often overweight and the boys lacking in musculature.

I remarked on the difference. "Given a chance, these young people could easily take over the world. They look superior to American kids in every way—health, happiness, enthusiasm—who knows what else. Maybe brains, too."

"Maybe that's why so many want to come to our country," Jessica responded. "They just need a chance to make something of themselves and be successful."

"They seem so confident. These kids act like they know their purpose."

Jessica let out a deep sigh and gave Emree another forkful of pineapple. "I wish I knew my purpose." A pickup truck loaded to the brim with pineapples rumbled past. "Look at these people rushing by. They know what they're doing, where they're going. Look at that guy carrying a ladder while he's riding a bike. That can't be easy, but he looks happy. Everyone seems so happy and confident."

"They really do," I agreed, watching a city garbage truck with gleeful men in yellow vests holding on to the sides. "Like those guys standing with their faces right over a pile of smelly garbage. They look like they love their job. Or maybe they're just thrilled to have a job."

"The people here seem to fit so easily into their environment. They know who they are, I think."

"They are a very connected society," I commented, thinking of how many of their houses and stores were connected like rabbit warrens. "No living in isolation. Everybody knows everybody else, which of course is what RJ complains about. No privacy."

"I'm a little jealous," Jessica mused. "How nice it would be to feel like that, like you fit in with those around you. I didn't feel like I fit in back in Salt Lake either. I tried, but I felt different from other women my age, the young married women."

"You *are* different, Jessica, but in a good way. You have sensitivity and maturity. You think about things deeply. I can't imagine any twenty-something young mom from my suburban neighborhood wanting to hang out with me. To walk to the store every afternoon, sit and watch people and discuss things of interest."

"Maybe that's why I wanted to come to Guatemala." Her large brown eyes were soft and tender. "Maybe I felt that far away from the fakeness and the social pressures to fit in and be like everyone else, I could find my purpose."

"Like a retreat."

"Yeah. I guess I hoped Guatemala would be a type of spiritual, emotional retreat for enlightenment. Like, open my mind to who

I really am, what I need to do. Or something." Her voice drifted away, and she attended to Emree, who was fussing.

"Me, I wanted a change of scene. To get out of the rat race, I suppose. To avoid us becoming helicopter grandparents for the next twenty years, hovering over our kids and their families. Waiting for them to need you like when they were little. And of course, Bruce hated the idea of retirement. I think it scared him to death, the fear of having nothing to do, no reason to get up in the morning. He jumped at the chance of an interesting job while helping Sally and RJ in the process."

Jessica rocked the heavy stroller gently over the uneven sidewalk. "Although I'm a foreigner and could never fit in no matter how hard I tried, I don't feel like a tourist." She paused to feed Emeree the last piece of honeyed pineapple from the little plastic bag. "Travis and I came here to help Sally, of course, but I think I needed this, too."

"I hope you can find your purpose, Jessica. There's something about the spirit here. I can't think of anyplace better to have a retreat." I watched her clean Emree's round little face with a couple of tiny napkins from Mercedes' stand. Guatemala food service offered such small, thin napkins. When she was finished, I stood up and held out my hand; Jessica handed me the shredded, crumpled bit of paper and the empty plastic bag.

"Thanks, Karen," she said as I dropped them in the trash.

We joined the crowd moving down Santander Street past Charo's. The expat woman's bike was still parked in front, and I wondered what was in there that she couldn't live without.

Beyond the Dispensa, the street led to the river and to a bridge that crossed from Panajachel to Jucanya, where Travis and Jessica lived. During the rainy season, the river flowed with water. When the rain stopped, the water dried up and people crushed rocks in the riverbed to haul away for gravel.

As we approached the Dispensa, Jessica said, "I really can't buy much, only a couple things."

"We don't have to go in. I don't need much either, although I could replace Paul's little cookies that I keep eating."

"I need eggs, milk and ketchup. We're out. It's just that I'm worried about money."

That didn't surprise me. What woman does not worry about money?

"This thing happened the other day that really upset me. RJ asked to borrow from Travis, and all he had was what RJ had paid him the day before. So, Travis handed it back to him. We hadn't even bought groceries yet."

"That's rather shocking."

"Travis told me not to worry, that RJ will pay him back."

"I hope so!"

"He said RJ has borrowed from him before and always pays it back soon after."

"If he doesn't, we can tell Sally and she'll send Travis the money."

"RJ pays Travis, usually late, then comes and takes it right back again. That leaves us with nothing for groceries."

"He apparently borrowed from Bruce, too," I said. "The other day he came by the apartment and gave Bruce 500 quetzales. When I asked why, he said RJ was paying him back."

Jessica jerked and lifted the stroller up the many stairs leading to the front entrance of Dispensa. She managed that thing like it was a little umbrella stroller instead of an oversized cart. Emree, securely strapped, laughed in delight at her wild ride. "What is RJ doing borrowing from all of us anyway?" she exclaimed. "Doesn't Sally send him his own money?"

"Yes, she does. They have an adequate budget for the hotel, Bruce said. I wonder if Sally knows he's borrowing from the family. Bruce works for free, and Travis works for quetzales. RJ shouldn't borrow from either one of them."

"We hardly have any money. We barely get by. People on the street always ask me to buy something from them or donate money or whatever. They think if you're American, you are super rich. They don't understand. We are here living hand to mouth like they are."

The automatic doors opened, and we entered the store. Jessica found the ketchup and we headed to the dairy aisle.

"Last week he came and took our tithing," she said.

"He took your *tithing?* How the heck did that happen?"

"He asked Travis for a loan, and Travis said he only had the tithing. He had it in his hand, and RJ grabbed it. Travis said, 'But that's our tithing. I'm turning it in on Sunday.' RJ said 'Don't worry, I'll pay it back.'"

"Good grief!" To grab money right out of Travis's hands, and tithing funds at that.

Jessica picked up the milk, and we each bought a dozen eggs. On the way, I grabbed an onion and a bunch of bananas.

As we checked out, I said, "Do you guys want to come to dinner tonight?"

"Sure! If you want us. You don't have to invite us every night."

"Oh, I know that, and sometimes I don't, like if I'm really tired or whatever."

Because of the pressure leading up to *Semana Santa,* the three men often worked late, making it difficult to plan meals around their erratic schedules. Bruce rarely missed dinner, but RJ always had a long list of things for Travis to finish.

"I'll do my best to get Travis to leave work at six, even if he has to go back later. Then it won't be that late for you."

"How about stir-fried vegetables and rice? Is that okay?"

Jessica's wide, happy smile lit up her pretty face. "That sounds great! Thank you so much, Karen."

On the way home, my thoughts were full of my next chapter. Once back in the apartment, I wrote until Bruce arrived home at five. I shut my laptop and went to cut up vegetables and start the rice. I mentioned our dinner plans and asked about RJ. "Is he coming by later?"

"I'm not sure. He wasn't at the hotel when I left."

"Jessica told me something weird today." I related the tithing incident.

Bruce stared incredulously and opened his mouth a couple times, but no words came out. I arranged the onion, celery, peppers, and mushrooms next to the cutting board. I thought of Mercedes and the fruit she handled with such loving artistry.

"Not to mention, they barely have money for food because RJ regularly borrows from Travis."

Bruce found his voice. "Travis will grow up fast working with RJ. This is an education he won't get at college."

"What if RJ wants to borrow from you again, Bruce?"

"He doesn't know when we get paid. If he asks to borrow a few hundred quetzales, I'll tell him I don't have it. I don't, not for that. His borrowing days are over."

"He knows when Travis has money though," I said.

"That's up to Travis. He is perfectly capable of managing his own situation. He can tell RJ no."

5
On Wings so Swift and Certain

God is our refuge and strength, a very present help in trouble.
Therefore, we will not fear, though the earth be removed,
and though the mountains be carried into the midst of the sea.
Psalm 46:1–3

The next morning, I called Sally on Google Chat about my concerns over the borrowed money.

"Yeah, RJ is real loose with money," she said. "He lends, he borrows, he spends, and then he refuses to spend. He can be weird with money."

"Apparently, he always pays Travis back, but it's hard on them. Especially on Jessica who worries."

"I'll check with RJ and make sure he's got enough. If he's borrowing from people, we may have to re-evaluate the budget. I can always send him more if he needs it."

"Thanks, Sally. I knew you would understand. There's no way you would want Travis and Jessica to do without their basic needs."

"No, of course not. Neither does RJ. It's just that he's impulsive and doesn't think things through. Don't worry, Mom. I'll talk to him. We'll handle it."

I disconnected the call feeling reassured. Sally understood RJ. She would manage the situation.

While on the computer, I checked Facebook and saw a message from my sister Becki. My youngest sister owned a health food store in northern Minnesota. A vibrant example of wholesome diet and vitamin therapy, she avoided doctors and hospitals, which is why her message surprised me.

> **Hi Karen. Just wanted to let you know I'm waiting to see a doctor in the hospital emergency room. I have horribly distended bowel and abdomen. Extremely uncomfortable. I am completely exhausted. I'll let you know what I find out. I'm prepared to be admitted. Not leaving until they fix me.**

A few hours later, my sister Jeri called me on Skype. The hospital had admitted Becki for tests and they were waiting for a full report, Jeri said, but it didn't look good. She and Gentz were driving up from Illinois to be with Becki. She filled me in on Becki's suffering before the hospitalization. "There were times she couldn't walk from her car to the house. A couple times, she had to drag herself on hands and knees in the snow and crawl up the steps to her back door."

As soon as we ended the call, I emailed Becki to see how she was doing and tell her I loved her. I spent the next few hours compulsively checking Skype, Facebook, and email for anything from her. When Jessica came by for our afternoon walk, I told her briefly what happened and that I needed to stay close to my computer in case a message came through.

Bruce came home late for dinner, full of reports about how well the hotel was shaping up for Easter week. I didn't mention Becki since all I knew was that she'd been admitted. It was a relief to shut my laptop and listen to my husband chattering on about plumbing and grout. Normal things to distract me from wondering why I hadn't heard anything more from Becki.

The next day, Jeri rang through on Skype with the results of the tests. It was indeed cancer, Stage 4, and it had metastasized in her bones. Becki was home now, meeting with the oncologist tomorrow about a treatment plan. Jeri and Gentz were staying at her house and would take her to the appointment. Our sister Julie was in Nevada visiting our cousin and looking for flights to return early to Minnesota.

"Keep praying for Becki and her kids," Jeri said. "They are devastated by this diagnosis." She promised to keep me informed, and we closed the call.

I set my open laptop next to me on the couch and stared out the line of high windows. I watched the legs of pedestrians passing by on the sidewalk. Time disappeared.

A few hours later, Jeri sent me a Facebook message:

Becki is getting worse right before our eyes. She is yellow and drawn. She asked Gentz to make her some of his whole grain muffins, which of course he did. He couldn't make those muffins fast enough, he was that glad to do something for Becki.

I visualized Becki sitting at the table with Jeri and Gentz as she picked at a muffin. It turned out to be her final meal.

I closed my laptop with a snap. It was late February and seventy degrees in Panajachel, probably well below zero in Aitken. I should be in Minnesota with my sisters. But how could I? Once there, I would want to stay long term until Becki improved or at least stabilized. Bruce would never complain if I left for several weeks, but I worried over his health. Without me, he wouldn't eat anything healthy. Too much disturbance in his environment and his blood pressure soared. He needed the peaceful regularity of home life, especially with the stress of getting the hotel ready for opening weekend.

I heard a key turning, the door opening. It was dinnertime, I supposed.

RJ came in with Bruce as he so often did. Talking fast and loud, he raised the energy level to intolerable. I escaped to the bathroom and shut the door, seeing my stricken image in the mirror. Cancer! What did that mean for my sister?

With clenched teeth, I listened to RJ go on and on. For someone who carried on about his privacy, he seemed oblivious to ours. His loud voice carried through the bathroom door. *The hotel. The paddleboards. Semana Santa.*

Finally, I came out and blurted, "I just heard from Jeri. Becki has Stage 4 cancer."

RJ stopped talking. He and Bruce both gaped at me.

"Jeri said it's metastasized to her bones. What does that mean? Jeri didn't seem to know anything. There's a meeting with the oncologist to discuss a treatment plan."

Although I directed my comments to Bruce, it was RJ who responded. He studied me with kindness and said softly, "That's not good, Karen. . . . It means the cancer is spreading through her body."

I had forgotten RJ was a registered nurse, because what sort of medical professional drags a sixty-five-year-old, overweight man all over town in the heat of the day? "Then it's bad?" I asked him. "What can they do for her?"

RJ hesitated before replying in the same low tones. "I think usually at this point, they will try to make her as comfortable as possible. It depends on how much it's spreading."

There was not much else to say. RJ left soon after, and Bruce made eggs for his dinner while I ate a packet of Paul's sandwich cookies. Quietly sympathetic, Bruce hovered in case I needed to talk. With so little information, there was nothing to discuss. We watched something on Netflix then went to bed.

That week, I could not focus on anything but Becki and my sisters in Aitken. I let work emails go unanswered. I skipped my walks with Jessica. I checked my laptop constantly for any word. Becki had sent me a brief email after her diagnosis.

Thanks for your email, Karen. I haven't had internet for awhile plus my brain is not working right. So Peter is typing for me. I went to the radiologist today and they took out 2.5 liters of fluid. We don't do anything tomorrow. They say I should feel better in the morning.

Love You
Becki

It was the last I heard from her, dated February 25th. Not yet a week ago but it seemed an age.

I thought about when I told Becki goodbye at our sister's reunion back in December. I had said this was my last trip to the north country. "Oh, you never know," she responded with that twinkle in her eye. "Something might happen to bring you back."

Recently, I read in a memoir about the sudden death of the author's husband, how those who die seem to have a subconscious premonition of it happening. It comes across in things they say or do, which their loved ones wonder about later. I wondered about Becki's statement, "Something might happen to bring you back."

It was the last week of February and things happened fast. Julie called me twice on Skype, although it wasn't her thing, having to sit at a computer to talk to someone. Julie, who had recovered from breast cancer twenty years ago, was upset that Becki had not gone in for regular mammograms. "I hope you're getting a mammogram every year, Karen. With two sisters having breast cancer, you and Jeri are both at high risk."

The cancer had come fast and spread aggressively. Within nine months, the oncologist estimated. Even with a yearly mammogram, it might have slipped through. Apparently, the cancer had originated in her breast and spread rapidly through her body. Tests showed it in her lungs, bones, liver, everywhere. No wonder Becki had suffered such pain in recent months.

Our youngest sister, age fifty-eight, stayed at the hospital for the remainder of the tests. There was little hope for treatment. Hospice was the recommended path forward. Becki, agreeing to enter hospice, knew what that meant.

Julie visited with her in the hospital. "She is worried about the cost of a funeral," Julie told me. "She knows cremation is cheaper but couldn't decide. I asked her which she wanted, cremation or a casket."

In her weakening voice, Becki had said, "I want a casket and to be buried here in Aitken next to Mother and Daddy. Only I don't think I can afford it."

Julie, who had more money than the three of us put together, firmly stated, "Becki, if you want a funeral, a casket and a place next to Mother and Daddy, that is what you will have. I don't want you to worry about the money."

Becki closed her eyes. "Okay, that's good," she murmured. "Thank you, Julie." She was ready for hospice. "I just want to go home."

The hospice staff brought a hospital bed and set up a room, previously her office, on the main floor of Becki's house. They arranged for an undertaker to come once she passed. They catheterized her and started morphine to make her as comfortable as possible.

Becki grew weaker by the moment. She wavered in and out of consciousness. The second day at home, she didn't wake up. Friends and family gathered to express their love and say their goodbyes.

Julie went into the room as Pete, Becki's first husband and the father of her kids, was finishing up his visit. He said, "Before I go, Julie, I want to tell you something that happened early this morning. It was maybe one a.m., and I woke up suddenly for some reason, heard a noise or something. And clear as anything, I hear your dad Bill say in an excited voice, "Lucille! Becki is coming!"

Their youngest daughter most certainly was coming. Only ten days after her diagnosis, our little sister died on March 2nd. Jeri was at her bedside when she passed. When Peter left his mom's room for a moment, Jeri went to sit next to her. Later, she told me about Becki's passing.

"It was about six-thirty p.m. when Peter left, after kissing his mom and saying, 'I love you, Momma.' I sat and held Becki's hand and talked to her, telling her Peter had left the room, that she was free to go and be with Mother and Daddy. Somehow, I knew Becki didn't want to die in front of her kids. She wanted to spare them that. 'Just walk towards the light,' I told her, and a few minutes later, she took her last breath."

Jeri stepped outside the door, caught Peter's eye and said, "She's gone, Peter." The family came in, cried, hugged one another and then circled the bed. Peter asked Gentz to say a prayer. Everyone held hands as Gentz prayed. Peter and Brekke were heartbroken, grieving beyond expression, bereft of the close companionship of the mother they adored.

"Seeing their grief was the worst," Jeri said. "There's nothing anyone can do to comfort them really." Afterward, Jeri and Gentz remained in the room. "There was such a sacred peace around Becki, I could hardly pull myself away."

The hospice nurse came to remove the catheter. When the funeral director arrived, the men gathered to lift and move Becki. "They wrapped the quilt around her and carried her out, that beautiful, thick hair streaming down," Jeri said.

The night after Becki passed, I woke up around two a.m., feeling the loss of my sister. Bruce was breathing peacefully at my side, in and out, in and out, to the rhythm of his CPAP machine. Becki and I had talked about strengthening our relationship this year, to have more frequent communication. She planned to visit me in Guatemala. As I thought of these things, I felt her presence next to the bed.

"Hi, Becki," I whispered.

"Hi, Karen." Her familiar throaty voice came clear and strong, the way an emphatic thought flashes through the mind.

"I can't believe you're gone," I said in this quiet thought language.

"I'm not gone."

"I'm sorry I wasn't a better friend to you. This was supposed to be our year."

"It's okay." I heard that note of humor in her voice and the little laugh.

"I love you, Becki."

"I know you do."

Then she was gone. She had come to say goodbye.

"I'm not gone." Those words ring in my ears to this day. *I'm not gone.*

What a tender mercy for Becki to come and comfort me, leaving me with a sense of peace and love. Despite my lack of communication through the years, she knew I loved her. I felt reassured that her two grieving children would also receive needed comfort. Their mom would speak to them in whatever way they would recognize.

Julie, Jeri, and Peter organized my flight with Becki's Delta miles, the ones she was saving to visit me in Guatemala. My flight to Minneapolis was difficult, patched together as it was with free miles. I brought things to survive an overnight layover in Atlanta: laptop for editing, notebook for writing, Kindle for reading. My night in the airport felt otherworldly with nothing open and hardly anyone around. I saw a few people stretched out on seats or the floor, using a backpack or duffle as a pillow. Some, like me, stayed awake with a laptop or tablet.

I found a comfortable bench near a diner. Prime real estate: a bench with back support, a side table, and a plug bar. A rare, open restaurant a few steps away.

At one point, a twentyish young man approached and said bluntly, "Can you move?"

It was three a.m. in the deserted Atlanta airport, a massive place with plenty of seating available. I stared at him in disbelief. "What?"

He stared back, expressionless. "Can you move?"

"What do you mean, *move*?"

He waved toward a chair. "Just move over there."

"No." I returned to my laptop. He wandered off. Get me back to Guatemala where people are normal, I muttered.

Becki's funeral was a sad affair. This small town, where Becki had lived and worked and been involved in community events for thirty years, was in shock over the rapid onset of her illness and sudden death. One minute she is running her store and going about town as usual, and next they hear Becki Jones passed away. *What happened?* Even those of us involved with the situation—in my case, though emails, Skype calls, and Facebook messages—could hardly process it.

She had worked through months of pain, thinking the sore back and shoulders came from muscle or ligament strain while lifting boxes at her store. She thought the bloating in her midsection was due to a developing dairy or wheat allergy. Only close friends and family knew she checked into the hospital for tests and diagnosis. Ten days later, she was gone.

February in northern Minnesota was below zero with deep snow on the ground. I borrowed boots and a winter coat from what Jeri had at their cabin. During the service, my sisters were surrounded by their families. Becki's many friends and family sat together, while I ended up alone on a bench with some other scattered people. Despite the warm coat, I was freezing cold.

My nephew John—Jeri's youngest—slid in next to me and kept his arm around me during the service. That helped me feel less alone, but I still felt strange. I didn't fit. Bruce was in Guatemala and none of my kids had been able to make the trip. Bruce and the kids were my everything. Without them, I would have no life. Such a scenario hit me as never before. I had craved adventure in a foreign country, new experiences, but to be alone like this? No, never. I shivered throughout the funeral in that heavy borrowed coat. I could not get warm. I wanted Bruce.

I was away for five days. Bruce and RJ were waiting for me at the airport, and I hugged them both, never happier to see anyone in my life. Pedro drove us back to Panajachel and dropped me at Paul's warm and sunny apartment. They went on to the hotel to finish out the day's work. I was fine with that, although Bruce asked if I needed him to stay for a while. Being by myself at home was nothing like the empty loneliness I had felt in Minnesota. "You go on with RJ, my love. I'll work for a bit, probably walk to the store and see about dinner. I might take a nap."

Each day Bruce went to work early and came home late, everyone focused on getting the hotel ready for guests by Easter week. People flock to the area for *Semana Santa* and hotels fill up fast. Left with whatever they can find, large groups often crowd into one room and sleep on the floor. Hotels can make a small fortune charging per person instead of per room.

I was alone for long hours in the cozy apartment and did not mind the isolation. Jessica came by daily to see if I wanted to walk with her and Emree. Although not feeling up to it, I went anyway. It wasn't healthy to stay cooped up writing at length in my journal and checking for messages from my sisters. They were helping to clear out Becki's house and do whatever else Brekke and Peter needed. I felt confused and conflicted and separated in my grief. I should have stayed another week at least. I had told Julie to make my ticket for only five days out of concern for Bruce.

Once there, I felt so out of place that only five days felt too long. What was wrong with me anyway?

Sunday at church, sadness overwhelmed me, and I left early. Shortly after, I heard a knock at the door. It was Jessica.

"I stepped away from church for a bit to come over and give you a hug," she said. We embraced and she held me tightly. "I'm sorry for what you're going through. I can't imagine how hard it must be to lose a sister. Are you okay?" Jessica had four sisters and one brother.

"Usually I'm fine, but today it just came over me. I needed to get away from people, I guess."

Between returning to the tasks of book publishing and writing my novel—which coincidentally was about a woman in a coma who visits the spirit world—I cried and prayed and pondered the mysteries of life and death. As I wrote the chapters about Helena in the great unknown, that world appeared real in my imagination. There dwelt Becki with our parents, our grandparents, and our family line who have passed on—those who Becki had always called her "people." Her third marriage had resulted in a costly, unfair divorce settlement that took nearly everything. Yet she maintained her calm, saying, "I'm going to be okay. My people are watching over me."

Despite work pressure with *Semana Santa* six weeks away and RJ wanting his crew available early and late, Bruce lingered at home in the mornings in case I needed to talk. He listened patiently when I shared my concerns over his health, his blood pressure, his Cheeto snacking habit.

When I bought my morning papaya at the fruit stand, I got fruit for him and stood by his desk to watch him eat it.

At home, we discussed how people die: accidents, sudden illness, slow debilitating disease. We hoped to go together one day in the far distant future, holding hands.

"Funny how everyone has their ideal plan of how to die," I said one morning at breakfast. "I watched this documentary once about healthy, middle-aged people with cancer, and their recurring theme was unfairness. How this wasn't supposed to happen to someone who exercised and ate healthy and took care of themselves."

Bruce stopped munching his granola. "Everybody wants to die peacefully in their sleep. But if everyone died in their sleep, we'd all be afraid to go to bed at night."

Death became real and present, no longer some vague far-away occurrence that happens to the old and the ill or to other people. Anyone can die at any time. Children, sisters, husbands. They don't even have to be sick first.

6
The Dance

The righteous shall be glad in the Lord and shall trust in him;
and all the upright in heart shall glory.
Psalm 64:10

While I kept to myself at Paul's, Bruce and RJ interspersed hotel labors with seeking our next home. Our time at the apartment was growing short with nowhere to go after. Other than back to the hotel, and none of us wanted that.

Pricing made no sense. One cramped, dark set of cement rooms was 2500 quetzales, or about $200 a month, what Paul paid for his nice studio at Macombo with its lovely, central garden. Still, I didn't worry. We belonged in Guatemala, and a house would come. Besides, RJ, who felt responsible for us as his in-laws, would not rest until we had a place.

A week before Paul's scheduled return, RJ banged on the open window and hollered, "Karen! Come on. I found the perfect house for you!"

I shut my laptop, grabbed my keys, and headed to the door. RJ joined me as I locked up. "My friend Lucas told me about it. He has the keys. He and Bruce are waiting out front in his taxi. Come on, let's go!" He strode through the hallway and pushed open the front doors.

"Is it in Pana?" I asked, stepping quickly to keep up. "I don't want to live in Jucanya or outside of town if we can help it."

"It's Pana, only a little north of here. It's perfect; you're going to love it." He stopped next to a beat-up brown sedan parked by the sidewalk. "Here we are. Bruce is in back."

I climbed in next to Bruce. "RJ wanted to come get you," he explained. "He figured it was faster than me going."

RJ slid into the passenger seat and pulled the door shut. He introduced me to Lucas behind the wheel. "Karen, meet Lucas. He'll drive people to the city for less than Pedro's van. Bruce already knows Lucas."

"He comes by the hotel quite a bit," Bruce put in.

Lucas turned and greeted me with a nod and a smile. *"Buenas 'tardes. Mucho gusto."*

I responded in kind, and we were on our way. Lucas's driving, like his vehicle, was rough and tumble, compared to clean and careful Pedro. He drove past the mercado, uphill into an unfamiliar part of town, nowhere I had walked with Jessica. I saw no churches or parks. The only stores were the scattered tienda or tortilla shop, although a corner bakery looked promising. People on the sidewalks and streets hurried about their business. I saw folks moving in and out of several narrow alleyways, like streams connecting to the main river.

"What are those little alley streets called?" I asked.

"Those are *callejónes*. They weave through town like a maze. People live there, and there's even small tiendas and cafés. This area is called Barrio Norte," explained RJ. "It's only a couple blocks north of the mercado. A good neighborhood and not as much traffic as closer in." He gestured left and drew my attention away from the *callejónes*. "Check this out, Karen. Nice, huh?"

Here were gated properties, with trees and flowers peeking above the walls, and Spanish-style houses rising behind them. Lucas turned left and drove down a bumpy lane with high concrete walls on each side. He parked outside a red metal double door.

"This is it," RJ announced. "Let's go."

We tumbled out. Lucas inserted a key into the brass lock. He pushed a button on the side to show us the intercom. *"Mucha seguridad!"* Opening one of the double doors, he gestured for us to enter.

"Big enough for a vehicle," RJ commented. "My truck can easily fit through here, Bruce."

Past the high red doors, a concrete and grass pathway led to the house. Manicured shrubbery surrounded a green lawn with a lime tree in the center. A covered patio the length of the house sheltered the front entrance.

Inside, RJ showed us around, as pleased as if he had built it himself. "There's two big bedrooms. Go check out the closet space! You've got wood beam ceilings, wide windows, and patio doors leading outdoors. You guys should take the bedroom with the patio door. You can lay in bed, open the doors to the garden, get the fresh air every morning."

I was impressed with the kitchen. It had an oven, a full-size refrigerator and decent counter space.

RJ opened the back patio door. "Look at this, Karen. A spacious back patio walled in for privacy."

I noted a clothesline and a sink. "A big sink like that outside?"

"It's called a *pila*," RJ explained. "For doing laundry."

"By *hand*?" So far, I had used the hotel washing machine for our laundry, carrying it up to the roof to dry on the clothesline.

RJ laughed. "This is Guatemala."

This was an actual house with a full kitchen, a dining area, even a fireplace. Such a pleasant contrast to the rough, two- or three-room cement apartments we had walked through. The rent was 3000 quetzales, or about $300, with the electric and WiFi extra.

"You'll need to get WiFi put in," RJ said, "but I know a guy who can do that."

"How much will it cost?" Bruce asked.

"Oh, a couple hundred Q a month, not much. It's Alex, Bruce, who installed Internet at the hotel. You've met him."

RJ was the only person I ever heard—local, tourist, or expat—who said "Q's." Everyone else used "quetzales," same as the national bird. At first when I called the bills "Q's," vendors looked confused, not understanding. I discovered it was another one of RJ's silly nicknames. Imagine Guatemalans coming to the U.S. and calling dollars "D's." We'd have no idea what they were talking about.

The house was for sale, which bothered Bruce. "What if we move in then someone comes along and buys it?"

According to RJ, the price was too outrageous for anyone to consider. "Morris, the owner, said he'd sell it to us for $72,000. Ridiculous. No one will pay that. Look at the work it needs. The floor tiles are in bad shape. The doors and windows are loose in their frames. Nah, don't worry about it, Bruce. Nobody's going to buy this house."

We left RJ to haggle with Lucas in the living room. Bruce and I wandered again through the rooms, peering into cupboards and closets.

"The price is right," I said.

Bruce agreed. "It's way better than anything else we've seen. I like how far it is from the hotel, gives me space away from work."

"Yeah, we should probably take it. It's dark though, despite so many windows and glass doors."

"It's the dark wood ceiling beams and the walls painted that deep tan."

"It's still cluttered from the last tenants."

"Lucas said his wife would come in and clean before we move in."

"Fair enough. Anyway, I know how to throw out junk and clean house."

"RJ and I looked at some pretty awful places," Bruce said. "I think this is a good deal. It will be nice to have a real home with distance from the workplace."

"Yeah, let's go with it."

Back in the kitchen, Bruce beckoned to RJ. "We'll take it."

"I knew you'd love it. Just wait. I think I can get a better deal for you."

The two friends negotiated while Bruce and I waited on the living room sofa. It was an animated performance of rapid dialogue and emphatic gestures spiced with jokes and good-natured name calling.

Lucas was one of those fit, compact older men one sees throughout Guatemala. Short as all the Maya were, typically five feet or under. At five-two, I often stood taller than the men, a strange sensation for me. He wore a fitted t-shirt tucked into blue jeans. His shoes, like his car, were scuffed and worn. Lucas struck me as a jack-of-all-trades type willing to do any job for the right price. He used his old but functional car for driving people, or at least friends of RJ, to outlying cities. Lucas had brought us to the house like a realtor, yet it turned out that he was also the gardener and general caretaker. RJ said Lucas could bring a load of firewood once we moved in. Was there any job this guy didn't do? I wondered if his scuffed shoes and battered car were merely the sign of a wealthy man who chose not to let the community know his status.

Observing the negotiations, Bruce commented, "It's like a dance. They know their parts, bargaining back and forth, one going this way, the other moves in sync then turns a different direction. Neither one loses the rhythm or lets up on the exchange."

I grew bored with the extended negotiations. "What's the big discussion? We told RJ we want it."

"Lucas gets a commission for signing us on, apparently a good one. RJ figures that gives him some wiggle room to reduce the price."

"Who cares! Let's get the thing done. Besides, what does it matter to RJ? We're the ones paying rent, not him."

"It's the game. RJ likes to play the game, do the dance."

Finally, they finished their dance and Lucas stepped outside while RJ told us the terms. "Your best price comes with a year lease," he explained. "If Morris sells it before the year is up, he gives you two free month's rent. Plus, if you pay three months at a time instead of monthly, Lucas says there's a ten percent discount. Sorry, that's the best I could do."

Bruce and I exchanged glances. "Wish we could afford to get the three-month discount," he said.

"It's okay," I replied. "The monthly rate is still good."

"Everything is laid out in the contract," RJ interjected. "Let's go take care of it. We'll meet Morris at the lawyer's office."

Lawyer's office? "Drop me off at home first, please."

Outside in the garden, Lucas asked me if I liked the house. *"Muy bonita, muy tranquila,"* he said.

I agreed but pointed to the opening in the fence at the back end of the garden, large enough to drive a small car through. It led to a vacant, weedy area and, beyond that, the fence of someone else's property. "What about that? *No es muy seguro.*"

Lucas brushed it off. "Nobody will steal from you. This is a safe town. If bad people come, we take them to the park and set them on fire." He lifted an arm toward the hills and gave a little hop and a laugh, like he was ready to go distribute Maya justice.

Justicia Maya kept out the gangs and thieves who might wander down from Guatemala City. I had heard about two recent incidents. Nobody set on fire, but when someone caught a woman stealing from a vendor, she had to crawl several blocks on her knees before they let her go. Another time, a few outsiders picked a fight at the mercado, and people threw hunks of concrete at them and their car. The police rushed in to protect the men from harm and take them into custody.

After six weeks walking around Panajachel, it felt safe to me. Perhaps Guatemala City was dangerous, but this seemed like a sheltered, comfortable small town. I took Lucas's word that I didn't need to worry about security.

Back in the car, Bruce said to stop at the ATM so he could withdraw cash for the rent.

"Drop me off at home first," I repeated. Paul's apartment was my refuge from the activity on the streets and from RJ's exuberance. Perhaps it was a grief issue, where I needed a quieter environment to process things, but since Becki's funeral, I felt more sensitive to loud noise and laughter.

I tried to tune RJ out when he was at the apartment. Jessica did the same. Neither of us, quiet and reserved as we were, could take much of his loud and lengthy monologues. On one of our recent walks Jessica said, "My goal today is to make it through the entire day without hearing RJ's voice. I need a break from it."

I had laughed at that, understanding perfectly.

"I took a break the other day, and it was nice," she said. "I made Travis leave the room whenever RJ called, because I could still hear his voice through the phone. Even that little bit was too much and gave me a headache."

Apparently, RJ's over-the-top personality was also getting on Bruce's nerves. He came home earlier than usual and on his own.

"You're home early for a change. And no RJ?"

"I think I've had enough of him for one day." He tossed the contract on the coffee table.

I shut my laptop, glanced through the paperwork and handed it back to him. "What a relief to have our house! Here, better put it in a safe place." Not that I had any concerns. Bruce was obsessive about keeping important papers safe. "I'll start dinner early. How about a vegetable omelet?"

"Sounds good, my love."

We ate sitting next to each other on the couch. Bruce finished his omelet and said, "I came straight home after signing the contract."

"You were there this whole time? It was hours! I figured you went to work after."

"Morris was already there, but we had to wait in line for the lawyer or whoever the guy was. Other people were ahead of us, and each group who went into his office took forever."

"I'm glad I didn't go."

"You would've hated it. What a hassle. When we finished, I told RJ I was cutting out early, and I came home."

"I bet you're exhausted, having to sit around and wait for hours."

"It wasn't that so much as earlier. When we stopped at the ATM, I withdrew the cash and RJ grabbed it right out of my hand."

"What? That's rather dramatic even for him."

"That was only the beginning. He played this game about how Lucas should take us out to lunch once the deal is done. Lucas gets this big commission so why not show his gratitude by treating us to lunch? I didn't get all the dialogue, but I got enough. Along with the expressions and posturing, I could tell what he was up to."

Patient Bruce rarely let anyone's behavior annoy him, unless he deemed it inappropriate with a clear line crossed. "Why does he have to carry on like that?" he continued. "It was embarrassing. Why not accept that Lucas earned his commission and quit trying to get something out of it for himself?"

"The culture, I guess. It's their way. At least, it seems to be RJ's way." I set our empty plates on the coffee table, wishing for dessert. We could share a pack of Paul's cookies.

"Well, it made me uncomfortable. Lucas wanted nothing to do with it, of course. He wasn't going to take us out to lunch! Why should he?"

"I guess Lucas won that contest."

"They kept going back and forth on who was cheap, who was going to do what, who owed who what. I was fed up with it, just wanted to come home and get a break from RJ's antics." He crumpled a napkin, took aim, and tossed it on his plate.

PART TWO

Barrio Norte

Better is an handful with quietness,
than both the hands full with travail and vexation of spirit.
Ecclesiastes 4:4

7

At Home in Guatemala

She looketh well to the ways of her household,
and eateth not the bread of idleness.
Psalm 31:27

We moved out of Paul's apartment several days before his return. Bruce, Travis and Dago came with RJ's truck to load it up and unload at the new house. After they left, I finished cleaning. Enjoying the peaceful stillness, I was in no hurry to go. I began a thank you note to Paul. He had mentioned in conversation that despite a religious background, he was no longer a believer. With respect for his chosen ideology, I sought to share how his home had been my spiritual retreat as I grieved for my sister. To me, it was like a temple, a place of quiet worship where I had come closer to God.

Taped to the wall above Paul's desk were his handwritten instructions to anyone who might find him unresponsive or lifeless. Due to this and to his health concerns, I knew that death was often on his mind. In my letter, I wrote about prayer and faith and how in his home I had sensed the presence of my loved ones on the other side. I thanked him for providing the environment where this healing was possible.

When I finished, I laid the letter open on his desk. I left my keys next to Bruce's on the kitchen counter. Setting the door to lock, I stepped out and shut it behind me. I walked through town and up the hill to our new home.

Later that week, Paul met me leaving the hotel. "I've been looking for you, Karen. I thought I'd run into you in town. You can be a hard woman to find!"

"I haven't been out much lately with moving into our house," I explained. "Was everything okay with your place? Did we leave it in good order?"

"Oh, yes, everything looked great. It's not that." He hesitated, and his eyes teared up. "I want to thank you for the note you left. I think I mentioned that my brother is a pastor. I was raised a Christian but am no longer a believer. In fact, I've called myself an atheist for years."

Perhaps I had shared too much, been insensitive and upset him.

Paul continued, "I understood everything you wrote . . . and I . . . I want you to know . . ." His voice faltered. "My health isn't that good. I don't know how much time I have . . . and your letter has given me great comfort." He asked if he could give me a hug and I said of course.

"Thank you for that letter. Thank you, thank you," he repeated as he clung to me.

Jessica and I had often joked about how much I liked the packets of sandwich cookies in Paul's cupboard. How I kept eating them. Replace, eat, rinse, and repeat. She said, "It's probably because with everything so different, you need to have something familiar and comforting."

When I think about Guatemala these many years later, I wish I could find those little packs of cookies again somewhere. They would remind me of Panajachel and of Paul and of the sacred month I spent in his apartment when heaven seemed so near.

⟨⟩

The first week in our house, the stove ran out of gas. A tienda across the street managed propane refills. You go tell them you're out and they call someone with a truck who appears soon after to fill your tank. Within the hour, we had propane again.

This tienda also had twenty-liter *garafones* of drinking water. The first time we emptied ours, Bruce went to exchange it for a full one. Since they are quite heavy, and seeing Bruce was gray-haired and not that fit, one of their young men stepped in. He insisted on bringing the jug across the street, up the lane, and into our house where he placed it on the dispenser. We used one or two of these water jugs a week, depending on if we had family around or not, and we always got the same personalized service from our neighborhood tienda. Their wide open doorway faced our lane, and they saw us come and go. They were watchful neighbors we could count on, providing us with a sense of security.

It was mid-March, six weeks since Bruce and I had arrived in Guatemala. *Semana Santa* was weeks away, when tourists poured into town on the days leading up to Easter Sunday. Our son Billy was coming the week before *Semana Santa* with as many friends as wanted to join him. Last I heard, five had expressed interest but only Billy and one other had bought their tickets. They would be Casa Colonial's first paying guests.

RJ saw dollar signs around the words *Semana Santa*. "Billy and his friends get first pick of rooms, then we'll fill the others," he said. "People get desperate as the week progresses. They pay 300 Q a head just to sleep on the floor."

Plumbing and electric were the two big hurdles to a smooth opening. RJ had recurring troubles with the cistern and its pumping system. How often I saw him half submerged in that deep pit in the back room, fiddling with pipes and pumps, the electricity shut off so as not to electrocute himself. More than once when I had carried our laundry in to wash at the hotel, Bruce greeted me with, "Electricity is off, Karen. RJ is in the cistern working on the pump."

At his most desperate, RJ called a technician from Quetzaltenango two hours away to come and assist with the latest plumbing catastrophe. The fellow stayed over in one of the rooms until the job was done.

Living farther away in Barrio Norte provided us with some distance from the drama and tension leading up to the Easter deadline. I stopped taking our laundry to the hotel. RJ didn't accompany Bruce home every night as when we were down the street. Our living space was no longer consumed by animated business discussions.

After Bruce left for work in the mornings, I did household tasks and opened work email. Afternoons, I dug into my novel. On laundry days, I wrote where I could see our fresh, clean laundry drying in the afternoon breeze. In my previous existence, I never would have imagined myself regularly handwashing full loads at an outdoor sink, let alone enjoying it. Washing clothes at the *pila* kept my hands busy while my brain worked out problems, either with my book or real life. Time disappeared in the sunny secluded patio with its high privacy walls.

Long flowing curtains graced the glass doors in our bedroom. Late afternoons, I sat on our bed with the door open to the front garden and watched the curtains drifting as I studied Spanish.

The other bedroom, which faced the back patio, was a favorite writing spot. There, I could look out the window at a profundity of life. Once I watched a spider build its web right outside the glass, fascinated as anyone will be who has the patience to witness a spider at work.

An enormous plant with beautiful red flowers grew close to the window and brushed against it. Like a gift, the flowers attracted hummingbirds. These mesmerizing tiny birds varied in color and in shimmering luminescence as well as in size, some as large as a sparrow and others so small they looked more like hornets than birds. Like the Maya, the hummingbirds were small and active, always in motion. They could have been the national bird instead of the quetzal. In my years in Guatemala, I saw dozens of hummingbirds but never a quetzal.

Travis and Jessica had moved recently as well. They rented a place owned by Pedro the van driver, in one of the maze-like alleyways several blocks from our neighborhood tienda. Pedro, his wife, and two little kids occupied their house, with this rental property behind their gate and up a flight of cement stairs. It badly needed work. The kitchen had only a sink, the cement rooms had no doors.

Travis and RJ devoted hours to cleaning and painting, then hung curtains for doors. They built a table and shelves for the kitchen. RJ had the idea of attaching high bamboo poles on the surrounding patio wall for privacy. He went to buy them somewhere near Sololá, then brought them back in his truck and went right to work on the privacy wall. Thanks to RJ's leadership and construction skills, as well as his tireless energy, these rooms became habitable. This was fit in among the many other tasks RJ and Travis completed for opening weekend.

After moving in, Jessica routinely stopped by with Emree and her stroller. The intercom Lucas had pointed out when we viewed the place never did work, although the buzzer did. When I heard it around one, I knew it was them. Down the lane I went to swing open the wide metal door and go for our walk.

Since Travis and Jessica lived close and I now had a real kitchen, we gathered again for the occasional meal. I planned a birthday party in March for Bruce; RJ brought the cake. On Sundays, I invited everyone over for dinner after church.

RJ thought I should hire household help. "You don't have to clean or cook or wash clothes, Karen. You can hire someone to do it for practically nothing. Plenty of expats have live-in maids." As hard as he worked on manual labor building or fixing things, RJ couldn't imagine anyone wanting to do menial household tasks. "If Sally and I lived here, I wouldn't let her do dishes. I'd hire a woman."

He introduced me to his friend Alicia, who wanted the job as my housekeeper. He arranged for her to make a dinner for all of us plus Alicia's family: her husband Ernesto and the two kids, thirteen-year-old Jacki and eighteen-year-old Felix. "A get-acquainted dinner," RJ said. "A trial to see if you like her."

RJ and Alicia decided what to serve, and she gave me a list of ingredients to buy at the mercado. The price came to 200 quetzales for chicken, vegetables, rice, and a few other items. I had sticker shock—two hundred quetzales for one meal? RJ and Travis brought in chairs from somewhere and set up a dining area outdoors in our garden. A huge production of time and money for such a simple thing as deciding whether to hire a housekeeper, but that was RJ. He never did anything halfway. It was all or nothing.

I welcomed everyone in Spanish and asked Travis to bless the food, as he had basic skills in the language. After my welcome, RJ said, "Wow, Karen, your Spanish has really improved. I better be careful what I say when you're around." He thought the meal was a bargain. "Look at all this food! There's plenty to eat later, and don't you think it's good? Isn't she a great cook? Imagine having meals like this every night for dinner, Karen. You could if you hired Alicia to cook for you."

I hired her to clean twice a week but not to cook. I liked making dinner for Bruce and me and had my own way of doing it, often simple meatless meals to save on cost. Groceries weren't as cheap as RJ seemed to think. Back in Utah, he said we could easily manage on "a thousand Q a month," or about $150. I struggled to keep expenses under 3000. We had food, rent, electricity, WiFi, and propane. Every ninety days, there was visa renewal, about 900 quetzales for two of us. We managed, but there was none of this "living like kings," as RJ had claimed.

As glad as we were to have found this house at this price, it suffered from a lack of natural light and from a termite infestation in the wood beams. Their debris dropped down from the ceiling; the tile floors needed constant sweeping. We regularly heard sounds of animal life on the roof.

Lucas had said he'd come twice a week to trim the garden and take the trash barrels down the long lane and out to the street. Instead, he showed up two or three times a month and never took the trash. Morris was paying him to care for the property twice weekly, but he said Morris was *barato*, cheap. Instead, Lucas did what I soon learned was typical among laborers, where they cut their time and effort to fit the pay. Not everyone did this, certainly not Dago. Alicia did though.

She and I agreed on so much a day, two days a week, at a rate of seven quetzales an hour for eight hours. She asked for ten an hour, but RJ said no, don't pay her that. Seven is good and bring her a treat or a meal now and then. Instead, Alicia finished in five hours rather than eight, thus boosting her hourly rate to ten since the custom was to pay by the day instead of the hour.

When RJ heard this, he said to pay her less for cheating and taking advantage of me. I couldn't have done that. Alicia did a good job and I liked her. Besides, she doubled as my Spanish tutor with her patient, friendly conversation as I stumbled to express myself.

When Lucas did come, he had the unnerving practice of glancing at me through the glass as he worked. One morning, I was in the living room with my laptop open, trying to ignore Lucas, when I heard louder than usual animal noises. It was a squirrel in the hall ceiling poking away to bite and claw an opening in the rafters. I watched with interest until he broke through to the inside.

I rushed out and called Lucas to come see, there's an animal in the house. I didn't know the Spanish word for squirrel, but Lucas came right away. *Animales* was the common reference to insects, rodents or any creature in or near the house that did not belong.

Lucas pulled the ladder around to the roof to assess the situation. He had grandchildren and a few wrinkles, but his fitness level and agility seemed undeterred by age. It was difficult to guess the ages of these local men; they stayed thin and muscular well past middle age. Lucas scrambled back down the ladder, gathered some scattered pieces of wood in the carport, and carried them up to the roof. Nailing them down, he closed the animal entryway.

Another time I saw what looked like a long, fuzzy caterpillar on the back patio. Fortunately, Lucas was there cutting the grass and trimming shrubs with his machete. When I showed him the snake-like creature, he said it was *muy peligroso* and hacked it to pieces with his machete. The pieces kept wiggling as, using the machete, Lucas flipped them into a plastic bag. *"No se preocupa. Terminado,"* he reassured me and carried the bag away.

When Alicia came, she did the housework and laundry. Sometimes her daughter Jackie showed up instead, when RJ called Alicia in to clean at the hotel. At those times, I had Jackie clean house and later, I washed the clothes. I couldn't bring myself to let a thirteen-year-old girl handle our underwear. Jacki worked faster than her mom. She finished everything in three hours, from nine to twelve, and rarely said a word. Shy and pretty, she wore stylish clothes—nice jeans, good athletic shoes, and feminine blouses. Both Alicia and Jacki dressed American style rather than in the traditional Maya skirts and blouses.

On Alicia's cleaning days, she rang the buzzer around nine, took an hour at noon to go home and fix lunch for Felix and Jacki, then came back to work until three or four. She swept and mopped the floors, washed our clothes and bedding in the *pila,* and cleaned the bathroom and kitchen. Before leaving, she made the beds with the freshly laundered sheets and set the folded clean clothes on top of the master bed. If I needed her to do anything extra, like clean inside the refrigerator or wash the curtains, she fit that in, too.

Alicia enjoyed conversation despite my limited Spanish. She asked questions about my family and talked about hers. She told stories about local life and about Jacki's teacher at school who charged money for grades. I wasn't sure I understood her properly. The teacher charged his students for grades?

"*Sí*. When they have a test, they pay him to not get a bad grade. What are we supposed to do? We give our kids money for the teacher, and he lets them pass their classes."

"I thought public education was free in Guatemala!"

"We don't have to pay tuition, but we pay for books and uniforms. And for the teacher when he is like that one. It costs a lot for our kids to get an education. When the teacher comes to school with a new pair of shoes or driving a new car, the kids joke about it. 'There goes our teacher with the car my mom bought for him.' 'No, I get better grades than you. My mom bought him the car. Your mom bought his jacket.'"

American parents would storm the principal's office or the school board, write letters and make phone calls to expose any teacher who extorted money for grades. Here, they felt powerless to change the system. It was corrupt and always had been, no matter what they did or how they voted. So, they adapted and made jokes.

I watched Alicia mop the floors with a broom wrapped in a wet towel or t-shirt, sprinkling Fabuloso as she went. She didn't use a mop or a bucket, instead rinsing the shirt out in the *pila* and going over the floor again and again until it rinsed clear water. The Fabuloso filled the house with its clean, fresh scent.

My questions about local culture or shopping or what to pay for a tuk tuk, Alicia answered with elaborate gusto and a few gossipy stories tossed in. I learned that the Maya will not pass through a group of people. "If you go between, you take on their bad luck. We walk around instead, even if we have to cross the street. Let them keep their own bad luck."

RJ eventually fired Alicia from the hotel due to gossiping. Bruce explained what happened. "I guess she told Dago how much RJ was going to pay her once the hotel was up and running.

How he promised her a salary and a retirement plan, and that he'd give her whole family jobs."

"Do you think it's true? Did he really promise those things?"

"Who knows," Bruce replied. "Either way, the end result is the same. Dago mentioned it to RJ and that was it for Alicia."

RJ kept his employees in line. If they didn't measure up, they were gone, and somebody else showed up in their place. Whatever he promised Alicia, he couldn't have her bragging about it to Dago, who no doubt wondered why he didn't have a salary and a retirement plan.

RJ made promises too easily and broke them as easily. He had fine qualities—like his willingness to help a friend without thinking twice and his outstanding work ethic—but trustworthiness was not one of them. At our dinner with Alicia's family, RJ introduced her son Felix as "the one who will run tours for the hotel." That sounded like a commitment, but for whatever reason it never happened.

I had considered letting Alicia go or at least cutting her hours to save money. I enjoyed doing laundry outdoors and could certainly clean my own house. After RJ fired her, I couldn't do it. Besides, I liked her cheerful countenance and talkative ways. I learned from Alicia, and I respected her as a fellow wife and mother. She kept asking me to please convince RJ to hire Jacki at the hotel. Jacki had afternoon school and could work mornings. In Pana, school was half days only. Kids went in the mornings or the afternoons but generally not both. This allowed them to take jobs or to help at home. I had no influence with RJ and stayed out of his business. Besides, he wanted nothing more to do with Alicia or her family, although I didn't tell her that part.

Whenever she mentioned it, I laughed it off. "It wouldn't do any good. He never listens to me. I'm only the mother-in-law. I don't have anything to do with the hotel."

It would've helped their family for Jacki to get that job. Working parents in Guatemala could barely afford food. A liter of milk cost ten quetzales or about an hour's wages. Imagine in the States working an hour for a quart of milk. A ten-ounce bottle of Pepsi cost seven quetzales. The abundance of fresh fruits and vegetables was for the middle class, not the poor or even the working poor. They ate tortillas, beans, and rice. The very poor and unemployed ate little besides tortillas with salt.

I generally supported local merchants at the mercado, except those who raised their prices for me. What expats call the "Gringo tax." When I complained about it to Alicia, she laughed. "They see you coming with your expensive purse, and the price goes up."

I stopped carrying my nice leather bags and changed to a backpack or my Guatemala shoulder bag. Nobody stays very long in Panajachel without buying one of those colorful, woven bags from local vendors. Bruce and I each had one. He took his Key Bank backpack whenever he went out, except to church. Then he left the backpack home and carried his scriptures, Kindle Fire, notepad, and pens in his Guatemala bag. He said it was nicer and more appropriate for church than the backpack, which no longer looked nice and new. Besides, these bags were what the other men at church carried. The women took their best purses to church, American style.

Looking American, vendors assumed I had plenty of money. It felt strange to have others think I was rich. I had never had much cash in my wallet, never had money left at the end of the month. How could I, with ten children? What didn't go for food went for everything else.

It bothered Jessica that people thought she was a rich American. "We live like the locals, in three cement rooms and an open patio with no privacy. We have curtains for doors. We pay rent to Pedro. He is nice and polite, but his wife pops upstairs whenever she feels like it. She doesn't say anything, just peers through our gate. Once she came through and looked in our bathroom while I was on the toilet! RJ pays Travis Guatemalan wages, and we can barely afford food. I wish people on the street would stop asking me to buy their stuff."

I bargained for the best prices at the mercado. "They expect you to bargain. Never pay what they ask," RJ said. Shopping at the Dispensa was easier since prices were set, and you paid the total at the register on the way out. Once a cashier charged me for four rotisserie chickens. It didn't sink in until I moved on and examined the unusually high receipt. I found a manager, pointed it out, and my money was refunded.

RJ said it was deliberate, and the cashier meant to pocket that 600 quetzales. I needed to count my change and pay better attention. "You'll see, once you've been here as long as I have. You'll see I'm not just saying this, I'm not exaggerating. You think they're your friends, how they smile and act so friendly, but they aren't your friends. Don't be fooled, Karen."

RJ's warnings and advice ran like a continuous thread woven in and out through those early months in Guatemala. We all got a little tired of hearing him carry on, and so like teenagers with a hovering parent, we learned not to tell him anything. Otherwise, we got the usual lecture. "See! See! That's what I've been saying. You can't trust them."

I was horrible at counting change and after the rotisserie chicken incident, I asked Bruce to handle the cash whenever we shopped together. If he got shorted, he noticed and called them on it. This kept us from losing a certain amount of slippery quetzales each month.

⁓

Since RJ's hotel tour guide job never happened, Felix wanted to go to America and find work. Alicia said, "I talk to him every morning to keep him from leaving."

I was confused. "Does he have his plane ticket?" If he already bought a ticket, why does she try to convince him not to go? If he doesn't have it, he probably needs to earn the money first. In that case, why is it a daily concern, since Felix didn't have a job?

"No, he doesn't have a ticket. How could he? *Son carrísimos!* He will walk. But I don't want him to go. *Es muy peligroso.*"

It suddenly hit home, blind and naïve as I was, this vast difference in our worlds. "You mean every morning Felix wakes up and wants to walk to the United States?"

"Yes. I argue with him every day. It's a bad idea."

"Does he know the way?"

She looked at me with wide-eyed amusement. "*Se va al norte.* Go to Mexico, then to the U.S. There are roads, buses, and then you pay people to get you through the desert and across the border."

"What people?" I was curious about how the details of this process would work for a kid like Felix.

"*Mucha gente.* Very bad people. *Es muy peligroso. Y el desierto es muy peligroso tambien.*" Alicia gestured in a vague way, either not knowing details or figuring they were obvious. I filled in the blanks with my own secondhand information supplemented with imagination.

Eighteen-year-old Felix desperately wants to head north, without money, passport, or visa. Once near the border, he will find his way over like others have done. In the U.S. he can find work and earn good money, if he doesn't get caught and sent back. What kind of hopelessness inspires a clean-cut, promising young man like that to set out one day and head north, risking the elements, crime and cartels, then cross illegally and hope it works out? If it doesn't, he could get disillusioned and swept into gang life.

Whenever I asked Alicia why things are so bad in Guatemala, whether it was the schools or no jobs or low pay, her answer was always the same. *Corrupción.* "The government is very corrupt.

We vote in a new government, and they are worse than the old one. The corruption never goes away."

Felix was a nice kid, polite and wanting work like his sister Jacki. Alicia's husband Ernesto had a job selling handmade native quilts to vendors. Felix had been in school, studying for a career in hospitality until he ran out of tuition money. Of course, his mom didn't want him walking to America. She would have fretted day and night, always worried.

Alicia eventually found employment with the city, an eight to five schedule Monday through Friday, a much better opportunity for her. She offered to clean for me on Saturdays and have Jacki come other days when needed. This arrangement worked for a while but in the end, I told Alicia we would take a break, that I wanted to do the work myself. If I changed my mind, I would let her know.

Afterwards, we remained friendly, stopping to chat for a few minutes whenever we saw each other in town. Our many conversations at home, besides improving my Spanish, taught me more about Guatemala than anything I might have read in a book.

8
The Tour Guide

A soft answer turneth away wrath;
but grievous words stir up anger.
Proverbs 15:1

When Billy saw our Barrio Norte house, he said, "You know how people say they're going to move to another country and get a house and live the simple life? *This* is the kind of house they're talking about."

Billy and his friend Larry, the first guests at Casa Colonial, flew in a couple weeks before Easter week. Billy had lined up several friends to make the trip, but in the end, Larry was the one who panned out. Pedro drove RJ, Bruce, and me to pick them up. Pedro's van—clean, comfortable, safe, and happy—signified family visits. First Billy, and then Sean and Erin coming in May. They already had their tickets.

My heart sang to see Billy and his friend exit the airport. They settled in Pedro's van for the scenic and companionable ride to Pana. Our tall, handsome son in Guatemala! I couldn't get enough of looking at him. He introduced Larry, a friendly guy with graying hair and a relaxed personality. Larry wore jeans, sport shoes and a button-up, short-sleeved shirt. In other words, dressed exactly like Bruce. Including the pen and small notebook in his shirt pocket. Larry was a thinner, younger version of Billy's dad, with surprisingly similar facial features and the same pleasant expression. Billy's dad and Billy's friend could've been brothers. They were instant friends.

Larry was an accountant nearing retirement age, obsessed with numbers and how much things cost. He frequently checked the money exchange app on his phone. On the way, he asked a few polite questions about our living expenses. Bruce and I were happy to share details, always willing to talk about how much cheaper and better we could live here than back home.

"Some might say it's exploitation, that American retirees are somehow victimizing a poorer country," I said. "I don't see it like that. Their economy helps us, and our U.S. dollars help them. Expats are essentially tourists that stay longer and spend more money."

Worried about his retirement fund, Larry said, "It might be nice to live somewhere like this, where money will go further."

Billy laughed at that. "Larry, you have more money saved than anyone I know. You could retire tomorrow and never get to the end of it."

RJ suggested we stop in Antigua, thirty minutes outside of Guatemala City, to visit a historical site, formerly a church, called Santo Domingo. Pedro pulled up to the street in front. We unloaded and agreed on ninety minutes before meeting him back outside.

Besides a luxury hotel with extensive public gardens, Santo Domingo hosted art displays, shops, an upscale restaurant, even an underground tomb with a skeleton laid out on its bed. It was a perfect stopover to meander through after a long plane ride. It focused on the Spanish era history of Guatemala, in contrast to the Lake Atitlán region which was all about the Maya.

As we viewed the lovely gardens and art displays, both modern and historical, Bruce and I resolved to make this a regular stop for anyone who visited.

RJ wasn't as enthusiastic, although coming here had been his idea. "Once they see this place, Pana and our hotel will look bad in comparison," he said.

But Panajachel and Antigua were different kinds of towns and so were the two hotels. This one was built up over decades with obvious wealth behind it. RJ's was a modest operation with no parking, no gardens or courtyards, and small rooms. This hotel charged $200 a night with every amenity. RJ charged forty dollars a night for a tiny room with sparse furniture, no TV, and street noise.

Initially, he had wanted to charge fifty, but Bruce talked him down to meet demand. "Maybe once people learn about it, but first we need to price competitively."

To my dismay, I soon learned that RJ was charging Billy and Larry forty *each* per night. Or eighty dollars for one shared room with two twin beds. For *family*, and before it opened. Bruce was aware of how much Billy got charged for the room. When I asked why he let RJ get by with that, he replied, "I'm choosing my battles. I don't like it either, but I can't challenge RJ on every little thing I don't agree with. Billy and Larry seem fine with it."

RJ made money off Billy and Larry with other schemes as well. Their third day, he arranged for a private boat tour to villages around the lake. Bruce and I went along, our first time on one of these boat tours that RJ praised as "a great deal for our hotel guests." The cost was fifty dollars per person, such a steep price that Travis and Jessica, as much as they wanted to go, had to decline.

At the first stop, RJ led us on a short hike through a wooded path that swerved up from the dock to a resort overlooking the lake. He took us around their garden and showed us their outdoor yoga room. We relaxed for a bit on a patio overlooking the water, then RJ suggested breakfast.

Larry said, "Well, I could use a coffee."

RJ herded us over to the restaurant. He raved about the quality of the food and said everyone should order something. Bruce never needed much encouragement to eat, but Billy and Larry seemed hesitant, having eaten before the tour. I rarely ate breakfast and ordered a diet Coke.

RJ kept insisting. "Their food is so good, you have to try it. Give you a taste of a real Guatemala breakfast." Finally, Billy acquiesced as did Larry. As always, RJ ordered for the table in his loud, fast, good ol' boy Spanish.

As they finished eating, RJ casually remarked to Billy and Larry, "You guys are paying for my breakfast, right? Because I'm the tour guide, and it's typical for guests to pay for their tour guide's meal."

Billy and his friend both kind of stuttered and looked at each other. "Sure, I guess," Billy said. He got up to pay the ticket.

I went with him to cover our share. What did RJ mean, saying he is the tour guide? He's part of the family and besides that, he's the hotel owner, not the tour guide. Not to mention, Billy had invested in the hotel, loaning money to help with construction.

"This isn't right," I fumed at the counter. "Dad will make sure the hotel reimburses you for RJ's food."

"Ah, it's okay," Billy replied. "It just took me by surprise. If you're going to expect someone to pay for your meal, then establish it in the beginning."

After breakfast, while touring the village, Larry bought a painting from a vendor RJ introduced him to. A few hours later in another village, RJ took us to a must-see hotel. We walked up three floors to a restaurant that had two walls of windows overlooking Lake Atitlán. This breathtaking sight gave us a clear view of the three imposing volcanoes, San Pedro, Atitlán and Toliman.

RJ gestured to a table by the windows and suggested we get drinks, since it hadn't been that long since breakfast. Then he looked at the menu and ordered an extra large pizza.

When the waiter left, I blurted, "So, RJ. Are you a tour guide right now who expects other people to pay for this? Or are you a hotel owner showing your guests a nice time? Or are you part of the family where we're equal?"

RJ gave me a sharp look. His eyes narrowed. "The reason I said that at breakfast is to show you and Bruce how the system works. It's customary to pay for the tour guide's meal." He didn't speak angrily, more like a parent or teacher instructing a child.

"I get that, only you aren't the tour guide. You're part of the family." I waved my arm in an inclusive gesture. "We are family here."

Billy lifted an eyebrow in curiosity and gave an amused smile, as though to say, "Well. What is happening here?"

"Not to mention, you're the hotel owner," I continued. "Maybe you should have bought *their* breakfast to show appreciation for your first guests."

Billy interjected, "I didn't mind paying for breakfast."

Larry added with a smile, "Everything is so inexpensive anyway. The whole bill wouldn't have bought one breakfast at a good restaurant in the U.S. Plus, we have a gorgeous setting. That's worth a lot. In fact, let me pay for the pizza when it comes."

Bruce pushed up his glasses and rubbed his eyes, rubbed his chin. Bruce sign language for, This is uncomfortable and I don't know what to do or say.

In clipped tones, RJ said, "This is Guatemala. Things are different and you and Bruce need to learn how it works."

"But you're setting the rules and changing them where nobody knows what's what. Are you part of the family? The hotel owner? That's what we thought, then suddenly you claim to be the tour guide and say your guests should buy you breakfast."

The pizza came as a welcome interruption to everyone but RJ and me. We locked eyes in a standoff. His flashing black eyes challenged me to go ahead, keep talking.

I tried to diffuse his anger. "I didn't mean to upset you. You're an important part of the family. We wouldn't be here if it weren't for you." Unfortunately, this came out as condescending.

RJ shook his head in disgust and gave a snort of derision. Shoving himself away from the table, he headed down the hall toward the kitchen. I heard him talking to the workers in Spanish, probably complaining about his *suegra* and poking fun at me.

Having skipped breakfast, I helped myself to a slice of pizza. The others, who had eaten two breakfasts, proceeded to wolf down their share. It was noon, when the morning fog had dissipated and left a random sprinkling of fluffy white clouds drifting across the vivid blue sky.

Billy and Larry engaged Bruce in conversation about the beauty of the area, how perfect the climate. "I dream about retiring to a place like this," Larry said. "My job is too stressful since the company was bought out. I'd like to live in peace and tranquility somewhere nice and inexpensive."

Bruce mentioned how wonderful the people are, concluding with, "You couldn't do better than retiring in Guatemala, and you could certainly do worse."

RJ returned and picked up the bill. "I'm paying for the pizza."

Larry pulled out his wallet. "No, I'll cover it, RJ. You didn't eat any."

RJ ignored him, lifted his bag off the chair and slipped it onto his shoulder. Larry set several bills on the table. "Here, let me at least contribute."

He left Larry's cash where it lay and huffed off to the cashier. We followed him down to the street, where the boat tour operator waited. As we explored the town, RJ was silent and angry, finding reasons to leave us alone with the boat tour operator—the guy we had originally thought was the tour guide. This fellow took us to different sites through the town, sharing information in Spanish which I roughly translated. RJ showed up at one point, told us when to meet back at the boat then took off again.

⌣⟶

The next day, I regretted my behavior and wished I had kept my big mouth shut. There we were, the five of us sitting around a table in this idyllic spot. The wide windows overlooked the still lake, misty blue and green, a tranquil setting to inspire pleasant conversation and companionship. Instead, I shatter the peace by calling RJ out on his silliness. If only I had taken a few minutes to think it over. His behavior did not always line up with his words. He liked to get free meals and other perks—to him, a harmless game. Why should anyone mind? Why should I mind? Nobody takes kindly to getting publicly criticized, especially not by their mother-in-law. Especially not a man, and not an alpha male like RJ Martín.

I went to the hotel to apologize. I found him on the third floor, sanding wood trim. He glanced up as I approached.

"I came to apologize for yesterday," I began. "I shouldn't have made such a big deal out of everything. I'm really sorry."

His mouth was a tight line, and he avoided eye contact. I waited, determined to stay calm, to let him have his say and not interrupt or argue. The opposite of yesterday.

Finally, he broke the silence. "This is how it works. You pay for the tour guide's meal."

"Yeah," I said.

"And when you take someone out and they buy something, you get a cut later from the vendor."

"Why would I want a cut from the vendor?"

"It's the way things are done. You're helping your guests by getting them a better price. When the vendor gives you a cut of the sale, you can give it away later if you don't want to keep it."

"You got a cut on Larry's painting?"

"Sure, and I intended to give it back to Larry. But when you started in with your stuff, I decided to keep the hundred I got. Why should I do anything for this family when that's how you see me?"

He must also have received a sizable kickback from the private boat owner he arranged to take us around to the villages. No wonder the price had been so high.

"When your sister comes to visit you," he continued, "you'll take her to San Juan to buy a painting. You'll get to know the artists beforehand and when you go there, they'll give her a better deal and give you some cash on the back end. You can keep the money for your trouble or give it to her later. Or buy her lunch or whatever you want to do."

"I don't think that's how I will handle things with Julie. Besides, I don't know anyone in San Juan, and I can't see myself going over there to meet people."

"Why not? It's how things are done. You'll learn. These people expect to share the costs of doing business with those who bring them deals. If you and Bruce expect to live here, you both need to learn how it works."

It seemed dishonest, especially with family, but I listened politely. When he finished, I apologized again. He snorted and grimaced and went back to sanding.

Downstairs, Billy was in the lobby with Bruce and Travis. "Hey, Mom," he called out. "Dad said you know where I can exchange more of my dollars for quetzales."

"Sure, my favorite little money exchange shop. Come on, I'll walk you over. I want to talk to you anyway."

When we exited the hotel, I brought up yesterday's incident and my recent conversation upstairs, including the part about RJ taking a cut of Larry's purchase. "I shouldn't have said what I did yesterday. I regret the whole thing."

"Except that everything you said was true, Mom. You wanted RJ to be clear about things. I don't mind anyone making a little extra money on the side, like he did with Larry's painting. Or no doubt with the boat operator. But he should have been open and upfront about it. He should have established earlier about paying for breakfast, for instance. Otherwise, it seems sleazy and sneaky and like my friend and I are getting scammed by my brother-in-law."

"That was my whole point! I tried to get him to understand but instead I made him mad at me forever. He saw it as disrespecting him in front of everyone. I can't blame him for being upset and angry."

"Yeah, probably would have been wise to back down when you saw his reaction instead of keeping at it like you did." Billy let out a chuckle. "Our family is used to your Mama Bear approach, and none of us are bothered by it. But RJ felt attacked and bit back."

"I should've remembered what Dad always says—'It doesn't cost anything to be kind.'"

Long after Billy and Larry had left, RJ avoided me for weeks. He no longer came to the house, and he skipped our dinners and gatherings. I called Sally for input. Apologizing had not changed anything. What else should I do?

"I don't think there's anything you can do about it, Mom. RJ holds a grudge forever." She paused. "I wish he could learn the meaning of forgiveness, that he can be forgiven and also forgive others, but it isn't something he understands. Too bad, since he'd be a lot happier if he could."

"I should have known better. Remember that time he got upset about the ketchup? He was mad because I handed him the nearly used up one from the fridge instead of the new one on the counter. He thought I was disrespecting him. He's sensitive to that sort of thing."

"He also worries that you and Dad judge him for not having a job to support me, and instead my job supports him and the hotel."

"Not at all! Casa Colonial is your shared business. His labor is his investment in its future. It's not like he sits there and does nothing. He's working constantly. Dad and I both respect him for that. We always have."

"I know that but he's still insecure about it. He feels like the man should support his wife, like Dad always has for you and our family. He really wants to make this business successful where he can finally get free of Panajachel and work in LA. He doesn't like that I have to work so hard."

Sally had mentioned this before. RJ's sensitivity to respect about employment and status was no doubt tangled up with his money issues. He could be very complex at times.

"My worry is one day I might say or do something where I'll fall off the pedestal and RJ will never forgive me," she said. "But he swears 'that will never happen because you always do the right thing.' That's what he says."

Sally gave me some parting advice. "Stay away from the hotel, don't give any opinions about the business or anything he does. Keep inviting him to dinners. If he doesn't come, send someone to the hotel with food. Eventually, he will come round. He won't forgive you or forget what happened, but maybe he will at least loosen up on his anger and hurt."

I followed her advice. After a few weeks of this, RJ must have given up his resentment since he no longer gave me dirty looks or avoided family dinners. It took longer, however, before he would speak to me again.

9
Nesting

Wait on the Lord:
be of good courage, and he shall strengthen thine heart.
Wait, I say, on the Lord.
Psalm 27:14

Sally wanted her husband back. In every Skype call with her dad, she repeated the same refrain. "Once the hotel opens and things settle down, then RJ returns to California and Dad, you run the hotel." This was, of course, the plan from the beginning. They had all agreed to it. Bruce had a list of things to focus on "once RJ leaves." After nearly six months on the job, he was ready to take over the work he had come to do.

But RJ lingered. Out of the empty framework of cement and plaster rooms, he had built an operating hotel with white pillars and patios on three floors. Tropical greenery in ceramic pots accented the open spaces. He had named it well. Casa Colonial. The colonial look echoed Antigua with its Spanish architecture. *Casa*, Spanish for house, added poetry and a sense of coziness. If it were me, I'd have lingered too, wanting to oversee the fruits of my labor. But it frustrated Bruce.

Billy and Larry enjoyed their stay, except for flooding in one of the empty rooms and subsequent shutting off water and electricity. Within twenty-four hours, however, it was back on with no further incidents, the troublesome cistern functioning and fully repaired. As the first paid guest, Billy gave a positive report. "Kind of like going to a live performance and everything behind the scenes is chaos. But the audience in front of the curtain doesn't see that. When the curtain is lifted, they see what they're supposed to see. We had a perfectly decent, relaxed stay. No complaints whatsoever."

Semana Santa brought in a few guests, but nothing like RJ had visualized with rooms overflowing and money rolling in. Good thing too, because his nerves couldn't have taken it. He showed visible distress when inquiring visitors came in. Awkward and nervous, like he didn't know what to do or how to act—jovial and friendly or professional and businesslike?

Bailey, the starved puppy he had rescued from the street two years earlier, hovered near, sensing her owner's tension. "Hey, Bailey, it's okay, girl." Petting Bailey, introducing her to people as though they had walked in to meet his dog rather than to ask about a room. Then he disappeared while Bruce and Dago handled the inquiries. No doubt leaving the confused people to wonder, Who the heck was that guy? And why did he introduce us to his dog?

Early one morning, RJ arrived at our house in a panic. "A bunch of people want rooms, Bruce, and Dago's not there yet. Come on! I have a tuk tuk waiting. We have to go *now*." He had no idea what to do with these people. RJ was more comfortable with those random friends who hung out in the lobby or kitchen and who occasionally snagged free lodging in exchange for favors. He'd rather fill his hotel with them instead of paying guests. I wondered if he could ever transition from "Sure, dude, you can hang out here" to "How can I best meet your needs, Sir?"

Meanwhile, at home in Barrio Norte, Bruce and I coexisted with our own freeloading lodgers. Termites lived above us in the wooden ceiling beams. Their debris dropped to the floor, the beds, the furniture. At night they swarmed the lights like moths.

They looked like flying German cockroaches. Once I saw a huge one, bigger than any cockroach, on the wall outside our bedroom. Hundreds and thousands must lurk in the ceiling beams, I thought. The wood likely held nests—eggs and babies, workers and great queens like the one who ventured out to our hallway. Killing them was futile. There were too many and they were too well established.

Jessica and Emree spent one Saturday evening with me while Bruce and Travis attended a church meeting in Sololá. After Jessica put Emree to sleep in the spare bedroom, she and I relaxed in the living room to chat. When it got dark, I turned on the overhead light. This brought the termites out for their flying dances.

Jessica glanced up. "What are those bugs? Moths?" When I told her, she looked horrified. "They won't crawl on Emree, will they?"

"Oh no, they aren't attracted to people. Only to wood, and at night they come out for the lights."

When Bruce and Travis arrived around ten-thirty, the patio swarmed with termites flying around the outside lights and crawling on the doors to find a way to the light inside.

Travis and Jessica left a short while later, Travis carrying Emree with a blanket over her head for protection. Jessica ducked and covered her hair. "Travis, hurry. Don't let them touch Emree! Travis! Careful!"

The next time Lucas showed up to work in the garden, I went out to explain how bad these bugs were and could he please do something about the problem.

"Ah. *Poliyas.* They go away during the rainy season."

I wasn't sure I understood. "During the rainy season, they leave the house?"

"*Sí.* Just wait for the rainy season."

Okay. The rainy season, not too far off. It was May and the weather was still dry. Every creature has its busy season.

Due to increased termite activity at night, Bruce and I left the patio lights on outside our bedroom and turned off the inside ones. We watched Netflix in bed, with the laptop propped against Bruce's knees. Termites were attracted to the brighter light outside and left the computer screen alone.

To sleep, I clung to my husband and used three pillows, two under my head and one over. I pulled the blanket over my face with a small space for breathing.

Bruce got out of bed for his final trip to the bathroom. When he returned, he said, "How can you sleep buried under all that? I sweat with just the sheet."

I scooted next to his big, warm, comfortable self and rearranged my pillows and blanket. "I sleep better knowing termites can't get at me. While you were in Houston, I went to bed every night at seven. I didn't watch Netflix, just read on my Kindle under the covers."

Bruce kicked at the sheet, leaving only his feet covered. "RJ offered to let you stay at the hotel. He didn't think you should be here alone that long."

"It was only three nights."

In April, Bruce had made a quick trip to our son's home in Houston to bring back some things we left there on our trip down. He went with an empty suitcase and returned with a full one, the usual expat routine. He also needed to renew his visa, that ninety-day bother to cross the border and get your passport stamped, then return a day or two later good for another three months. Mine got renewed when I went to Minnesota. Now with his Houston trip, we were closer to the same visa schedule. We would pay someone to renew for us in July. Three months later, in October, we were flying to Utah to visit family.

"I don't believe Lucas about the rainy season," Bruce said. "The termites have it good here. They aren't going anywhere. He only said that to keep us off his back. Lucas doesn't like being bothered."

"I wonder what the owner pays him for taking care of the place."

"Probably not enough to suit Lucas. That's why he only does half the job." With that, Bruce turned over, and I snuggled close to him. We drifted off to the rhythmic hum of his CPAP machine.

Every morning, I saw termite wings on the floors and in the curtains. I swept up piles of droppings and debris. Why would anyone build a house with wooden ceiling beams in the heart of termite country? Travis and Jessica lived in three cement rooms; they didn't have termites.

During my losing battle with nature's wood eaters, our son Sean and his wife Erin came for a week in May, a month after Billy. They stayed at Casa Colonial, of course, to enjoy the restaurants and shopping stalls on Santander Street. Developed for tourism, this area had everything colorfully Maya and interesting to see and to do. They were the only guests at the hotel, except for a friend of RJ who was leaving soon. He was supposed to have gone before *Semana Santa*. Since the demand for rooms had not been as great as anticipated, RJ let him stay through the holiday and beyond.

An elderly Japanese man lived in Pana and drove around town on a bicycle with a front basket. He sold and delivered Japanese food cooked at home. Sean saw him one morning in front of the hotel and waved him down, bowed, and surprised the man by greeting him in his own language. Japan was where Sean had served his two-year church mission at age nineteen. In Japanese, they discussed the menu. Sean ordered several dishes for the following evening, asking for delivery to Casa Colonial.

My son, I thought proudly. I enjoyed this brief scene more than any first day of kindergarten or piano recital or high school graduation. This one moment felt like the culmination of everything.

When the man delivered the order, I again witnessed the exchange. The two of them greeted each other politely in the Japanese custom, both bowing slightly.

To me, Sean sounded brilliantly fluent but later he complained, "My Japanese is awful! I've forgotten so much. I make too many mistakes."

We gathered around a table on the third floor balcony to eat the food. RJ and Travis had arranged the setting for eight people, a tight fit, but it worked. Two-year-old Emree sat perched on a stool like a tiny but well-postured grownup lady, her big brown eyes bright with joyful excitement. *A party!* To me, it brought back the happy memories of when we first came to Pana and shared so many meals together. We had not done that much since the hotel opened.

Sean opened the boxes and named the food: *gyoza* (pot stickers); two orders of *yakisoba* or fried noodles with meat and vegetables; miso soup; and *chahan* (fried rice). The small boxes didn't hold enough for our crowd. "I wasn't sure how much to order since I didn't know how large the portions were. The main thing is to get authentic Japanese food, even if it's a sample."

"Never mind," I said. "If we're still hungry, we can go up the street to the pupusa ladies. They start cooking about now."

"And there's the pie lady," Bruce added.

We finished the scanty but delicious meal and decided to go see if the pupusas were ready. Everyone went except RJ, who said he had things to do. With *Semana Santa* over and business dwindling, RJ had returned to what he most enjoyed—construction tasks to repair and beautify —the building of the hotel over the actual running of it. And, above all, his collection of paddleboards.

The pupusa restaurant was outdoors under a large canopy. At six, two ladies and their male helpers came to set up and start cooking. When they closed at nine or ten, the men returned with their truck and took down the tent, the griddles, the tables and chairs. They hauled everything off until the next evening.

Pupusas are a traditional dish from San Salvador. The ladies pressed the dough into thick tortillas with a choice of fillings:

cheese, meat, or beans. They turned them over on the grill, pressed and turned them again and again until they were melty and crispy. They sold three pupusas for fifteen quetzales, or about two dollars.

Travis ordered three, one each for him, Jessica, and Emree. Bruce checked with me to see if we wanted to share an order. "Let's each get a full order," I suggested, knowing what Travis ordered wouldn't be enough for them.

Sean and Erin got two orders as well for a total of six pupusas. "I'll eat what Erin doesn't," Sean said.

We found a double table where we could sit together without crowding. Each table had a gallon jar of the relish—a shredded mixture of pickled cabbage, carrot, onion, and jalapeño. There were tongs for serving it to your plate. A girl brought our steaming pupusas over on plastic plates. She handed out napkins and plastic forks, one thin napkin per person, a challenge considering how messy pupusas are. I kept one of mine and passed the other two over to Travis and Jessica.

"Thanks, Mom!" said Travis. "You don't want these?"

"No. One is plenty. My favorite thing is the relish. It's like a salad."

Bruce ate two and asked Travis if he wanted the last one.

"Sure, if you don't. I'm still kinda hungry. I can't believe Emree ate an entire pupusa by herself!"

The evening air was sweet and balmy. To be out at night like this was a rare treat. Bruce usually felt too tired after work to go anywhere but home. I could have sat right there forever in heaven with my family, against a backdrop of Santander with its noisy excitement. Clusters of tourists passed on the sidewalks and spilled into the street, weaving in and out among the cars, bikes and tuk tuks. I never tired of watching this scene. People came from faraway to visit Pana, but we *lived* here.

Finally, we vacated our table and joined the throng.

"Let's head back to the hotel for board games," suggested Sean. "On the way, we can stop for that pie Dad's been raving about."

The pie lady was Bruce's favorite food vendor. As wide as she was short, her size was unusual for a local lady. Each evening around seven, her men came to set up a long table with the pies displayed in their pans. She then cut the pieces according to order. Bruce's favorite was lemon. Once I tried it and the cheesecake, but neither tasted that good to me.

We approached the table where she had positioned herself on a stool. Bruce greeted her and praised the selection. "They look so good I can't decide." He ended by ordering lemon like always. Sean and Erin got a piece of banana cream to share, while the rest of us declined.

Bruce stood near the lady, eating his pie where she could see how much he enjoyed it. "*Muy bueno!*" He patted his belly expressively.

She smiled and thanked him.

"That's the best pie," he proclaimed as we left. I wasn't sure about that, but she was by far the best pie lady. Bruce never passed her table without buying a piece and complimenting her with his enthusiastic, "*Muy bueno!*"

On the way back to the hotel, Bruce and I lagged behind the others. "Look at those brothers," I said, "how much fun they're having together. And Jessica and Erin get along so well, too."

Instead of basking like me in the glow of our shared family success, Bruce was distracted. "RJ needs to return to Los Angeles," he said. "Sally wants him home. The hotel is open, he's finished enough paddleboards. What's the hold up?"

"He can't let go, I suppose. He's been in and out of Pana for most of his adult life. As much as he complains about it and says he wants to leave, it's familiar to him. He's been here too long to break away easily."

"Once Sean and Erin leave, that's going to change. There's things we can do to bring in more business, and if he's not interested, I will make those decisions on my own. I'll just need to be subtle about it."

"Sneaky?"

"No. Subtle. Two completely different approaches. Let him work on his paddleboards if that's what he wants to do. I'm moving on without him."

With Sean and Erin in town, the family met every morning for breakfast at a restaurant on Santander. Occasionally, RJ joined us. Their menu had a wide selection of American favorites, like crepes, pancakes or waffles, bacon and eggs. The orange juice was freshly squeezed and their fruit licuados were cold and tasty.

Travis and Sean kidded each other and joked around when they got together. I delighted in their antics and laughed at their silliness. Bruce ignored it the same as he did when they were teenagers. Their wives tolerated it and rolled their eyes.

It was a sad day when the week ended, when Sean and Erin left Panajachel in Lucas's taxi. That became our pattern; pick up family visitors in Pedro's van, stop at Antigua, ride in relative luxury to Pana. They return to the city on the cheap in Lucas's taxi—holiday over, magic ends, they save a few bucks.

Afterward, the four of us carried a pall of sadness. Bruce and Travis went back to the hotel, Jessica waiting there with Emree until Travis finished work. I trudged up the hill to Barrio Norte with a heavy heart. Family visits were over. At least I still had Travis, Jessica and Emree.

RJ and his hotel settled back into the pre-Easter routine. A few guests wandered in over the weekends; RJ always found improvements or repairs to keep Travis and Dago occupied. Bruce spent less time at the hotel, going in later and coming home at five instead of six. While there, he worked at his desk, on his computer. Being subtle, I figured.

Meanwhile, RJ focused on his paddleboards. A dozen of the long sleek boards monopolized the open room next to the lobby, like killer whales lounging on a tourist beach. They were in various stages of production. Nothing made RJ happier than to run his drill and his electric sander and open a can of the smelly varnish to brush on the surface. Things he couldn't do with guests around.

No wonder he insisted on pricing the rooms beyond competitive rates. No wonder he turned off the pretty, inviting outside lights at night. No wonder he let street dogs wander into the lobby and Bailey curl up on the furniture. No wonder he invited his unkempt friends to lounge about the place.

Real guests, those who paid to stay, interfered with his paddleboard construction.

10
Leaving

By the rivers of Babylon, there we sat down,
yea, we wept when we remembered Zion.
Psalm 137:1

Jessica and I made our way down the Barrio Norte hill. We passed the tortilla ladies rhythmically patting the masa balls, clap clap clap, as they shaped and flattened tortillas to press onto the hot griddle.

"*Hola!*" Emree hollered out to them.

"*Hola!*" they called back, smiling.

Emree sat forward in the stroller and lifted her hands to show them her skills. Clap, clap, clap, turn hands, clap clap clap, quickly back and forth. The ladies laughed in delight and waved. Emree sat back satisfied.

"I'm still trying to figure out my purpose," Jessica said.

I paused a moment before replying, "I know my purpose. To finish this book and then write another one."

"I wish I had a clear vision like that, about what I want from life. I'm trying to settle things in my mind."

"I'm not so great on follow through," I admitted, "since there's other purposes as well. To keep Bruce healthy and maintain contact with the family back home. And there's the publishing business."

"It seems like you're always writing though," Jessica observed.

"I have good intentions but there's so much to interfere. Housework, of course, and working on other peoples' books."

"There must be something special for me to do here, maybe some service or someone to help," Jessica continued, "but what can I do? I don't speak enough Spanish to get to know people."

As we approached the mercado, the sidewalk grew crowded and pedestrians moved to the street, where they coexisted with vehicles in the shared space.

"That American lady with her grown kids, the Jehovah's Witness family?" Jessica said. "She's friendly and always stops to talk when she sees me in the street."

"Oh, that's nice." Thank goodness she doesn't stop and talk to me when she sees me in the street, I thought.

"She invited Emree and me to lunch a few times. I guess she realizes I seem a little lost and in need of a friend."

"You know, when we planned this move, I thought all of us would get together more than we do. Every night for dinner kind of thing, like when we first moved to Paul's apartment. Or we'd go out and do things, to see more of Guatemala."

"That would be great, but Travis works too much. RJ has always kept him there until nine or ten at night."

"Remember RJ's promises about how much money Travis would make if he came to work for him?"

"It's enough to pay rent and keep us from starving but not to go out much or save for school," she replied. "That's okay though. Travis and I decided before we came it wasn't for the money. It's for the experience and to help Sally."

"Does RJ borrow money like he did before?"

"No. He stopped doing that after I told you about it."

"Sally must have put a stop to it. Sent him a bigger allowance or something."

"Karen, did you know RJ left last night for California?"

I stopped, causing a man with a crate of eggs on his shoulder to nearly bump into my left side. "What? Are you serious?" It was the second week of June, a few days before my birthday. "This is the best birthday present ever!"

Jessica laughed. "Yeah, it's true. What a surprise, right? Bruce and Dago had gone home, but Travis, of course, was still there when it happened. RJ told him he was catching the night bus to the city for an early morning flight. He said, 'Travis, you know the plan. Your dad's in charge but keep an eye on Dago. Your dad's too soft on Dago.'"

"What is his problem with Dago? Does RJ know how lucky he is to have Dago? He does everything he's told and then some."

"I know. Dago is great, and RJ takes advantage of him," Jessica agreed.

"Since he takes advantage of everyone, I guess it's no surprise. Bruce thinks the world of Dago. It's not that he's too soft, it's that Bruce respects him. He listens to Dago. They both want the same thing, for the hotel to succeed and make money. Unlike RJ who acts like he's given up on that idea."

Jessica made a move to turn the big stroller left toward the Dispensa. "We're going this way, right?"

"Except I feel like celebrating! Let's go to Mercedes' fruit stand. I'll treat you and Emree to pineapple." With us living in Barrio Norte, Mercedes' stand was out of the way, and we had stopped going there together.

"Just like old times," I remarked once we positioned ourselves on the bench. "I'm glad our seat was empty."

"It was waiting for us." Jessica broke off a piece of pineapple for Emree.

"RJ gone!" I said. "Two months past *Semana Santa,* and finally he slips out under cover of darkness."

"Yeah, he can be weird. So secretive and private about certain things. He doesn't want anyone to know his business."

"He's been carrying on forever like it's imminent, making sure everything is in order and Bruce knows what to do. Bruce has been ready since Easter. He wants the hotel to make money.

'Once RJ leaves, I'll run this place like a business and not a bachelor pad,' he says."

"Travis and I have a list of what we can do now that RJ is gone. Travis has been saving money for us to enjoy Guatemala a little bit."

"What a slave driver." The injustice of that situation irritated me. "Let's get together for my birthday. Bruce and I will probably go out to lunch, but you guys come over for dinner. I'll cook a special meal."

"And I'll bring dessert," Jessica added, "so don't make a cake."

That evening, Bruce got home by six, an hour later than his recent pattern. "Are you walking on air?" I asked when he came through the door. "Jessica gave me the news."

He laughed. "Maybe a little. I'm ready to get busy and turn Casa Colonial into what it's meant to be. A boutique hotel with competitive pricing and full occupancy every weekend. There's a lot to do."

"Hopefully you won't be a boss like RJ. Travis needs some time off to enjoy life."

"As long as the job gets done, Travis can take as much time off as he wants. First, we clean the place up."

"RJ really is gone? For good?"

"Sally called me this morning on Skype, giddy with excitement, to say he had boarded the plane to LA. She reaffirmed the plan. He will get a job as an RN then move up to traveler as soon as he can. With the two of them earning traveler wages they'll double Sally's current income and pay off the construction debts."

"Let's hope it plays out that way."

"I see no reason why it won't. I met with Dago and Travis today to emphasize our priorities: cleanliness, professionalism, and competitive rates. 'We're letting go of the side hustles,' I told them. 'Nobody is interested in renting bikes or paddleboards or taking guided tours from us. They want a room. That's where the money is.'"

Before long, the three of them transformed Casa Colonial. They cleared out clutter in the back room. They repaired and sold the collection of bikes, except for RJ's, one for Dago, and a couple additional ones. Old fans, extra paint, random duplicate parts and tools were either sold or thrown away. Travis finished the construction RJ left for him. Bruce refined his office area and added shelves. Dago went to Santander Street every afternoon to talk to tuk tuk drivers and local businesses, to let them know Casa Colonial had rooms available. He offered a referral fee when someone they sent over took a room.

And, of course, the outside lights went on every evening to make the hotel beautiful and inviting.

Travis, Jessica, and Emree came for dinner another Sunday and this is when we got their news. Good news and bad. The good news was another baby on the way. The bad news was they planned to return to Utah for the birth and for Travis to continue his education.

"I'm not excited about leaving," Travis said, "especially now with RJ gone when I can work and have a life too. But I feel like I need to be responsible and get back to school. Besides, the hotel is shaping up so well now. I'm not really needed here like I was."

"We've been discussing it for a while," Jessica added. "We didn't want to say anything until we knew for sure whether to stay or go, but finally we got the answer to our prayers."

"There was the pregnancy," Travis said. "Could Jessica go through that in another country, not knowing the language?"

"Yeah, I was nervous about it. But if the answer was to stay, I knew it would be okay. Lucy Jensen had her youngest in Guatemala. She would help and advise me, I'm sure. Maybe go with me to appointments and translate."

Travis explained further, "I felt so conflicted about what to do, about what was best. I took a long bike ride to clear my head. I got the strong impression that we could stay if it was what we both wanted, but going back to school was the better decision. The more responsible choice."

They planned to leave in July, three and a half weeks away. Before they left, they wanted to eat at restaurants they hadn't tried and to revisit their favorites. They invited us to join them in their marathon. Taco Kid, the Pupusa Ladies, the Tostada Table and the Pie Lady covered all our favorite street food stands. Bruce and I introduced them to the little Italian place. There was the break-fast restaurant, a couple pizza places and ice cream shops and, of course, Smoky Joe's, the BBQ place run by an expat couple and only open on Saturdays.

For their departure, Bruce hired Pedro's van. "No Lucas taxi for them," he said. "They deserve to return like royalty, and the hotel is paying for it."

They had a one-thirty p.m. flight, and we left before dawn. "Too bad it's still too dark for one last glimpse of Lake Atitlán," I said as we left Pana and drove up the hill towards Sololá and beyond.

"At least Emree is going back to sleep." Travis adjusted the blankets around her. She lay quietly next to him on the seat. Jessica and I sat on the second bench row, and Bruce was in his favorite side seat with the extra leg room.

"This is so sad, leaving," Travis added. "I hate that we were only here for six months. I have such mixed feelings. My heart aches knowing it's the last time we will drive through these hills."

"I can hardly bear to think of it," I said. "I wish you weren't going."

"Oh, I know. It was the right choice, no question, but I still don't like it. We wanted to stay a year," he said. "Although we're at peace about our decision. I only wish we could have seen Tikal.

I can't believe we spent six months in Guatemala and never made it to those ruins."

"I wonder if Dad and I will get to Tikal."

"You have to. Maybe Jessica and I can come back and go with you."

I had researched the journey awhile back. A rough trip of several days on a lot of different buses, on bad roads and through isolated areas. The Tikal nature reserve is in the middle of a jungle wilderness, with not much else around it.

I turned to Bruce, who was falling asleep. "What do you say, Bruce? Do you want to go to Tikal?"

"Not if we have to travel five days on a chicken bus."

"RJ said the best way is to fly out from Guatemala City to Flores," Travis said. "Then you catch a van from Flores to the park."

The rising sun turned the sky a light pinkish orange, softly blending into the gray morning fog behind the layered peaks. We rode in silence as the sun shed its new light over the land.

"What a magical place this is," Jessica said in a slow, dreamy voice.

Travis and I murmured in agreement. Emree and Bruce were both asleep. Time no longer mattered. We moved in a dream as Pedro's van rolled through the misty hills.

"I'd give anything to see the sun rise over the temples of Tikal," Travis said.

Sadness permeated the van like a funeral service, deeply moving and sacred, sorrowful yet inspiring.

"I wonder what it is about Guatemala, what gives it those feelings to move your heart," Jessica said.

"I wonder, too," I responded. "People from everywhere sense it. 'What is it about this place?' they say. Expats refer to *pachamamma,* but I think it's more the spirit of the Maya themselves than some ancient goddess."

"I learned so many life lessons here," she said. "Especially how freeing it is to not try and be like everyone else. I knew I never could fit in here, so why worry about it? I loved the feeling of freedom that came once I stopped thinking about the differences between me and everyone else."

"Did you ever decide on your purpose, Jessica?" I asked her.

She laughed and said, "No, but that's okay. Whatever it was, I'm sure it will change when we're in Salt Lake."

"When I got off my mission, I always wanted to go back with the girl I married, if not to Africa then to some other third world country, and together serve a mission," Travis reflected. "Sure, senior couples can serve, but it's too far off when you're young. I learned so much from my mission. How wonderful it would be, I thought, to go back and start our married life with that transforming experience. To me, Guatemala was the realization of that dream."

When Pedro left the jungle road and reached open ground and the main highway to the city, we knew the end had come.

"This is the last time we drive that crazy road, Jessica," Travis said.

"It's sad," she responded. "Maybe we will come back one day."

"I think you will," Bruce said, waking up and stretching. "Together we will go to Tikal and watch the sun rise over the pyramids."

Funny Bruce. How often it seemed like he wasn't paying attention when he heard everything, even in his sleep.

Emree woke up and needed snacks. It was back to life as usual.

Arriving in the city, Pedro pulled into the airport and parked. After unloading the luggage, he stayed with the van while we headed to the entrance. Travis thanked us again for going with them and hiring Pedro's van. "You didn't need to do that," he said, giving his dad and me each another hug.

"Of course, we did," Bruce said. "We wanted to send you off in style."

"And spend every last minute with you," I added.

Outside, we said our final goodbyes while slowly moving along with the crowd toward the entrance. With Jessica holding Emree and Travis maneuvering a luggage cart, they reached the door, showed their passports, and went through. They turned back, and we waved goodbye. With teary eyes, I watched them disappear into the airport.

The drive had taken less than three hours. The roads were clear, and we had met no eventualities such as blockades or detours or breakdowns. No traffic on the outskirts of the city. It was only nine a.m. Pedro asked if we wanted to make any other stops, as we often did on a trip to the city. Bruce and I looked at each other. Walmart? Price Club? Home Depot? No, let's just go back.

Pedro dropped us off at the hotel around noon. Bruce said he'd make eggs for lunch. Did I want any? Stay and eat with him?

No, because I couldn't bear the thought of stepping into the hotel right now without seeing Travis or Jessica. They had always been there, since the day Bruce and I first arrived in Pana.

At home, I built a fire for comfort. Carrying in wood and creating a blaze in the fireplace always improved my outlook. I curled up on the sofa and watched it and fed it and felt somewhat useful and productive. I thought about Travis, Jessica, Emree and their new baby. About the future ahead of them, this dear little family who had interrupted their lives to help Sally and RJ. How I would miss them.

While gazing and ruminating in front of the perfect fire, I felt a sudden drop in my center. A sense of loss cycled through me. I checked the clock. "They've lifted off," I said to no one.

11

Boat Taxis, Bicycles, and the Chicken Bus

The Lord will preserve him and keep him alive;
and he shall be blessed upon the earth:
and thou wilt not deliver him unto the will of his enemies.
Psalm 41:3

With everyone gone and Bruce now spending more time at the hotel, I made sure to get myself out several times a day. Not only for shopping, but to explore the town.

Three blocks from the hotel was a dock where the boat taxis transported people to the towns that hugged the shores of Lake Atitlán. After discovering it, I sat on a nearby low stone wall to observe the action. The passengers were the same type I saw daily on the streets of Pana. Local folks, moms with children, vendors with their unwieldy boxes and overstuffed sacks, tourists with backpacks and woven Maya bags.

The boatmen and their young assistants directed people to board or disembark. Older men in official white polo shirts oversaw the operation. They guided people to the correct boat or gestured for them to wait, the one they wanted wasn't there yet. No, no! Don't get in this line, wait over here.

The boats were like the one RJ rented for our private tour with Billy and Larry—large motor at the back, benches lined up in two rows on either side, a tarp overhead to protect from sun or rain.

I didn't know about this public dock back when RJ arranged our excursion. "It's the only way to see the villages around the lake," he had claimed. "The public boats are dangerous. You don't want to go anywhere on them."

Watching now, I doubted that was true. These men lived along the lake, probably born here like generations before them. This was their livelihood. They would know the boats, know the lake and how to manage in any condition. Sun or rain, rough water notwithstanding, travelers lined up to climb into the boats. When everyone boarded, no matter how crowded the seats, the boatmen pulled away from the pier.

One Sunday at church a family with five children was visiting from the States. Two of the girls attended my Primary class. The older one, age eleven, said they had come to do humanitarian work for three weeks. "We live in San Pedro," she offered.

"How do you get from San Pedro to Pana?" I asked her, knowing they must have crossed by boat. It was the only way, unless they had a vehicle and wanted to drive an hour and a half on a circuitous, bumpy ride through the hills, which nobody did.

"We take the boat. It's pretty fun."

"You like it?"

"Oh yes, unless the water is rough. Then you can get wet and cold." She touched the two blond braids twisted around her head in a crown and held with a bow. "I got wet this morning!"

I smiled at her enthusiasm over her lake shower and asked how much it had cost?

"Twenty-five quetzales a person. Kind of expensive when it's our whole family. That's why we only come to Pana when we have to, like for church or if we're going to do something else important."

They seemed like a normal, responsible family with four young daughters and a toddler son. If these parents felt safe taking their children on the boat, why shouldn't I?

Walking home from church at noon, I mentioned it to Bruce. "Let's try the public boat one of these days. You can take a full Saturday off work and we could visit another town, maybe San Pedro."

He seemed doubtful. "Didn't we see those towns when Billy was here?"

"Yeah, but we could do it without RJ bossing us around. Or without the guide hovering where you never know if you're supposed to ask him questions or feed him lunch." We turned off Santander to follow the street that passed the park and the mercado. Then up the hill to Barrio Norte.

"Maybe when family comes again, we can do it," Bruce suggested. "Weekends are the busiest times for the hotel. If I want my Sundays, Dago needs at least part of Saturday off."

We passed by the mercado crowd. People in their colorful Sunday best thronged to the stalls. It was still the same patterned clothing in the same traditional cuts—for the women, wrap around skirts with cloth belts plus decorative blouses—but the fabric looked brighter and fresher, not as worn as their everyday skirts and blouses.

"Julie plans to visit in January or February," I said. "Maybe she'll be up for a boat trip from the public dock."

"Julie? I can't imagine your sister wanting to get on one of those rickety things." Bruce looked around for a tuk tuk, usually plentiful around the mercado. "Why is it so busy today? Every single tuk tuk is full of people."

I was fine walking, especially after sitting in church for three hours. "Let's keep going and flag an empty one when we see it. Anyway, Bruce, the boats aren't rickety. If they were dangerous, the locals wouldn't get on them day after day."

"They have no other choice when they work in another town. Their livelihood depends on it. Man, it's getting hot!"

"Those guys on the docks are experts. RJ probably criticized them to get us to rent the private one because he keeps a cut. How much is fifty dollars in quetzales?"

"About 350 quetzales."

"We paid that *per person* for RJ's stupid private boat. Compare that to twenty-five for the public ones."

"Quite a difference," he agreed. "I'm not sure it was worth what we got charged."

"RJ never liked us doing anything or going anywhere without him along to protect us. He thinks everyone is watching us. 'They know where you go, where you live, your routine, everything about you,' he says. 'Don't give out any information or they'll tell everyone else.'"

"RJ is paranoid about his privacy," Bruce said. "Before he left town, he kept telling Travis and me not to tell anyone where he went. He didn't tell me in advance, that's how paranoid he is." He picked up his pace, apparently giving up the tuk tuk idea. "I'm hungry. Let's hurry up and get home."

"People are always coming around asking for RJ. How do you not say where he is?"

"If they ask outright, I'm supposed to tell them, 'He's out for a time,' and then redirect by saying, 'What do you need?'"

I laughed. "How like him to prep you in detail for any scenario like you don't have a brain."

"I'll say whatever he wants if it keeps him away. Business is better than ever now. We've been full nearly every weekend with half-occupancy during the week. More than double the business since RJ left."

At the steepest climb of the Barrio Norte hill, Bruce leaned over, panting. "I need to rest a bit." He plopped down on the same wide step where he always stopped when we trekked home together.

I sat next to him. "I took the bus to Sololá this week, to the mercado."

"You did? By yourself? Why didn't you tell me?"

"You're always working and by the time you get home, we're both ready for dinner and too tired to think. I went at ten. It was fun and cost just a few quetzales."

"Those buses are too cramped and uncomfortable."

They were old school buses from the States, repainted and repaired. "I like them. I think they're comfy and cozy, especially the window seats. I always felt jealous of the farm kids who got to ride a bus to school."

"I lived in the country and rode them every day. They're nothing special. They were uncomfortable back when I was a kid. Now they're miserable."

"It makes me happy to get on a chicken bus. I'd like to go farther than Sololá though."

An ancient, stooped lady in Maya dress approached us. Small and thin, she was the size of a six-year-old American child. She held out her tiny, claw-like hand, palm up and said something indistinguishable. I caught the word *comida*. Food.

"Bruce, you have any change?" He dug some coins out of his pocket and placed them in her open palm. She pronounced a blessing on us and wandered away up the street in her leathery bare feet.

We sat awhile in silence until Bruce felt ready to continue up the hill toward home. As we climbed, he said, "I've ridden one of the hotel bikes around town a bit. I'd like to get fit enough where I can ride it up and down this hill. There's a women's bike left. You want me to fix it up for you?"

Bruce had been *exercising*? "There's so much traffic on these streets. I'd be nervous dodging cars and weaving in and out like people do here. It's been years since I rode one."

"If you don't want it, I'll sell it. The hotel can use the extra cash."

I hesitated. Maybe I shouldn't turn down a free bicycle.

"Bikes are a hot commodity here, Karen. Even the old used ones are expensive."

"I don't know if I still have the skills. I haven't ridden a bike since college."

"We could go on rides together," he suggested. "Not on Santander since it's so busy, but there's a few side streets I've practiced on that have less traffic."

I wanted to encourage his desire to increase fitness, and I also liked the idea of us going out on rides. We didn't go anywhere together except to church on Sundays and shopping for groceries on Saturday. I agreed to try the bike.

A few days later, Dago rode it up to our house, parked it on the patio then walked back. It was a sturdy girl's bike with yellow fenders, no hand brakes. I liked how it leaned against the wall like it belonged. A sassy girl's bike.

When Bruce arrived home that evening, he asked, "Have you tried the bike yet?"

"No. I'm too nervous. I'm afraid of being wobbly. What if I hit someone on the crowded street? Or if I lose control and run into a tuk tuk?"

"Ride around the patio to get a feel for it. I'll adjust the seat to where it's comfortable for you."

"Maybe later."

On Saturday morning, he suggested we go for a ride together. "I have to take care of some things first but why don't you come down around eleven. We'll try the quiet street not far from the hotel."

It wasn't often Bruce initiated a date or any kind of joint activity. He used to plan Saturdays out for the family back in our younger years in Illinois. Day trips to Nauvoo or scenic drives through farm country and river towns, with picnics at a roadside park. As he approached fifty, he got tired and heavy and ran out of ideas.

"Okay," I agreed. "I'll come down around eleven."

I ended up walking the bike most of the way, since I wasn't used to it yet. While waiting for Bruce, I rode on the street in front but felt silly and conspicuous. RJ's voice ran through my head. "They watch you. They know everything about you. You think they're so sweet and nice, minding their own business, but you'll see once you've been here longer. They talk about you behind your back. They make fun of you with their friends."

This watchfulness isn't a bad thing, I thought. So what if they're watching me. It contributes to the safety of the neighborhoods. Lucas had said, "You don't need to worry about anything. If bad people come, we take them to the hills and set them on fire." The Maya were peaceful, quiet and friendly as long as you weren't there to fight or steal or interfere with their families, especially their children.

"Don't ever take a picture of one of their kids," RJ had warned. "They'll break your camera and maybe worse."

Dago arrived for the afternoon shift and waved at me before going in. A few minutes later, Bruce stepped outside. I pulled up and stopped the bike without difficulty. Maybe this wouldn't be too bad. Maybe the two of us could do this regularly.

"After our ride, let's drop the bikes off here and stop at Smoky Joe's for lunch on the way home," he said.

Wow, an entire date planned by Bruce! That rarely happened, not even on special occasions like my birthday or our anniversary.

He wanted me to ride ahead where he could see I was okay, but I felt more comfortable with him in the lead. We set off. I felt steadier but worried about my companion up ahead. I observed a few awkward moments where he stopped pedaling, his bike coming to a standstill. Somehow he managed to not fall.

"You almost tipped over there, Bruce."

"I need a lighter bike with hand brakes. We got this one ready first, but I think I'd do better with hand brakes."

My own difficulties came from weak leg muscles, despite the daily walks. My neck and shoulders ached with tension.

At the end of the side street Bruce stopped, properly this time. "We can turn to the right toward the bridge. It's not busy that direction either."

"I'm too out of shape to enjoy much of a ride," I admitted. "Let's go back and try again another day. Hard to believe that in college I used a bike instead of a car."

We returned the way we came and stopped to cross a busy street. Bruce headed across the intersection while I waited for another break in the line of cars. Once across, he did his strange pause, trying to defy gravity and cease pedaling without tipping over. He fell in a heap on the sidewalk, half over the curb, the bike under him. Where the area was vacant seconds before, people came rushing out of a tienda, a shop, a couple houses. One or two cars stopped, and a passenger hurried over to help.

By the time I reached him, a half dozen kindly folks had gathered round, assisting him to his feet, lifting the bike and holding it upright. *"Cuidado, cuidado. Está bien?"*

We thanked them profusely then walked our bikes away from the scene.

Finally, I broke the silence. "Have you fallen before?"

"Only a couple times."

A couple times! That meant three or four since of course he would minimize it.

"It's when you brake and don't get your leg to the ground. Is it because of your knees?"

"I don't know. I think I'd do better on the lighter one with hand brakes. I'll try that as soon as I fix it up."

"It's too risky! I can't stand the idea. You could've been hit by a car. Or broken a bone."

Bruce did not respond. I thought about a couple we knew. They had retired early and moved to southern Utah to enjoy a more relaxed, outdoor lifestyle. Until the husband crashed on his bike and was never the same again.

"Please promise me you're done with the bike, Bruce. Any bike. It's too dangerous, especially with your knees. Never mind hand brakes or no hand brakes. Walk or take a tuk tuk—it's only seven quetzales. That's a dollar to get you anywhere in town."

We dropped the bikes at the hotel and then followed Santander Street to Smoky Joe's. On the way, I talked about our friends in

St. George, the charming Southern Utah town with its many trails and mild winters, their dream destination for an active outdoor retirement. "He falls soon after and is disabled for life. That turns out to be his last bike ride. And he retired early like you which makes it a very long time to not do what you want."

Bruce knew the story. There was little he could add to the discussion. That man had been healthier and in better shape than my husband by far. "You could have crashed into a car and gotten seriously injured. Even killed!" On and on I went until we arrived at Smoky Joe's. "I don't want a bike. Period. Sell them both."

End of rant. I calmed down as we entered the open air space, converted one day a week to Smoky Joe's grill. Open Saturdays in Pana, Sundays in San Pedro. We stepped in line behind the expats and tourists who frequented the place. It was cheap for Americans but too pricey for those who survived on local wages.

We chose our sides, ordered our steaks, and found a table to wait until Joe hollered, "Hey Bruce!" Once, when Bruce wasn't feeling well, I came on my own for to-go dinners. I gave them my name but when the order was ready, Joe still called, "Hey Bruce!"

The stress of the bike ride behind us, we relaxed in this perfect, temperate climate, sharing American comfort food of steak, potato salad, green beans, cole slaw. It was late July, and the weather felt like a beautiful spring day. The rain usually started around one and ended at four or five. Right now, though, it was clear and sunny, with a slight breeze. We talked as always about how much we love Guatemala and how lucky we are to live in this remarkable land. And weren't those people nice who helped you today?

"This is the best steak," Bruce said. "Joe sure knows how to cook a cow. He says it's the wood he uses. He gets it somewhere up in the hills toward ChiChi."

"We should go to ChiChi one of these days, Bruce. It's a long bus ride, but I hear it's through gorgeous mountain scenery. Their mercado is famous, only open a couple days a week. They shut down half the town to set it up."

I didn't mention how much I worried over Bruce's health, my fears about him working too hard and wearing himself out and dying too soon. Or he didn't mention his concern over my increasing restlessness, afraid I might take off on a whim and get myself into trouble where he couldn't help me. He rarely mentioned his anxieties, but I knew. As he knew mine for him, even if I didn't go on and on like I did today. Even if I never said a word about it, he would know.

We had been together so long and knew each other so well. Neither of us could imagine a life without the other.

12
Evicted by Termites

*This poor man cried,
and the Lord heard him,
and saved him out of all his troubles.*
Psalm 34:6

Rainy season in the highlands begins shortly after Easter and ends around November. December through April or May are the dry months, the tourist season.

By mid-June, the rain was consistent but not excessive, perhaps a few hours in the mornings or the afternoons. Enough to say, *Hello again. Are you ready for this?*

By the end of July, the heavy rains began in earnest. Once, after raining hard day and night, the lane outside our gate was a muddy stream. Water rushed down our lane to the street, which ran like a river. Elsewhere, it was worse. The heavy downpour had pushed rocks down from the hillsides, and muddy water flowed around boulders in the road.

When the rain ended, city workers arrived to shovel out dirt and debris. They moved the boulders, enabling traffic to proceed. Before long the sun shone brightly, and fluffy white clouds again danced across the blue sky. The usual stream of vehicles and pedestrians filled the streets and sidewalks.

Our termites did not leave with the rain. I told Lucas to fix the problem or we would move. I supposed he would spray or something while we left for twenty-four hours.

When Lucas reported back, he said Morris wanted him to treat the wood ceilings and replace the most infested sections. It required tearing out and replacing ceiling beams in the two bedrooms, the areas of greatest infestation. Other areas he would treat with poison that brushed on like paint. Since this involved powerful, toxic chemicals as well as construction work, we needed to pack our clothes and vacate the house for *"unas semanas."* A few weeks, as I interpreted it.

Bruce suggested we move to the hotel for the short term. With RJ gone, our presence would increase security. Due to the rainy season, occupancy was low. Two rooms had monthly tenants, a couple of single guys, but everything else was vacant, other than a few rooms rented occasionally on the weekend.

We took Rooms 4 and 5 on the second floor, located opposite each other at the end of the hallway. I positioned three large potted plants across the hall as a barrier, to create a private garden. "This is the manager's suite," I proclaimed.

"We won't be here that long, a few weeks according to Lucas, but call it whatever you want," Bruce responded.

We slept in Room 4 and used the bunkbeds in Room 5 for extra storage. I put my camp chair in the corner for a writing area. Room 4 had a kitchenette consisting of a counter, a mini fridge, a portable propane stovetop, and a sink. Our bed, closet, and side table filled the rest of the space. It was too crowded and awkward to navigate cooking. A few bottles of diet Coke went in the minifridge.

Our cozy rooms suited me. I liked being close to Bruce and to the center of activity in town. I imagined us staying in our manager's suite and never moving back to Barrio Norte with its creeping darkness and sense of isolation. I thought Bruce might enjoy the convenience, but no. These tiny rooms were too uncomfortable for a big guy.

Whenever the bell rang late at night, Bruce got out of bed and went downstairs to answer it. Somebody might want a room, and the hotel needed the business.

The young man from Guatemala City in Room 2 always came in at midnight and rang the bell. Bruce woke up to let him in because, "I'm not about to give that kid a key to the outside door." The kid often had his giggling girlfriend with him, which annoyed my traditional, upright husband no end. "What kind of place are we running here?" he muttered as he came back to bed.

Our projected two or three weeks away turned into four, with no sign of the termite treatment ending.

Bruce grew irritable and short-tempered. He missed his home and his uninterrupted sleep. He missed my home cooking to welcome him at the end of each workday.

Mornings, he showered, dressed, and went downstairs to let Dago in at seven. I stayed upstairs until ten or eleven. By the time I ventured down to leave on a walk, Bruce was trapped into one of his lengthy Skype calls with RJ or doing accounts and spreadsheets on the computer. Or he and Dago were deep into conversation, usually involving bouts of pantomime like a game of charades.

"Kindle, Mr. Bruce," Dago pointed, when neither words nor gestures made sense.

Bruce would pick up his Kindle, translate English to Spanish on the app, show it to Dago. Problem solved. There were chuckles and congratulatory pats on the back, along with deepening bonds of friendship as they relished their victories in achieving mutual understanding.

With me, however, Bruce seemed stressed and unhappy. He refused to talk about it, except to snap, "Because I can't get away from work! I can't relax at home."

"You couldn't relax there either, always talking about work or Skyping with RJ and Sally. Coming home late, especially once RJ left. Living on site should be easier. I don't get it."

"Never mind. It doesn't matter."

Four weeks turned into six, and our house was still not ready.

I focused on my own work and left Bruce to figure things out for himself. I was at the best part with my novel—the wrapping up edits. Thinking about a cover design. Looking forward to launch.

We ate either lunch or dinner out, sometimes both. Certain places didn't open until after eight, making it late for dinner. One of these was a footlong hot dog stand. Besides the usual onions, tomatoes, ketchup, and mustard, they came topped with a unique blend of coleslaw, mayo and picante. Each hot dog cost fifteen quetzales or about two dollars. A cheap meal but not the best choice before bed.

Another after-eight café on Santander served grilled beef or chicken with sides of grilled green onions, refried beans, rice and tortillas. Their chicken tasted as rich and tender as pork.

Eating out challenged our budget. We still paid rent and utilities on our house. At the outset, when I asked Lucas if we had to keep paying rent, he laughed like it was a joke. "It won't take long," he said. "Don't worry."

About once a week, Bruce said, "Let's grab a tuk tuk and go check the house." It was his favorite thing to do.

As we approached the end of our second month out of our house, we went again to check on progress. The smell inside was poison. Lucas, who wore a gas mask, said it would air out and disappear. *No se preocupa.*

Another time, we saw him and his wife on the roof. He hollered and waved at us. I told him not to bother coming down. We only came to grab something from the kitchen.

Every surface of our bedroom, including the bed, was covered in debris and scraps of wood. I couldn't imagine returning to this mess.

Bruce went through the rooms, inspecting the ceiling beams. "Looks like he's doing a good job. Very thorough. I'm impressed."

"You know what, Bruce? Lucas should paint the walls while he's at it. With the whole house clean and repainted, maybe I could stand it."

He ceased gazing upward. "Paint the walls? There's another two, three weeks at least."

"Yes, paint over these dark beige walls. It will look like new, termites gone, fresh paint. Now's the time to do it, while we're out."

"We've been gone eight weeks already, Karen. The hotel is getting busy again. We need to move out and leave Rooms 4 and 5 for paying guests."

"That's because of our garden enclosed space at the end of the hall. As soon as people see such a pretty, separate area, it piques their interest. I've heard them talking and asking Dago about it. Our manager suite makes the entire hotel more appealing."

Bruce gave me a doubtful expression. "Did you get what you need? Let's go outside in the fresh air."

"Yep." I held up a bag of storage containers.

We left, waving goodbye to Lucas on the roof. "Really, our exclusive suite helps business. It attracts paying guests," I continued.

"We were full last night. We had to turn people away, four sets of people wanting rooms."

"See? That's good news! It's about time." In the front garden, I looked up to the distant hills. If we moved from Barrio Norte, I would miss that view.

"People are hearing about us around town," Bruce said as we walked down the lane toward the street. "Those outside lights are stunning at night. They attract attention and bring people in. RJ used to keep them off to save electricity. One more way the place feels like a real hotel with him gone."

"We'll leave the hotel soon enough. Once our walls are painted. It's a small thing, Bruce, and will make such a big difference."

"We need to act like a hotel, and here we are using up two rooms. We even had Room 9 rented out last night." Room 9 was unfinished, a catch-all space with a bed, no bath.

"All the more reason for you to stay on site."

"I don't need to stay on site. I hired Jacob as guardian. He can wake up and let that kid in every morning at one a.m." Jacob was an American teenager, the son of the friendly Jehovah's Witness lady who lived in Pana off and on with her three kids.

We flagged a tuk tuk back to the hotel and ceased discussing this circular argument going nowhere.

I decided to take matters in hand. I saw Dago in the lobby and asked him to tell Morris we want Lucas to paint the walls before we move back. We would buy the paint if Morris paid for the labor. Bruce overheard the conversation and understood enough of the Spanish. He scowled at me. We had not agreed on this.

That evening he worked through dinnertime and so did I.

At ten minutes to eight, he came up to Room 5 and said in a whiny raised voice, "You've been in here for two hours! What about dinner?"

After a full day of writing, I felt pleased with my progress. I glanced up from my laptop, waiting for him to continue, maybe make a dinner suggestion.

"Just come down when you're ready." He huffed out, leaving the door open. That's him being passive aggressive, I thought. He knows I never work with the door open.

Ten minutes later I descended to the lobby. He kept me waiting for twenty minutes while he talked to Jacob. Again, passive aggressive. When I got upset, I got angry and loud. Bruce showed his temper in more subtle ways. Sometimes I wondered how we managed to stay together.

Next week would be our anniversary. Forty-five years. I knew how it would go. Bruce working late until at day's end, he notes our anniversary. "Where shall we eat dinner? It's our anniversary (whiny voice), we should go somewhere nice." We, or rather I, would figure out where to get food and then we'd watch Netflix to mark forty-five years.

Well, forget that. I would not plan anything. Let *him* take the initiative for a change.

When the day came, we went about our routines the same as always, neither of us mentioning the event. At nine p.m. as we silently prepared for bed, he said in a humble tone, "Do you want to go with me for hot dogs?"

"Okay." I would stay in my pajama pants and add a hoodie and flipflops.

Without speaking, we walked up Santander to the hot dog stand. We ordered and sat on the plastic stools to wait for our food.

Bruce broke the silence. "I feel so stupid. Forty-five years and we're eating hot dogs. Why can't I ever think of anything nice to do for you? Especially when it's a special event."

My heart overflowed with love, and I instantly forgave every slight. "It's okay. These hot dogs are special, and we don't get them very often."

⌒

Dago did everything from hanging sheets on the line to cleaning rooms to hauling out trash, but in hospitality he came into his own. He and Bruce shared the same vision for the hotel, and they both liked people. Their energy level soared when weekend guests poured in, which they did whenever the rains slowed down.

Besides daily Skype calls with Sally and RJ, Bruce emailed them a weekly report along with a current spreadsheet showing profit and loss. He reported on each extra expense, approved in advance by them, such as the clothes drier and the electrician to finish wiring Room 9. The hotel was not yet self-supportive and needed Sally's continued financial support for a few more months. The good news was, according to Bruce's figures, that with careful management of funds, it would soon support itself and then turn a profit within a year. Sally was encouraged by that and said of course she'd keep sending the amount they had agreed on.

I overheard the call while waiting for Bruce so we could go to lunch.

RJ didn't want Sally to continue payments through December. He had told Bruce to get the drier and the electrician, but apparently had not expected to pay for them. RJ wondered why the hotel couldn't pay for these things along with any other extra expenses. Bruce must not be charging enough for rooms. Bruce was hiring too many of Dago's family—his sister Graciela to clean, for example. Why can't Dago do the cleaning?

"Why pay Jacob as guardian when you live there?" RJ asked. "You can be guardian."

Bruce did not respond to that. His unpaid job was to manage the place, not to also work nights as guardian. Instead, he ended the discussion by saying he would compromise by cutting Graciela's hours. And having Jacob stay over only when guests were in, although it meant Bruce still had to answer the doorbell at midnight.

After an unseasonably dry and consequently busy August, business died in September when the rain started again. The weather turned cool and wet. Some days were overcast both mornings and afternoons, cold and gray and dismal with the sun behind the heavy cloud bank above the mountains. That's when I missed *one thing* at Barrio Norte: the fireplace.

By the first of October, Bruce and I had made it through three months living at Casa Colonial, much of one rainy season, and forty-five years of marriage.

Lucas finished the termite work but refused to paint, because Morris was *barato*. Morris found someone else. We hired Lucas and his taxi to drive us to Xela to buy the paint at Walmart. I chose white.

"Everything white?" Bruce questioned, as we stood with our cart in the paint department. "Won't that look boring? You normally like colors."

"Trust me. It is exactly the thing with so much dark woodwork. Load up twice what you think we need. It'll take several coats to cover those ugly brown walls."

On the drive home from Xela, Lucas sang one hymn after another in a clear tenor voice. He said he needed to practice because he sang in the choir at his church. He hoped we didn't mind. Mind? Of course not! It was a lovely way to pass the hour drive.

Three weeks later, the walls had two or three coats of white paint. Our house was finally ready. To move us back, Dago called a guy he knew with a truck. RJ's truck, parked in front of the hotel, was out of commission, there being no extra funds for repairs. Dago and his friend loaded and unloaded everything for us.

Our lovely, bright home with its fresh, white walls smelled like Fabuloso from Graciela's cleaning. The brick-red tile floors gleamed and reflected light. On the patio, Graciela had organized the firewood into two stacks built up into a cluster of connected houses. The October weather was cool, damp and dreary. A fire in the mornings would be delightful, but what a shame to break down Graciela's little houses. I decided to wait a bit before using the fireplace.

That evening after dinner, Bruce and I sat together on the living room couch in one of our favorite cuddling positions. "I never thought the white paint would look this good," he said. "I like it."

"Me too. The place looks like new."

"It's good to be back, my love. This feels like home."

"I wish we had more time to settle in and enjoy it before leaving for Utah," I said.

We had planned a ten-day visit. Travis and Jessica's baby boy was due the end of October. Nathan and Brenda's little boy had arrived in September, and they invited us to stay with them. If we timed it right, we could manage to meet both new grandbabies while renewing our visas for another three months.

Bruce wrapped his arms around me. "I almost wish we weren't going. Things are shaping up so well at the hotel, I hate to leave now. Dago and I are anxious to really push business once the rains end and people flow back into Pana."

"Like *Semana Santa* only without RJ."

"Without RJ neglecting to pay the bills, despite Sally sending the money for it." An atypical note of anger sounded in his voice.

I wish I had never mentioned RJ. It spoiled the moment. "Bills like what, utilities?"

Bruce ran a hand through his hair. "No, he can't get by with that or they shut it off. It's the local and national fees for running a business. RJ doesn't want to pay what his accountant says he's required by law to pay. The accountant comes by the hotel regularly asking for RJ and telling me IVA is past due. I know him well enough to trust him, especially since he sticks by his guns despite RJ's arguments. I've checked his paperwork, and it's up-to-date and legitimate. Whenever I pay enough to catch up the past due amounts, RJ gets mad at me."

"Kinda irresponsible to not pay your business fees."

"Yeah, the government can fine him, shut him down, but RJ doesn't care. Says that will never happen, that I'm paranoid and don't understand how things are done in Guatemala."

"His old refrain of 'how it works here.'" My attention wandered. The hallway outside our bedroom looked empty and bare. That wall needed something.

"Maybe IVA never will come after him. Maybe he's right about that, I have no idea." Bruce raised his voice in irritation. "What I do know is if you run a business, operate lawfully. Pay your bills. Pay your taxes. Pay Dago the minimum wage the law requires instead of trying to scam him as well as the government."

At least Bruce was talking again instead of holding it inside. It was good to be home.

"Let's bring back the kids' wedding photos, Bruce, and hang them in the hallway. With their matching wood frames, they'll go perfectly with the woodwork." It was the wall where I had seen the giant termite queen.

Bruce agreed. "Good idea. It's time for us to hang pictures and make this permanent."

13

Bad News

He shall not be afraid of evil tidings;
his heart is fixed, trusting in the Lord.
Psalm 112:7

We were not twenty-four hours back in our house when Sally rang her dad early on Skype. "RJ doesn't want Dago left alone at the hotel while you guys are gone to Utah. I'm coming to Guatemala with him to stay for five days. Can we crash at your house?"

The unspoken but implied message was that although our daughter was coming for five days, her husband would stay on. Not a message Bruce wanted to hear, I saw by the expression on his face. The call was short. Sally, exhausted from working her four nightshifts in a row, had rung from bed. "RJ's at the gym. I'm going to put on the Harry Potter audiobook and go to sleep."

When Bruce signed off, I couldn't hold back. "I hate the idea of RJ in our house taking over everything while we're gone. Trouble follows wherever he goes!"

"Me neither but what else could we do?" He gathered his things and headed for the door.

"Nothing else," I said. "It's our daughter."

I knew what Bruce's stony look meant: *I don't like this one bit, but I better figure out how to deal with it.* For him, the larger issue was RJ staying on in Pana to take back hotel operations.

Why does he have to come back now? We barely return to our pretty house after three months stuck at his stupid hotel, and we don't get one week of enjoyment without him barging in. I don't believe the story about not wanting to leave Dago in charge. RJ used to leave Dago in charge for weeks at a time, well before Bruce came into the picture. *How is this any different?* We're gone for *ten days.* Dago can certainly manage on his own for ten days.

I grabbed the broom and swept vigorously from one end of the house to the other. "Believe it or not, RJ, Dago is way better equipped to handle the hotel than you are. Whenever real people, *not* your personal friends, rent a room—*paying guests*—you act like a fool, all nervous and anxious. You'd rather fill the place with your pals and with Bailey's fellow street dogs instead of people with money."

Ever since Billy and Larry, I didn't trust RJ's motives. He didn't get a nursing job because apparently "California isn't hiring nurses right now." Ha, fat chance! He's using our absence as an excuse to get back to where he feels useful and important.

"Nobody feels good about themselves while on a job hunt, RJ. I get it—humbling yourself at an interview, feeling like a loser waiting for someone to give you a chance. Coming back to Pana frees you from the embarrassing job search, doesn't it? The uncomfortable interview process, the potential for rejection."

I finished sweeping, glad to see very little termite debris. Whipping our sheets off the bed, I marched them out to the *pila.*

In Panajachel, RJ was somebody. A hotel owner, a businessman, an entrepreneur who hired people. I filled the sink with water and poured detergent on top, swirled it fiercely around and pushed in the billowy sheets. The fresh graduate on a job hunt didn't fit his grandiose image like staying in Pana did. The guy who struts around town at night flexing muscles in his black wifebeater. Or daytime dressed in Dockers and a button down shirt, wearing his trendy wire rim glasses, going to meet with his accountant and stopping in at the bank.

I didn't believe a word of Sally's statement that "RJ doesn't trust Dago alone at the hotel." Maybe she believed it, but I knew it was bogus. He couldn't have come up with a better excuse than *that*?

They arrived the day before our flight and got to our house at four-thirty. I was glad to see my daughter at least.

Sally had the olive complexion of her dad. Her long, straight, dark brown hair had reddish highlights, also like her dad. She had hazel eyes same as Bruce, with curly thick lashes, perfectly shaped nose and lips, and smooth skin that tanned easily. Next to RJ, she looked as Latin as he did. They made a handsome couple.

I had dinner ready—a hash of hamburger and vegetables, and fresh fruit mixed with yogurt. RJ complimented the food and the house, how nice it looked with the white walls. After dinner, he cleaned up the dishes while Sally kept up a running monologue of positivity. She was happiest in Guatemala with her husband. Too bad they couldn't live here and run Casa Colonial, and Bruce and I would go do something else. Only she made too much money in LA to justify leaving.

RJ expressed concern over the condition of the mountain roads. "If it rains through the night, it can get bad. Mudslides, rockslides, roads blocked." He paced and worried. "It's dangerous when it rains like this. You don't have any idea."

Sally tried to calm him down. "They'll be fine, honey. Pedro is careful and knows the roads."

"What time is he picking you up again, Bruce?"

"At three-thirty in the morning," Bruce responded. "Our flight's at eight. I confirmed the schedule with him this afternoon."

RJ pulled out his phone and rang Pedro. "Okay, it's settled. He's coming at two to allow more time."

Even that schedule change didn't stop him from circling the room and fretting about the stormy weather.

Bruce and I finished packing and set our luggage by the front door. We said goodnight, needing to get to bed early. Sally suggested we have a prayer together and pray for everything to go well in these potentially dangerous driving conditions. We gathered in the living room, and Bruce asked her to say it. After the prayer, RJ seemed calmer. Bruce and I went to bed.

In the end, our prayers were answered. The pre-dawn trip to the airport was safe and uneventful.

In Utah, we stayed with Nathan and Brenda and their now four children. We had a big turkey dinner and gathered with the other Utah families for "an early Thanksgiving." A few days later, everyone came to Nathan's again for one-month-old Milo's baby blessing.

On November ninth, Jessica had their baby—Miles—giving us the happy opportunity to stop at the hospital before our flight and hold the newborn. Then we were back in Guatemala, our visas stamped for another ninety days, Pedro and his van waiting at the airport as though he had never left.

"*Bienvenidos!*" he greeted as always, shook our hands and loaded our bags. Bruce and I climbed in and took our usual seats.

"Welcome home, my love," I said.

"It's sure good to be back, isn't it? I don't want to leave again for a good long time."

"We shouldn't have to for a year at least, when we go for Don and Lauren's wedding next October." There were other ways to get the visas stamped besides flying home.

"Unless Forrest gets married before then," Bruce said. "There's always that possibility. It seems like he's dating a lot at the U."

"Yeah, funny how he has so many girlfriends, when he didn't date much in high school. He has become such a handsome, confident young man."

As Pedro deftly maneuvered the van through the city traffic, Bruce and I reflected silently on our own thoughts. Feelings of homesickness at leaving our family lingered in my heart. Bruce soon dozed off, while I gazed out the window at the rich display of activity rolling past as though on a screen.

When Pedro dropped us off at our house some three hours later, the signs of RJ were everywhere. In the short time we were gone, he had found the money to repair his truck, now parked inside our gate. Paddle boards cluttered the patio in various stages of completion. Our living room was his workshop, with furniture moved out of his way. RJ had set up sawhorses in the middle of the room for sanding and varnishing boards. Spots of varnish had spilled and dried on the tile floors. Dust was everywhere.

"I'll get this cleaned up, Karen. Don't worry," RJ said, reading my mind or perhaps my expression.

I looked around in dismay. "Why not do this at the hotel? Why haul it to our house?"

"I kept getting interrupted. This is better. Nobody bothers me, and I got so much done."

I headed to the bedroom. "I need a nap."

"I'll make an early dinner," RJ called out. "You guys rest and unpack. I'll take care of it. I'll clean this up, Karen, don't worry."

Bruce joined me, and we both went right to sleep. After an hour, I felt better, not as upset about the house.

True to his word, RJ had cleaned up at least part of the mess. For dinner, he sauteed a tasty concoction of chicken, potatoes and onions. While we ate, he gave us the bad news. "Morris came by showing the place while I was here. But don't worry. He'll never sell it. He's asking too much."

"Of course he sells the house after we get it nice and fixed up!" I lamented.

"This house has too many problems. Anybody who agrees to pay $75,000 for it is a fool," RJ scoffed. "That was the asking price when you guys moved in. Morris paid $40,000 for it a couple years before. The neighbors laughed and said he got ripped off."

"Did the buyers see the paddleboard construction and all that mess?" I asked.

"Yeah, I didn't have enough notice to clean it up."

"Good! Hopefully they don't want it."

"If he sells, our contract gives us two months free rent," Bruce said.

RJ changed the subject to his favorite topic: paddleboards. He would take everything to the hotel and finish up there. He explained where he was with each board and how little time it would take to finish.

"Karen, I have a couple of boards ready to try out tomorrow. You want to go? It will prove that an older woman who's never gone paddleboarding before can have fun on the lake."

Well, this was unexpected. "You think I should, Bruce?"

"You're in better shape than me. I can't see myself getting on one of those things. If you want to give it a try, sure why not?"

Living in Guatemala was my big adventure, doing things I never would have done if we were still in Utah. "But you'll give me a training lesson first, right, RJ?"

"Sure, sure. I'll help you. We'll take it slow and easy at first. You'll see, it's not as hard as it looks."

RJ and Bruce reviewed the plan. Set off from Jucanya tomorrow morning around nine or ten. From there, paddleboard to one of the towns around the bend, where Bruce picks us up with the truck and drives us back to the hotel. Simple, straightforward, and carefully considered. What could go wrong?

14

Burned

He sent from above, he took me, he drew me out of many waters.
He delivered me from my strong enemy, and from them which hated me,
for they were too strong for me.
They prevented me in the day of my calamity:
but the Lord was my stay.
Psalm 18:16-18

For Karen's Big Adventure, I wore loose, white linen pants, a short sleeve cotton shirt, flip flops and, of course, my sunglasses. I never stepped outside without sunglasses.

The three of us and Bailey took the truck to the launching place in Jucanya. RJ said it would take about twenty minutes to paddleboard from there to Santa Catarina, just around the bend. Or an hour to continue to San Antonio. "Santa Catarina is good for your first time on the board, Karen," he concluded.

Twenty, thirty minutes sounded great to me. Santa Catarina it would be.

"A nice trial run," he added. "Bruce will meet us at the dock."

It was clear and sunny with no sign of rain, being the end of the rainy season. It seemed more like a gorgeous June morning in Utah instead of the second week of November.

I waded into the shallow water up to my knees. RJ held the board for me as I managed with difficulty to climb on. I felt awkward, heavy, and old. "You can sit or kneel or stand, whatever feels most comfortable," he said by way of training.

I tried kneeling but the rough surface hurt my knees. No way could I stand or I'd tumble right off. I ended up sitting with my legs straight out in front of me, using the paddle like an oar. I did know how to row a boat.

Once I got settled, Bruce took pictures with his silver digital camera. Way too many pictures. I waved and smiled as directed.

"Lift your paddle in the air like a victory salute," he instructed. I lifted my paddle to salute the doubtful victory of having struggled onto the board and stayed there.

Bailey took a flying leap from the shore to RJ's board, and we were off. Farther out, the water was slightly rough and choppy, although not so much as to interfere with my rowing rhythm.

RJ hollered out to ask if I was okay, if I enjoyed it and wasn't this the greatest thing ever? We were too far apart for him to hear my response. He kept saying, "What? What?" So, whenever he hollered in my direction I simply waved and yelled back, "It's great. I'm fine."

To finally get on this lake thrilled me no end. I was practically *in* the lake really, with the board floating on top and the cool water splashing over my bare legs. I had rolled my pants up to the knees.

The long flat board moved with the waves like it belonged there. Suspended between wind and water, it carried me along. RJ and I were alone out here, except for the occasional far distant boat taxi. We had launched from a rocky deserted beach, not a high traffic area.

I paddled from side to side as with a kayak, following RJ as we bobbed along. I glanced at my watch, surprised to see it was after eleven. We had left the house before nine, probably on the lake by nine-thirty. We should have reached Santa Catarina by now. RJ had said it was the first cove. I saw no cove, no village or dock, only the lake surrounded by sloping hills of thick vegetation. Ahead was the cone shape of a volcano silhouetted in the distant sky.

"How much longer?" I yelled, tired of the endless rowing on a lake that appeared much larger from this vulnerable angle.

"It's not far." RJ stood easily on his board with Bailey in front. He lifted his paddle and pointed straight ahead. "We might as well go on to San Antonio. It's the town in the next cove."

I wasn't sure what he meant by "the next cove." Did he mean the first cove or the one after that? Like on a Monday when someone says, "next Wednesday." Do they mean in two days or Wednesday of next week?

"I don't see anything," I hollered back. "Are we almost there?"

RJ pointed to a jutting segment of forested land. "The cove is right past there."

"Oh, good! That's our dock?" I paddled with renewed vigor seeing an end in sight.

"It's Santa Catarina. I guess we may as well pull in there. Santa Catarina is closer than San Antonio, and it's where Bruce is gonna meet us with the truck."

Then why ask me if I want to go to the next town if you already arranged for Bruce to meet us in the first one? RJ often changed plans without notice and left people hanging. Bruce was used to it, but with me out here, he would be concerned if we didn't show up on time.

Where the land jutted out was farther than it appeared, but finally we reached the cove, the *first* cove, and turned in. I saw Bruce at the end of the dock, a small figure in the distance but unmistakable in his cowboy hat. He waved with both arms. As we approached, he took more pictures. Our boards slid forward quickly on the glassy smooth surface of this protected area. How nice if the whole lake had been like this.

The moment I reached the dock, Bruce stretched his arms down to help me up. I couldn't get hold of either his hands or the side of the pier, because the board kept slipping away. RJ moved his board next to mine and held it steady while Bruce pulled me upward to dry land. Stiff and numb, I needed every bit of assistance.

Bruce let RJ manage the boards while he hovered over me. "I'm glad to see you guys. I've been waiting over an hour, thought you'd be here in twenty minutes. Are you okay? You feel okay, Karen? How was it? I was getting worried."

"I'm fine but stiff. It took longer than I expected. RJ said twenty, thirty minutes, and what's this? An hour?" I checked my watch. It was almost noon.

"Nearly two hours," Bruce said.

"*What?* No wonder I'm worn out. I was so glad when we came around the bend and I saw you waiting."

RJ tied the boards to the dock, and the three of us climbed a wooden stairway leading to a restaurant that overlooked the lake.

"It'll go faster on the way back, don't worry," RJ assured me. "The wind was against us coming over. That's why it took so long. It'll push us forward on the way back and take thirty minutes, tops." We entered the restaurant. "This is where our tour guides can bring people on the paddleboards, Bruce. It's a great place, has the best empanadas."

A lady in full Maya dress greeted us. RJ at his friendliest and most outgoing explained who we were and promised her a lot of business with our paddleboard tours. She smiled and nodded in the shy, humble way of the Maya women, then invited us to follow her to a table.

"Karen, take pictures of us. Bruce, come on, give Karen your camera." He directed me to get shots of the three of them together and several with him and the lady. Quiet, polite and smiling, she complied with each request.

RJ stepped away and gestured for Bruce to move in next to her. Bruce was visibly uncomfortable with such carrying on, especially when RJ said, "Don't stand so stiffly, Bruce. Put your arm around her." He hesitated but couldn't refuse without appearing awkward.

The photo shoot ended, and I took a seat at the table.

"How are they?" RJ asked. "Did they turn out? Do we have enough?" I checked the camera and replied yes, the pictures are great.

RJ kept on kidding around in Spanish with the lady, who responded with quiet friendliness. He said she should give us a free meal or two in exchange for the future business Casa Colonial will bring to her restaurant. She shook her head no with a little chuckle.

Bruce, sitting next to me at the table, muttered, "That photo shoot was embarrassing. Now look at him trying to get free meals."

"It's how he is. Remember the act with Lucas?"

"Don't remind me. I hate this kind of stuff, but RJ is all about snagging favors and commissions and whatever he can for free." Bruce opened the menu.

"I'm still not hungry," I said, "only thirsty. But I guess I better try one of these famous empanadas."

RJ suggested we get a plate of empanadas to share. I ordered a diet Coke and a water bottle. He requested a bowl of water for Bailey, who stretched out on the cool tile floor beneath our table.

The empanadas came six on a plate, were smaller than a toaster pastry and little more than a snack. They tasted dry with sparse filling that looked like frozen mixed vegetables heated and baked inside the dough. Nonetheless, my thrill of accomplishment was not dampened by a poor lunch. Sure, it took us two hours instead of twenty minutes. But we made it, Bruce was waiting, we were eating the famous empanadas.

Our table overlooked the Santa Catarina cove with the lake beyond. I noticed white caps on the choppy waves farther out and pointed them out to RJ. "It looks rough out there now."

He glanced out the window. "The wind is going toward Pana. It was against us on the way over. That's why it took over twenty minutes. The way back will go fast."

I wasn't sure what he meant by "the way back." I thought the plan was to land, meet Bruce and visit the restaurant. After lunch, we load up the boards and drive back in the truck, right?

We finished eating and filed down the hill back to the dock, where I supposed we would untie the boards and carry them up to wherever Bruce had parked the truck. Instead, RJ stepped onto his board and called Bailey, who acted hesitant to join him. Normally, Bailey jumped right on, ready to go anywhere with her favorite person.

While RJ coaxed his dog, I said to Bruce, "I'm not sure I want to take the board back." The idea of returning with RJ instead of Bruce didn't feel right. I'd been so relieved to see him waiting on this dock, how could I leave him now? Besides, I had accomplished the task, done the thing. I saw no reason to get overzealous and stretch it out for longer.

RJ looked at me. "Are you coming?"

I felt confused and nervous, much like Bailey who wanted nothing to do with the board.

Bruce spoke up. "She's not sure she wants to get back on the lake."

RJ thought he meant Bailey. "Ahh, she just needs encouragement. Come on, Bailey, come on girl." Finally, Bailey jumped on.

My board floated next to the dock, ready for me. In the restaurant, RJ said the trip back would be shorter, that the wind was against us before. Surely, I could do an hour back to Jucanya. I had taken a break, drunk water, eaten a dry empanada. Why not finish this adventure?

I turned to Bruce. "Well, I guess I'll go."

"Are you sure?" he said.

"Yeah, I might as well."

Getting on the board from the pier was easier than climbing on from the water. The ease of it encouraged me. I adjusted myself to the kayak position and waved goodbye to my love. He didn't take pictures this time.

Once out of the cove and past the jutting bend, I realized that the wind must've been *with* us on the way over. Now, it was hard against us. Paddling to Santa Catarina had taken three times longer than RJ predicted, but it had not been difficult. This time, however, we had to paddle against the wind and the rough, churning water. Naturally, I struggled more than RJ did, although he no longer stood on his board. He went from kneeling to occasionally sitting, with his legs hanging over the sides. Bailey kept looking over at me with canine anxiety, the worry and fear of a sensitive dog recognizing danger in the pack.

After two and a half hours of this unbelievable effort, three o'clock on my watch, we were not halfway. I obsessively checked the shoreline for a suitable landing where we might pull in and rest, wait things out, maybe have RJ call Bruce to come pick us up.

Lake Atitlán is like a deep bowl. It has no way out, no stream or river leading away from it. Each rainy season the level rises a few inches up the surrounding hills, a bowl with its sides angled upward. Ancient cities lay buried beneath it. Homes and businesses are lost every year as the crater fills and the shoreline gives way. I saw nowhere to dock, no way to stop rowing. There were only the steep hillsides, thick with tropical vegetation and enormous boulders, rising sharply above the shoreline.

At four o'clock I felt the sunburn. Rolling my linen pants up to the knees had been yet another bad idea in a day full of bad ideas. I had no sunblock. I never used it unless I planned to be out in direct sun for over two hours. Otherwise, I didn't burn. I unrolled my pant legs and splashed water on my feet and arms to cool them.

I noticed a slightly open place where perhaps we might dock. I asked RJ about pulling in. No, that's impossible. I can't call Bruce, there's no minutes on my phone. There's nowhere to pull in the boards, no way for Bruce to get the truck down to us. We'll go a little farther. It's not much longer.

While battling the swerving, unruly board and the choppy waves, I punctuated my efforts with mutterings against RJ's carelessness, his impulsive foolhardy ways. He always carried on about how the lake is ideal for paddleboard tours, how successful that will be, how people will flock to Casa Colonial for his paddleboards. Did he have the slightest clue about this lake? Or about these angry churning waves that emerge so unpredictably?

The sky was clear, with a few fluffy clouds in the distance. The lake should be calm on a day like this, except this lake didn't react to typical weather patterns. It moved according to some force within itself, some hidden inner turmoil. Lake Atitlán has no tide like a normal lake, does not answer to the sun or the moon, does not empty into the ocean. It is a vortex, filling higher every year, swallowing the shoreline and creating new ones as it creeps upward.

Stupid RJ ignores reality and believes in whatever fantasy suits his picture. Furiously, I rowed.

White caps on a lake mean it's not safe for small craft, not row boats or motorboats, certainly not paddleboards. Years of vacationing with my family in Midwestern lakes should have taught me not to get on this thing. What an idiot I was. I wasn't even wearing a life jacket. The hotel didn't have them.

I hate him, I hate him, I hate him.

Between regretting my bad decision or fuming about RJ—the clueless moron in his fantasyland of cool board dude making a fortune—I prayed for endurance and protection. *Somehow, somehow, God, please get me back to Bruce in one piece.* I had an overwhelming desire to give up and quit rowing, to let the wind and the water take control while I hung on until someone rescued me.

The beach where we set off that morning, hours and hours ago, came into faraway view. I hollered at RJ. "Isn't that where we started? Shouldn't we head that direction?"

"Yeah, but we can't pull in there. It's too far to go for a phone. I have to find a tienda and use their phone to call Bruce."

Of course! Because he brought a cell phone with NO MIN-UTES. What if we had a life-threatening emergency, if one of us lost a paddle or if I got cramps in my arms and couldn't row?

When I asked him, he responded glibly. "That's okay. I'd pull you in."

Right. The all-powerful RJ.

It took all my strength against the churning waves to keep the board straight and headed in the right direction. Every minute took torturous effort. *I hate him.*

"Or we could kick back and relax on the boards and let the current take us to San Antonio. We'd have a drink, call Bruce and he'd pick us up there."

Of course, since the current so agreeably goes in exactly the right direction. With us "kicking back on our boards," without paddles, the lovely lake would deliver us right up to the San Antonio dock. What an idiot.

I hate him, I hate him, I hate him.

At long last, we arrived where RJ said we could dock, where stores were nearby for him to find a phone. It was five-thirty. Five hours since leaving the Santa Catarina restaurant. I stumbled off my board and sat on a rock under a tree, leaving RJ to manage the rest. Numb. Skin burning. Dehydrated. I wanted Bruce. Bruce would take me home.

RJ muttered something unintelligible about what to do now. I snapped back, "I'll wait here." He went off to find a phone.

Before long I saw the pickup truck with my beloved behind the wheel. To take me home, away from this crazy person and his big ideas. I climbed in next to Bruce. RJ stayed in back with the two boards and Bailey.

"I was so worried," Bruce said. "I hovered near the desk phone for the past three hours, afraid to run to the bathroom in case I missed the call. You guys were out there for five hours. I was sick with worry." He asked if I was okay and what took so long, but I was too wrung out to say anything.

Five hours. In the heat of the afternoon sun.

Bruce pulled into our lane and parked. I climbed out with difficulty. I limped through the high gate, across the lawn and the patio and through the front door. I had to stay in motion until I could shower and put on my pajamas. If I stopped I wasn't sure if I'd ever move again.

When I came out of the bathroom, Bruce and RJ were in the living room, watching me.

"Are you okay?" Bruce asked.

I limped my way to the kitchen. "I need a water bottle. I'm going to bed."

In my cool, cotton pajamas and my wonderful comfy bed, I felt better knowing this ordeal was finally over.

Only it was not over. Not even close to over.

15

Dexter and the German Mercenary

In the day of my trouble, I sought the Lord.
My sore ran in the night and ceased not;
my soul refused to be comforted.
Psalm 77:2

In the morning, I could not stand. When I stepped out of bed, sudden shooting pains up my legs knocked me off balance, and I fell back into bed. I called for Bruce, who held my arm as I inched my way to the bathroom and back.

I sat at the edge of the bed while he went to get his crutches and adjusted them to fit. They were awkward and troublesome. I dropped back into bed.

"Never mind about the crutches. I'll stay in bed and work on getting up without falling over."

Bruce brought me a plate of scrambled eggs. I gobbled them down, feeling starved. He rushed back to the kitchen to make more. I drained my water bottle, and he refilled it for me. I polished off the second plate of eggs. He set the water bottle on my bedside table. "Or do you want it next to you in the bed?"

"No, it's fine right there. Thanks."

"You want more eggs, Karen? I used up what we had, but I can run to the tienda and get more. It will only take a few minutes."

I handed him the plate and fork. "No, I'm done. Those were such good eggs."

"Because I made them with love." He stood next to the bed holding the plate and watching me struggle with my pillows. "Here, let me stack them for you." Setting down the plate, he fluffed and arranged the pillows. "Try that."

I leaned back. They felt cool and billowy.

"You need another one?"

"Maybe on the side."

Bruce brought me another pillow and a blanket, "in case you get cold." He shook out the sheet to air before pulling it gently over my legs. The blanket he folded at the end of the bed. He brought his bottle of Ibuprofen and directed me to take four now and four more at noon. Finally, he left for the hotel, promising to come home early.

I had no desire to leave this bed. When I stood, the intense shooting pains went up and down my legs, bringing me close to collapse. After a few minutes of remaining upright, the pains abated. I managed to get myself to the bathroom, along the way checking the kitchen to see what we had for easy meals.

Bruce was home by four, two hours earlier than normal, and ready to start dinner. Except he had no idea what to make. I suggested he boil spaghetti, drain it, then open a box of plain tomato sauce to pour over. About as simple as it gets. I waited in bed with my legs stretched out. When the meal was ready, he brought our plates, mine on a cookie sheet laid over with a dish towel to dress it up. He carried in a dining room chair to sit next to me.

When I praised his spaghetti, he scoffed. "I boiled water and opened packages."

"How did you manage two years on a mission without learning to cook anything except breakfast?"

"It was the Southern states. In Georgia, we picked peaches off trees as we walked by. They were everywhere. We ate lunch out of boxes and cans; macaroni and cheese, instant pudding, canned soup. Members and nonmembers alike fed us dinners. People were always feeding us. You wouldn't believe some of the meals they laid out. You want more spaghetti?"

I declined, and he went to get seconds. He returned with a small serving on his plate. "I didn't know how much of the noodles to put in. Are you sure you don't want more? This is what's left but I can share."

"No, I'm full. I had a big breakfast, remember?"

"That was seven hours ago!"

"Yeah, but I didn't move much today." I lifted the tray off my lap and turned to see him better. "Tell me about those Southern feasts."

"Always two kinds of meat for dinner—pork chops and fried chicken, for instance. Greens, like collard greens or chard, whatever was in their gardens, I suppose. Then potatoes or grits, and fresh vegetables like sliced tomatoes or green onions, maybe a cucumber salad. Usually a dish of something pickled they put up themselves, weird things like fruit and vegetables you wouldn't think about. They liked to pickle everything, it seemed. They served hot vegetables like green beans, corn cut fresh off the cob, okra, squash. They fried okra, too. Sometimes they boiled it but more often the okra was fried. Boiled okra can be slimy so that takes some getting used to."

"Tell me the story about when you ate two Thanksgiving dinners in a row."

"That was the fullest I got in my entire life. My companion and I could barely walk back to our apartment, we were so stuffed. You can't tell those Southern ladies no to any dish or second helpings, or it hurts their feelings. We ate it all, including seconds on the pie. We had the first dinner at two. The next one was for five."

I had seen pictures of Bruce before his mission, tall and skinny as a rail. In his return home photos, he was twenty pounds heavier and a handsome young man instead of a skinny kid. That was who I met and fell in love with—six two and a half, one hundred seventy pounds, a year back from the mission. The kindest person I ever saw was my first impression of him. How I knew that I have no idea, but it turned out to be true.

By the third day, seeping and oozing blisters covered my feet and lower legs. My face and arms were burned but not blistered. They soon healed while my feet and legs got worse. The blisters filled with fluid and grew larger, spreading over the skin. Standing brought the awful shooting pains. Bruce helped me when he was there. When he wasn't, I maneuvered awkwardly on the crutches.

"RJ says he's leaving soon to spend the holidays with Sally," Bruce said one morning before work. "Do you know, when we were in Utah, he only rented three rooms in those two weeks. He raised the rates by fifty per cent, up to 300 quetzal a night, nonnegotiable. He turned away customers rather than adjust the price. Totally lost income. When Dago asked about negotiating rates for proven regulars, he refused."

"What an idiot," I grunted.

"You know what he says? That it doesn't matter, the big money is in the paddleboard business." Bruce slid his Kindle and yellow notepad into his backpack. "I'd rather stay longer with you, Karen, but somebody has to keep an eye on the place. Left on his own too long, RJ will run it into the ground."

"It's fine, Bruce. It's not like you can hurry up the healing. This sunburn is worse than childbirth. Different, but worse. Just constant burning. It lasts longer too, and there's nothing anyone can do." I turned gingerly to one side and closed my eyes.

"I'm sorry, my love. I feel like it's my fault. I should have listened to you when you said you weren't sure. I should have been more aware."

"How could you know?" I murmured. "RJ said thirty minutes going back."

"You were hesitant, and I didn't pay attention."

Before he left, Bruce filled a spray bottle with olive oil and melaleuca then sprayed my legs and feet to cool and hydrate them. He gave me Ibuprofen and Aleve, but they didn't touch the pain.

While Bruce was gone, I watched *Dexter,* the series about the psychopath killer of criminals that I'd discovered on Netflix. I consumed one episode after another, gratefully sucked into the intensity of a storyline I never would have enjoyed otherwise.

At night, I dozed in bits of five or ten minutes before the pain woke me. This compelling series of depravity and misery provided an escape from my pain-filled insomnia. It distracted me from the burning, blistering, swelling legs and feet. I binged on *Dexter* episodes day and night.

After five days of constant pain and no sleep, I was desperate for relief. Surely Bruce could pick up something stronger than Ibuprofen at the pharmacy. After all, they sold medication over the counter that needed a doctor's prescription in the U.S.

Through my insomniac brain fog one long night, came the image of Doc Lewis, a tall, blond man with a clinic across the street from Casa Colonial. He had NGO funding to treat local folks who couldn't pay. The expat community used him, too, as he was well known around town and fluent in both English and Spanish. One time at the Dispensa, when there were long lines at check out, I heard someone yelling in Spanish to open more registers. It was Doc Lewis in his scrubs, holding a couple items he wanted to buy and not wanting to wait twenty minutes for it.

Employees responded immediately and additional lines opened. Doc Lewis could help me get past this misery.

As soon as Bruce woke up, I asked him to please go see Doc Lewis today. He should have something to at least help me sleep.

That afternoon, Bruce returned with a nameless brown card of eight little pills. "Doc Lewis said to start with one and go to two if you need it, but no more than that every four hours. He didn't charge me, but I gave him a donation of fifty quetzales. He asked if I was sure you will take them. Too many expats won't take his meds, he said, because they're not herbal or natural or whatever, and these are too precious to waste on someone who won't take it."

I swallowed one and thirty minutes later another. Exactly four hours later, I took two more and experienced relief. After a week of no sleep except for intermittent catnaps between episodes of *Dexter,* I finally got an uninterrupted five hours. Then right back to sleep until morning. God bless Doc Lewis. I took his meds as instructed until they were gone.

My feet and lower legs swelled up to three times normal size. The blistering was worse around the ankles; they looked like two huge wraparound blisters. Bruce took pictures and emailed them to the kids, although I specifically asked him not to.

"What's wrong with letting the kids see? They care about us and want to know how we are, like we do with them and their families."

"I'm embarrassed. I'm ashamed of myself for letting this happen."

Bruce sat on the bed and took my hand. "It's not your fault, Karen."

"I saw the white caps. I knew it was a bad idea to go back on that lake. I ignored my common sense. And why didn't I bring sunblock? Or roll down my pant legs sooner."

"Don't blame yourself. If anyone is responsible, it's me. You said you weren't sure, and I didn't listen. I should never have let you get back on that board."

When Sally saw the pictures her dad emailed, she texted me on Google chat. "I feel awful, Mom. Like it's my fault."

"Your fault? How is it your fault?"

"I don't know. It's how I feel."

Between Sally, Bruce and me, we each felt responsible. The one actually at fault never uttered a word of consolation or apology. He went along his merry way.

On the lake, I was furious with him. Afterwards, I blamed myself. None of us called RJ out for so badly misjudging conditions and putting me at risk. What good would it do? After ten months in Guatemala, Bruce and I knew him too well. RJ was the fifteen-year-old kid with no license who takes the family car out on the freeway. He brings along a friend, and they end up swerving into a ditch while the friend yells, "What are you doing, you moron? You said you knew how to drive! We almost died!"

⟨⟩

I thought my legs might not return to normal, that I might never walk easily again. I was afraid they'd stay discolored or have underlying damage.

Bruce made up ice packs to arrange on them. He sprayed the cooling, soothing olive oil-melaleuca mixture. At home, he hovered close, anxious to provide whatever I needed. I made him a list of things to get at the store and we survived on easy, basic meals.

When night came and my gentle companion fell asleep, I had Dexter.

After a few weeks, the swelling subsided, the blisters healed, and I could walk again. Lingering effects were the shooting pains if I stood too long in one place. Gradually, that symptom lessened as well, although it took nine months before they stopped completely. The only permanent changes were freckles on my legs where I never had them before. Years later, I still have those ugly freckles.

Even RJ was gone, back to California. At least for the holidays.

One December evening, Morris dropped by with a man and a woman. They were the ones he had shown the house to when we were in Utah, the ones RJ said would never buy it. Well, they did. They had just signed the paperwork. Morris apologized to us profusely, although clearly thrilled to have closed the deal. He and the man were both tipsy and happy.

No wonder Morris was celebrating. A couple years earlier, he paid $40,000 for it. He sold it to this couple for $100,000, we found out later, when Lucas told Dago and Dago told Bruce.

Morris showed the couple around, asking what furnishings they wanted to keep and what they wanted removed. The man was German, his wife Norwegian. He spoke both English and Spanish but to her, he spoke German.

In English, he told us, "She fell in love with this place. We looked at a lot of properties, and this is the one she wants."

The man was tall and slender, probably in his early to mid-fifties, with deep lines in his face and short cropped, reddish-brown hair. He looked and sounded like a chain smoker who had lived rough. His English was heavily accented and due to his alcohol-induced, slurred speech, I barely understood him. He directed his conversation to Bruce. I paid little attention, too distracted with this bad news to care anything about the couple buying our home out from under us.

I did notice how solemn Bruce appeared. He watched the man silently and without expression, not cracking a smile as the fellow chattered on. About what, I couldn't hear and didn't care. It was unlike Bruce to be that unresponsive to friendly conversation. I figured maybe he, like me, was upset about this sudden change in our situation.

As they viewed the rooms, Morris didn't seem to notice or care about any paddleboard resin on the tiles. Why should he? He had made an astounding profit. He gave us one month's free rent. The contract allowed for two months if the house got sold, which he would honor if we stayed through January. I couldn't imagine staying two more months because as of this night, it no longer felt like our home. The new owners were eager to move in and hoped to celebrate Christmas in the house.

"Any chance of that?" asked the German guy.

I doubted we could find a suitable rental in such short time, but we would try. "Maybe by New Year's at least," I said before they left.

The German man nodded and smiled. "We'll get together. My wife and I want to take you and Bruce out to eat, to make up for everything. Once we move in, we'll invite you over for dinner."

When they were gone, I mentioned how nice the guy was, inviting us to dinner and regretful about causing us to lose our home.

Bruce responded, "I don't want anything to do with them."

My gregarious husband didn't want anything to do with a friendly guy who spoke English and offered to treat us to dinner? "He sure seemed to like you. He kept cornering you into conversation."

"He was explaining how he came to Guatemala as a mercenary during the war. He said, 'I'm one of the bad guys.' And I knew it. I could tell."

In the 1980s, the Guatemalan government brought in mercenaries to supplement their army during the thirty-year civil war,
to quell rebellion and wipe out the indigenous population who
they saw as the problem. These mercenaries were key players
in committing atrocities and genocide against the Maya villages.
During our tour to the lake villages with Billy and Larry, the tour
guide (not RJ) took us to a church in Santiago, where local folks
had been held captive and a priest killed during the war.

"That was wrong to bring war into a church," the guide told
us. "Our people will never let this happen again. Next time, we
rise. We fight. Everyone fights. We are prepared for next time."

"This German was one of *them*?" I asked Bruce.

"I can believe it," Bruce said. "Did you look into his eyes?"

"No."

"Well, I did, and I don't want anything to do with him."

Photographs

We arrive in Panajachel

Casa Colonial

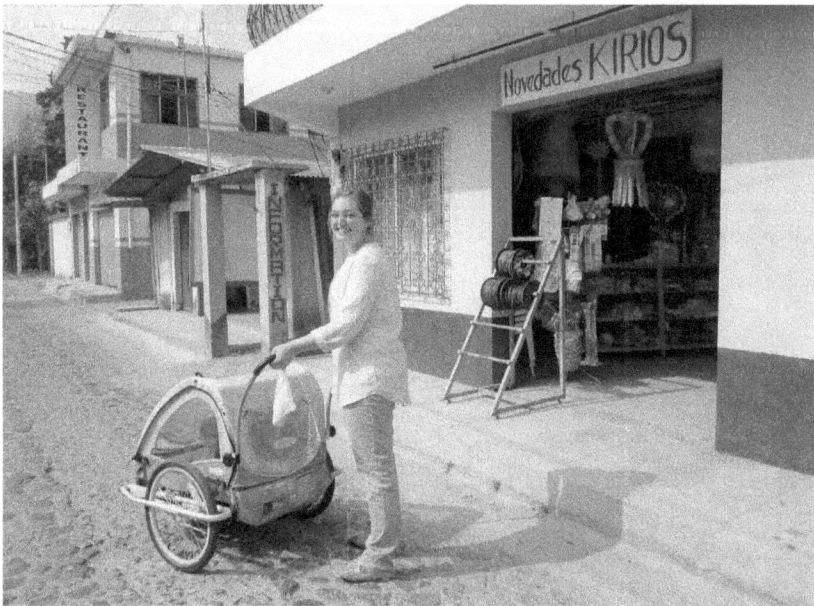

Jessica with Emree in the stroller

Bruce at work in his office

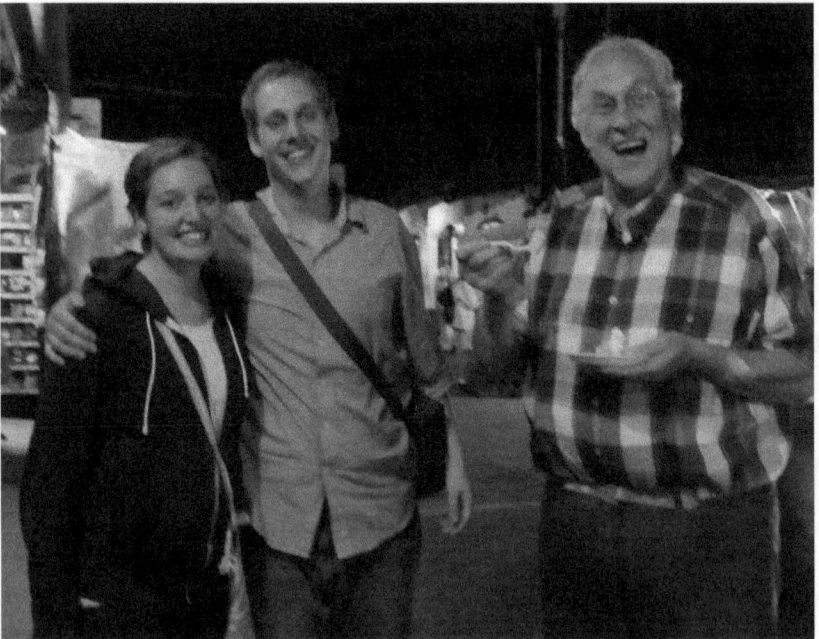

Enjoying street food on Santander with Jessica and Travis

Left to right: RJ, Lucas, Bruce, and Dago in front of Casa Colonial

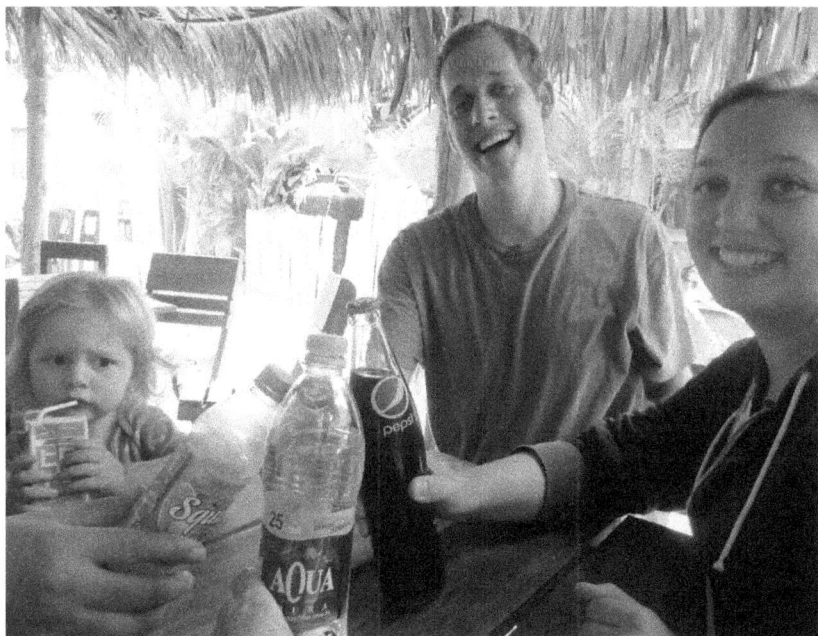

Travis, Jessica, Emree at Smoky Joe's

Karen in front of our Barrio Norte house

Bruce on Santander

Billy at the Pana Nature Reserve

Enjoying Japanese food on the balcony of Casa Colonial

RJ and Karen first setting out on the paddleboards

The back of our Pana house

After a baptism at our church. Hermano Juan is second from right.

The elders with Hermano Juan in our front garden

Bruce waiting for transport at ChiChi

Mother and baby on chicken bus

At Big Burger in San Pedro
left to right: Erin, Sean, Tommy, Forrest, Karen, Bruce

Leaving San Pedro

Saying goodbye to Guatemala

Celebrating our anniversary in San Cristobal, Chiapas

PART THREE

The Pana House

—◌

Be thou humble;
and the Lord thy God shall lead thee by the hand
and give thee answer to thy prayers.
Doctrine & Covenants 112:10

16
Pam the Expat

Let the wicked fall into their own nets,
whist that I withal escape.
Psalm 141:10

Before RJ left for the holidays, he told Dago to "take care of Mr. Bruce" and "help him find a house." Dago, always ready and willing to help Mr. Bruce, got right on it. He sought out rentals and made phone calls, with a lot of unreturned calls and appointment cancellations. We did visit two or three unsuitable properties that we declined.

I checked with two expat families, the Jensens and the Kellys, in case they knew of anything. No, they said, good furnished home rentals are hard to find in Pana. The Jensens lived in a mountain area far from town, and the Kellys in a luxurious townhouse north of Barrio Norte that rented for $800 a month. I asked Paul if his building had anything available. He didn't think so but promised to ask. Later, he reported that the waiting list was long as ever.

I kept my eyes open around town and searched the Facebook Panajachel Expat Group. There, I found a listing by a woman named Pam, an expat of twenty years who lived in nearby Jucanya. The house, in central Pana the ad said, rented for 1000 quetzales a month, electric included, a third of what we paid for rent alone at Barrio Norte.

Bruce called her on the hotel phone for an appointment. They set it for Sunday at one in the Catholic Church courtyard. From there, she'd take us to see the property.

After church on Sunday, Bruce and I walked the few blocks over to the Catholic Church. We arrived a half hour early and sat on a low stone wall in the courtyard. A sunny day with blue skies and a slight breeze made waiting pleasant.

I looked around at the neighborhood. "This is a pretty area, Bruce. I like that it's closer in than Barrio Norte."

"I hope it isn't far to the house," replied Bruce. "That was a long hot walk up from church, and here we are sitting in the direct sun."

Interesting what opposing tracks our thoughts followed. Comfortable and relaxed sitting in the sunshine with my favorite companion, about to go see our potential home, I felt happy anticipation. While Bruce, too warm in the glaring sun, was miserable and impatient, dreading another walk.

A woman came down the street on a bicycle. "There she is," I said.

"You know her?"

"No, but she's got the look of the female expat. The t-shirt and knit pants, long hair in a ponytail. Riding a bike to get around."

As she approached, I recognized her as the same woman who had yelled "Damn tourists!" at Jessica and me in front of Charo's. "Plus, I've seen her before," I added.

After proper introductions, Pam led the way to her house, proclaiming her political views sprinkled with profanity as we walked. A real character, probably difficult to deal with, I concluded. Not sure I want to rent from her.

Pam turned down a *callajón*, an alleyway too narrow for RJ's truck and barely wide enough for a tuk tuk. "No way will RJ get his truck through here," Bruce said.

She stopped at a high security gate, unlocked it and took us through a vegetable garden, past an orange tree, and on to a squat, square cement house with four rooms. The kitchen had a shelf full of old dishes, bottles, and pans, and a table with three plastic chairs. In the two bedrooms, I saw sunken beds with raggedy bedding. The bathroom was okay, with a toilet, sink, and shower.

Bruce and I said nothing. Pam, no doubt sensing our hesitation, offered, "Of course, I will have someone come in and clean the place and clear out the junk. I can bring in a stove and fridge from storage." This was the first of many lies.

We went outside, where I breathed sweet, fresh air. Pam pointed past the garden to a winding stone stairway lined with trees and plants. It curved up a modest hill to another building. "That's included. It's new and not quite finished." We followed her up the garden stairs.

She unlocked the front door. It opened to a long, wide room lined with windows on one side and an unfinished kitchen on the other. The space was clean and bright. Now *this* had possibilities. We could use it as our apartment while fixing up the little house below. Afterward, it could be my writing room and a guest apartment for family.

Pam must have taken note of our pleased expressions, because she quickly upped the price. "If you take this house too, the rent will be higher, like 1800 quetzales. And there's electricity; you've got to add that in. I won't pay the electric."

Her Facebook ad said electricity included. Ignoring this red flag, I mentally excused the rate increase, supposing the ad meant the one small house. 1800 was still a good deal, half what we paid for Barrio Norte, and this property was larger and more interesting.

Outside the guest house, Pam pointed down to the two bodegas set back from the path, halfway between the front gate and the small house. Bruce's eyes lit up seeing the bodegas, each one enclosed and as big as a garage. We went down to take another look.

Pam unlocked the bodegas to show Bruce while I explored the garden pathways. Behind the house, I discovered a papaya and an avocado tree, both fully grown.

When I came back around, Pam asked me how I liked the garden.

"It's lovely! The orange tree, an avocado and a papaya tree. Plus, flowers and vegetables. It's a beautiful garden."

"You must not have noticed the lime and banana trees." She gave me a doubtful, almost hostile expression. Maybe she didn't think I was the type to appreciate a fine garden or get my hands dirty. Since we had come straight from church, I wore a Sunday dress and nice shoes. I had straightened my shoulder-length hair and put on makeup.

"I want that garden well taken care of," she emphasized with raised voice. "Nothing better die, and I need access to my native plants." She described her native herbs and vegetable plants in detail. They would die out if it weren't for people like her maintaining the seeds in their proper environment. Her work was crucial to life itself. She belonged to a gardening group of locals and expats who kept these endangered species alive. She told us about plants and seeds and the problem with Lake Atitlán and about the Maya way and how long she has lived here and how much she knows about this area and her grown daughter who doesn't care about her or anything important.

Bruce kept bringing her back to the subject at hand. "We'd want to clean and improve both houses with paint and so forth, perhaps building cabinets for the kitchens."

"Sure, that's fine, as long as you pay for it." Pam grabbed the three chairs from the kitchen and set them in front of the little house. "Here, let's sit down outside."

Bruce, who hated to stand, took a chair with relief. I was hungry, thirsty and ready to go home and lie down. Hadn't we seen and heard enough by now to decide?

"I will pay for certain improvements, things I already planned, like adding a fireplace to the kitchen." Another lie. She had no intention of paying for anything.

Pam and Bruce discussed the possibilities of fixing up the two houses. He mentioned the bodegas. His tools, of course, he'd keep there. He didn't have the collection he used to have before moving to Guatemala, "but what I do have I value and take care of."

"I mostly let young people, hippie-types, stay here while they work for me. My interns." They assisted with her film projects and the lake restoration and local sewer issues, especially with those ongoing fights with the big hotels along the lake who don't care about anything but money. "Expats who come here without getting involved don't belong. They shouldn't be here in the first place."

I listened, trying to look like someone who cares, and asked a few polite questions. Bruce kept bringing her back to the property, away from her outside projects.

Pam waffled on her initial quote about price, about improvements, and about who would pay for what.

"We aren't here to take advantage of you," Bruce reassured her.

"Okay, I see you're good people." She explained further about her projects and her opinions. More words, so many words. Finally, she concluded with, "We will work it out to everyone's satisfaction. It will be fair, and we will all get along." Ending with the biggest lie of all.

Two hours later, Bruce and I moved at last toward the gate. We will think about it, we told her. Outside, I flagged down a tuk tuk that miraculously appeared before I fainted dead away from hunger and dehydration. Pam got on her bike to ride back to wherever she lived across the bridge in Jucanya.

At home, I threw together pancakes from a quick mix. Bruce, energized, called the little house a "cottage" and the other building the "guest house." He was enchanted by the idea of a project, a fixer upper. Something to do outside the hotel and independent of RJ.

Spatula in hand, waiting to turn the pancakes, I verbalized my concerns. "I'm afraid she will get overly involved, a micromanager, and won't let us do anything our own way."

"I agree she has that tendency, but I think it will be fine. I know how to handle her."

I stacked the pancakes on a plate. "I can see her coming over too often and drawing you into endless, repetitive conversations like the one we recently endured."

Bruce set the table, retrieved butter and syrup from the fridge. "I don't think it will be a problem. Today we were getting to know each other. She needed to feel comfortable about renting to us. It sounds like she has a lot of things going on. I doubt she has the time to hang with us."

We blessed the food and dug in. "As long as the guest house is fixed up where we can live in it," I said, "then I guess I'm okay with this. I can hide out there when she shows up to check on her native plants."

The guest house and the gardens were what enchanted me. For Bruce, it was the bodegas, a place to keep his tools, collect a few more, and fix up a house like he used to do in our early years.

That evening, he emailed Pam to accept her offer of 1800 quetzales a month for both houses. She didn't reply but friended us on Facebook.

Pam's email reply came first thing in the morning. "She is adding the electric at 350 a month to the rent," Bruce reported. "Total will be 2150."

"Okay . . . I guess she did warn us about adding that."

"She's also worried about workers coming in and 'tearing everything up,' as she puts it. I responded that we only want to clean and paint."

By the time Bruce finished his breakfast, Pam had sent him more anxious emails. We needed to understand her expectations about the garden. December was deep into the dry season, she wrote, and she didn't like this January move in date. Her plants would die without water until January. We could paint in December, but we would also have to water. Without agreeing to water her garden, the deal was off.

Bruce responded that he would be fine with watering in December. That sent, he closed his laptop and went off to work.

The next morning upon opening my laptop, I saw several lengthy Facebook messages from our prospective landlady. She was done with email because "I have to wait too long for a response." And, "I was up all night trying to figure out how this would work. I don't see how it will work."

I texted her back repeating what Bruce had already confirmed. Happy to water, won't make any unapproved changes. She continued to message me expressing the same fears, and I wrote back with the same responses. Writers have no problem saying the same thing a hundred different ways.

She agreed to meet and finalize the rental contract.

By the time Bruce came home, I had serious doubts about whether to go through with this. "We need to go into it with our eyes wide open, Bruce. She's the worst kind of micromanager and won't leave us alone. How bad do you want it?"

He *really* wanted this place. "It can be an escape for us, Karen. An ongoing project to distract me from Casa Colonial. RJ won't be able to park his truck or bring his boards onto the property. I can collect my tools from the hotel and keep them in the bodega."

Christmas was two weeks away. We could celebrate the holiday in Barrio Norte and move after New Year's. We agreed to meet Pam Thursday at ten to pay the rent.

Even then, sitting on those rickety chairs around the kitchen table, Pam was ill at ease. Again, Bruce promised to water regularly in December and to run everything past her. "We buy the paint and pay for the labor, is that okay?"

She softened somewhat. "Sure, and we can work out a deal where some of the work comes out of the rent, to be fair." These words no sooner left her mouth than she added testily, "How much is this going to cost me? Labor is cheap here. I can see you overpaying for labor and then charging it to your rent, and I'm losing money."

She didn't trust us, probably didn't trust anyone.

"Although you seem like good people, I'm used to having kids, hippies, staying here. They don't care about making changes. They only want to be left alone to drink booze and smoke pot."

I blurted, "Let us give you the rent money for January, before you change your mind again."

She laughed. "All right. You need to water though, or the garden will dry up."

How many times did Bruce have to tell her yes, he would water. The problem with liars, I have come to learn, is they think everyone lies. That's why they don't trust a living soul.

Bruce reaffirmed our terms. "We'd like to have our guys come paint the guest house before we move in."

Pam agreed, and I paid her the 1800 quetzales. She scribbled "January rent" on a piece of paper and handed it to me. We got up to leave. But first, she wanted to show us more of the garden, more of the guest house, and the rest of the property. Oh, dear God, I prayed. Not two hours again.

When she opened the bodegas with their extensive storage, I saw everything on Bruce's face. The thrill of once again having a workshop, a place of his own to keep tools, repair things, sit in a chair and ponder the complexities of the universe while he thought about how to fix what was broken.

We managed to escape in under an hour. We had our instructions, our keys, our new home.

Bruce kept his agreement to water, going every other day according to Pam's request. He hired a few of Dago's brothers to paint the guest house, where we'd live while making the cottage habitable. Dago expressed concern about the weeds and trash around the cottage, saying it allowed *animales* into the house. He had his brother Walter clear out the weeds first thing.

Either Bruce or Dago let the brothers in and locked up once they finished. Dago's brothers were as trustworthy and hardworking as he was. Bruce, who knew them, let them do the job with minimal supervision.

One evening as I closed my laptop to start dinner, a series of angry messages shot in from Pam. She saw the men working unsupervised and was afraid they'd steal from the property. Also, they left trash around.

These people won't clean up after themselves. They won't work unless you watch them. I am not willing to put my property at risk. Maybe we should call the whole deal off. And by the way, the tomatoes looked dry, and I told you to water them.

"How can we live with someone like this, Bruce?"

"I'll respond to her message. She's just insecure and a micromanager."

"Exactly what worries me, someone trying to control everything once we move into her house."

"Let me use your computer, Karen. Mine's at the hotel. I'll send a reasonable, well-thought-out reply." He carried my laptop over to the table and signed into Facebook under his own account. While he composed his message, I went to the kitchen to chop vegetables. There was a bit of leftover beef; a stew might be good.

Bruce took his time writing a long message. "Take a look at this, Karen. Does this hit the right tone?"

I read his message twice through. "It's good, Bruce. Thorough, clear and way more agreeable than she is."

"Clicking send," he announced.

Before the simmering vegetables were tender, more messages came rushing in. Bruce, still at the table, read them aloud while I stirred the stew.

> **I don't want your workers throwing ANYTHING of mine away, not the bottles in the cottage or a single cardboard box. If you give them permission to throw things out, they will take items home for their own use.**

Bruce wrote back:

> **They are doing simple basics like clearing out weeds next to the house and removing the trash. I see no problem with this, since the property is not livable as is. You said so yourself. You knew and agreed that we did not want to live in squalor.**

Pam whipped out another series of messages about how the rent was too low.

> **These improvements make the property worth more. I have no option but to raise the rent.**

Bruce laughed at this and shook his head. "Let's eat. I've said enough for now."

While we ate, we heard dings from Facebook coming in one after another. "Good grief! What's she complaining about now?" I got up from the table and scanned through the escalating angry accusations filling the message boxes.

"Listen to this one, Bruce."

You are not only taking advantage of me, but you are also letting your workers run rampant on my property.

That did it for him. He slammed down his fork. "Enough of this psycho woman and her accusations. Three weeks after paying January rent, her guest house is fresh and clean with its new coat of paint. Trash in and around that cottage cleared out! Her garden watered regularly. I went every other day before work to do it!"

Bruce whipped out a terse message, saying—among other things—

The deal is off. Please return our 1800 quetzales, in cash, to Dago at Casa Colonial Hotel. And I won't charge you for what we spent on paint and hiring painters.

It was back to the house hunting business. Morris and the new owners expected us gone right after New Year's. We had ten days.

17

The Opposite of Pam

Through wisdom is a house builded;
and by understanding it is established.
Proverbs 24:3

A few days before Christmas, I noticed a for rent sign on a large property near Casa Colonial.

Bruce wasn't crazy about living that close. "It's too convenient for Dago or RJ to come over with a question or problem. I'd never get time off." RJ was due back after New Year's. "Besides," he reasoned, "it's probably too much money. Look at the size of it. The property wraps around the corner and takes up half a block."

Still, we were intrigued by what lay hidden behind that vast expanse of bamboo fence. Cracks between the wood provided glimpses of the house. Bruce and I had always been suckers for a sizeable property and the grand scale that stimulates imagination.

"Let's meet tomorrow for lunch and then see what we can do," I suggested. "Maybe the manager next door at the Bungalows can tell us something." I mentioned the little Italian place around the corner. "We ate there before seeing Paul's apartment, remember? It might bring us good luck."

The next day, after lunch at the Italian café, we walked over to the big house. The gate to the nearby Bungalows entrance was wide open, as though welcoming us in. We entered and saw a man in the front garden, doing laundry at a *pila*.

In Spanish, I asked him where to find the manager. He pointed to a line of cottages behind him and said in English, "Number 3."

The door of #3 stood open. A plump, middle-aged woman sat on the sofa in the front room. What luck! We introduced ourselves, and I explained we needed a house to rent for January.

Her name was Helen, and she offered to show us around the enclave of cottages called the Bungalows. These were nicer than the cottages in Jucanya, also called the Bungalows, where Travis and Jessica lived when they first came to Pana. Helen took us to a recently vacated unit ready for January occupancy. The rent, same as our Barrio Norte home, seemed too high for this smaller house.

Helen explained, "The price is because of the garden courtyard and the central location. I never have any problem keeping them rented."

Pleasant and talkative, she spoke English well and answered every question in a straightforward manner. I liked her at once, finding her a refreshing change from the unhinged Pam.

After a brief tour of the cottages, I asked Helen about the big house next door with the For Rent sign.

"I take care of that too. I can show you if you're interested. But the rent is higher than the cottages."

"We'd like to at least take a look," I said, "as long as we're here."

She led us down the gravel drive back toward the street. Halfway down, veering off to the side, stood a high metal security gate connected to the bamboo fence. Helen unlocked a padlock and inserted a key in the metal lock box. She pushed open one half of the wide door to reveal a grass and gravel driveway. This led to a sprawling yellow and white, ranch-style adobe home centered in a sizeable yard overgrown with high weeds. First, we went around back.

The back yard had two broad palapas, each one with a concrete floor. Helen pointed out fully grown fruit trees around the palapas and the house: grapefruit, orange, lemon, even a banana grove. One could barely find the narrow walkway through the overgrown vegetation. Outside the back door stood the *pila,* three connected sinks on a concrete pad. Near a side wall of the house, a lime tree grew alone in a sheltered area.

Helen unlocked the back door for us to go through to the inside. The interior rooms were crammed with furniture and clutter. There was an unpleasant odor throughout. The monthly rent at 4500 quetzales was higher than Barrio Norte, no gardener provided.

After the tour, we thanked Helen for her time and I said, "I think it's too much house for us."

At home that evening, Bruce and I discussed it. "What a project that place would be!" I exclaimed.

The longer we talked, however, the more attracted we were by its potential, especially Bruce, who had not felt as disgusted as I did while viewing the inside.

"Karen, did you notice the attached workroom?" Bruce said. "I could keep my tools locked there and use the palapa for big projects."

"No, I didn't see it."

"It was on the side by the two banana trees."

"Helen seems agreeable and easy going," I reflected. "At least she would leave us in peace."

"It has too much potential to dismiss outright," Bruce said. "But we don't want to jump into another mess like with Pam."

We decided to pray about it over Christmas before deciding anything more.

The day after Christmas, we decided to view the property again. Bruce tried calling the number on the For Rent sign with no luck. Twice, I went to the Bungalows. Although I found the gate open, nobody answered at #3.

Five days later, Bruce happened to see Helen walk past the hotel. He flagged her down and asked if the big house was still available. Unfortunately, it was not. We dropped that idea and went back to looking. We toured another place down the street from Helen's. It was okay, with a yard and house only half the size of hers. Dago tried to connect with the owner for more information but he never returned Dago's calls.

And then Helen popped into the hotel to tell Bruce the renters she had lined up fell through. If we were still interested, she would like to show it to us again. They set up an appointment for Friday, the day after New Year's.

When we met Helen at the gate, she explained about the previous deal. "I found out the people were going to use it for a restaurant and bar. The owners don't want that."

"We only want it for our home," I assured her. "We have a big family and need space for them to visit."

Smiling and nodding, she said, "The rent dropped since you looked at it. Not 4500 a month anymore, down to 3000 a month."

While Pam had raised the rent, Helen did the opposite, dropping it by 1500 quetzales. This was $300 a month less than Barrio Norte!

Once through the gate, we noticed the grass and weeds were cut, providing shape to the surrounding gardens. Inside, the house was clean and tidy, the furniture rearranged instead of piled up blocking pathways. In the living room, an area rug was under a coffee table and the sofa faced the fireplace. Two matching chairs with side tables finished the look of cozy elegance. All the junk must have been hauled out since we looked at it, and nice things brought in. Even the bad smell was gone.

We inspected the three spacious bedrooms, Helen pointing out the full bathroom connected to each. Down a short hall off the living room was the fourth bathroom, the only one without a shower.

In the back, light streamed through the high windows into the spacious dining room off the kitchen. Such a comfortable country home! The wide galley kitchen led to an open pantry, a sunny square room with a window that faced the banana grove. Under it stood a sturdy but worn farm table. The rustic table beneath the window made an appealing visual. If I were an artist, I would paint the scene in oils.

"We'll take it," I said.

Bruce and Helen both turned to me in surprise. He asked, "Are you sure? Maybe we should think about it for a day or two."

"No, this is perfect. We'll take it."

Bruce seemed pleased. He wanted the house, too, I could tell. Maybe more than I did. He would have an entire bedroom and bath for his office! An outside room to organize his tools and keep them safe. I asked Helen if we could bring the rent on Monday.

"Monday I'm not available. We can meet again on Friday, same time as today." Disappointment flooded over me, until she handed me her set of keys. "It's fine if you move in before Friday. I trust you for the rent."

We had our house!

Bruce rushed to tell Dago, who was thoroughly relieved. Mr. RJ was expected soon, and he wouldn't be happy if Dago had failed in his duty to "find a house for Mr. Bruce."

Bruce arranged with Dago and his brothers to paint walls, and for his wife Rosa and sister Graciela to deep clean, especially inside cupboards and closets. The paint was what remained from Pam's guest house and the Barrio Norte job.

"Everything will be settled and done before RJ comes back to put his nose in," Bruce said with satisfaction.

We set our official moving day for Saturday. Morris was fine with that, of course, since by rights we had the full month of January to vacate Barrio Norte. I supposed the German mercenary was impatient, but that didn't concern us.

Finalizing the one page contract on Friday went quickly. We stood outside the front door of our new home with Helen, the three of us smiling and joyful. I asked her how long the contract was for—a year, two, three years?

"Oh, five years." She waved her hand vaguely. "Or as long as you want."

"Forever!" Bruce said.

Helen laughed in delight. She truly was the opposite of Pam.

We did feel like we could stay forever in this home. It was spacious, filled with light, and centrally located, unlike the dark Barrio Norte house up the hill. I had felt sorely cheated out of that situation. We had waited so long for the termite problem to get resolved and then bought paint and waited for that to get done, only to have the house sold out from under us. Yet look what blessing followed.

Our new home had a few plumbing issues, which Bruce had already noticed and asked about when we signed the contract.

Helen responded, "If you take care of them, I will only charge you 2500 quetzales a month for the next six months. Bring me receipts to show what you do." She handwrote the lower price on the contract and handed Bruce back 500 quetzales of the 3000 paid. This house had gone from 4500 quetzales down to 3000 and now to 2500. Again, the opposite of Pam.

Bruce and Dago took care of the plumbing within a few weeks, while the rent advantage went on for six months, saving us way more than we spent on plumbing supplies. The 1800 quetzales rent money thrown away on Pam, which she never did pay back, was multiplied and returned to us each month with what we saved on the Pana house.

18

Hermano Juan

The hay appeareth, and the tender grass sheweth itself,
and herbs of the mountains are gathered.
Proverbs 27:25

Bruce and I stood at the open back door, gazing out upon our yard. The air, cool and fresh as it was every morning of every day in Pana, was filled with bird songs. The expanse of lawn lay dead and dying from lack of water. The rainy season ended in November, and it was January—sunny, gorgeous and very dry January.

Bruce ran his hand over his chin. "This property needs a lot of maintenance, and we have no lawnmower, no edger, none of those tools I used to keep things in order back in Utah."

"I'll start by watering a section of lawn each morning and bring it back to life," I said. "At least we know how to take care of grass."

"Sure, but those trees need pruning. The banana grove looks overgrown, and there are dead sections. I better figure out how to prune a banana tree. And the lime tree, something is wrong there. The fruit is small and dry, and there's not much of it."

"Well, I can at least buy a hose and sprinkler for watering."

After doing that, I got educated about the Pana water supply.

Our cistern filled with city water piped in every morning. As it poured into the tank, I turned on the sprinkler and gave everything a thorough soaking. After the cistern filled, the city water shut off. However, if I kept the hose running, city water kept pouring into the tank. Perfect timing of water in, water out made a fun game.

I began each day in my writing room, the front bedroom, with the windows open to the fresh morning air and to the sounds of nature waking up to the world. The birds sang out their early calls. Hummingbirds and butterflies flitted about the flowers.

When I heard water splashing into the cistern, I went outside to turn on the hose and set the sprinkler, moving it every thirty minutes. I had about two hours of strong water flow coming in with the hose running. Once the flow ended, I shut off the sprinkler to avoid emptying our supply. Before I figured out the system, I ran it dry a couple times, leaving us without household water until the city water poured in again around five. It didn't always come twice a day. Evenings were not regular like the mornings.

Soon the grass turned green and plants flowered. Besides fruit trees, we had numerous other trees and shrubs. Tropical plants and flowers grew next to the house and bordered the fences. I watered all of it, turning our yard into a lush tropical garden.

We needed a gardener, at least to mow the lawn. They didn't use lawnmowers here to cut grass, only a machete, the universal tool. As for the lime tree, thorny, woody vines wrapped tightly around the trunks and branches of it and the orange tree. At first look, they seemed a natural part of the tree, except that the vines had thorns. The thicker the vine the bigger the thorns.

Bruce approached one of his friends at church, Jaime, who didn't have a job. He offered to hire him for the day, perhaps one or two days a week, to help tend the garden and prune the fruit trees. Jaime agreed to come on Monday and take a look. When he arrived, Bruce pointed out the lime tree, saying, "*No es bueno.*"

Jaime hadn't brought his machete and asked if we had one. No machete. "Okay," he said and made a sawing motion, giving us a questioning look.

I thought "bread knife." It wasn't sharp but serrated and long enough for sawing.

What Jaime lacked in sword power, he made up in strength and determination. With the bread knife, he cut off entire branches that had succumbed to the thorny vines. "It feeds off the tree and kills it," he explained. "It is a cancer." He used the English word, making me think *cancer* must be the universal word for a destroying force. Something that attacks its host and sucks the life out of it.

"See these branches? It's too late for them. Already they are taken over by the cancer."

Bruce and I watched him cut and slash at the deadly vines, the lost branches of the lime tree falling in piles on the ground. "It is good we do this now. Another season and the tree is dead."

Finishing with the lime, Jaime moved the ladder over to the orange tree. It was tall and fully grown, twisted with larger cancer vines and their vicious thorns, thick and sharp. Jaime made little progress with the bread knife. He would need his machete to finish the job.

Bruce found Jaime's effort more interesting than whatever work awaited him at the hotel. With a simple bread knife, the man had pruned an entire lime tree. Having to give up on the orange tree, he descended the ladder.

With gestures and broken Spanish, Bruce explained about our supplemental water tank, the one next to the side fence and high in the air. "It's meant to catch rainwater. Karen, can you ask him while he's here to climb up there and see why it's not working?"

Jaime moved the ladder to the tank and soon disappeared inside of it. He lifted up a couple birds and a squirrel to show us. "*Muerte!*" he said laughing, then dropped them to the ground.

He scrambled back down and asked for a few items—a broom, a bottle of bleach, a pair of pliers, a bucket and hose, a tarp with ropes. I gathered the household things while Bruce brought the tools and tarp, our usual division of labor. My household tools were related to cooking and cleaning, Bruce's to maintenance and repairs. We were old-fashioned that way.

After draining the water, Jaime rinsed out the tub with bleach and fresh water. He adjusted the pipes and valves to enable it to get both city and rainwater. It was smaller than the in-ground cistern but would dribble its supply into the main tank once the city water stopped its fast pour. To me, it seemed insignificant and not something to count on, but Bruce was pleased as anything to have it cleaned and operating. It satisfied his need to see everything in our environment functioning properly. He couldn't tolerate unpruned trees, overgrown gardens, sagging fences, or broken equipment.

Jaime covered the cistern with the tarp and tied it down. Impressed by what his friend accomplished in a few hours, Bruce offered him the job of gardener once a week, or twice if his schedule allowed.

"*Tengo que pensar,*" Jaime replied. He would think about it. "But I will bring my machete on Thursday to finish the orange tree."

On Thursday, Jaime didn't show up. Early Friday, another man we knew from church, Juan Molina, rang the bell at our gate, machete in hand. He and I greeted one another in the way typical of Latin members of our church.

"*Buenos días, hermana.*"

"*Buenos días, hermano.*"

"Hermano Jaime told me about the gardening job. He can't do it, but I will work for you. Is it okay?"

Hermano Juan was a smiling but timid single man who always came alone to church. He was small and thin, a good fifteen or twenty years older than Jaime and not as strong looking. His clothes hung on him. Like many of the thin men and boys, he cinched his belt with folds of extra trouser material gathered around the waist. His shirt was tucked in to appear neater. Juan

Molina and his clothes were old but clean; he was willing and ready to go to work.

"I can work one or two days or whatever you want."

I invited him in to see the property. While he checked things over, I popped my head in the back door. "It's Juan Molina, Bruce! Jaime sent him."

Showered and dressed for work, Bruce was mixing yogurt and granola for his breakfast. "Juan Molina? I like that guy." He set down his bowl, and we joined Hermano Juan in his inspection of the grounds.

After circling the full area, he said, "Two days is better. *Hay mucho trabajo.*"

Bruce replied, "Well, let's start with one day a week and go from there. Pay is seventy quetzales plus lunch."

Juan countered with seventy-five.

Bruce chuckled. "I like your spirit. Okay, seventy-five a day plus lunch."

Juan Molina and his machete went to work. He whacked his way up the orange tree cutting away the cancer, as thick in places as the largest branches. His machete was like an extension of his arm. Hermano Juan was no bigger than a twelve-year-old boy, but he was vigorous and focused.

By the lunch hour, I had no doubt this scrawny, tiny muscle man was the right one for the job. Dago's brother Walter was also working at our house that day, painting one of the bedrooms. I sent Bruce out to get fried chicken, fries, tortillas and a couple two-liter bottles of orange soda while I made a tomato cucumber salad and set the table.

Juan Molina cleared every morsel off his chicken bones. He ate a stack of tortillas. Bruce and I held back to make sure he and Walter got enough to eat and drink; especially Juan, outside in the heat, crawling around in our treetops and expending thousands of calories.

A few weeks after Juan Molina started with us, the missionaries approached Bruce at church and asked if he could possibly loan money to Hermano Juan. Behind on his rent, Juan was in danger of getting evicted from the small room he rented in the back of a house. He would pay off the loan a little at a time as he worked for us.

Bruce asked these young elders how much was needed, what is the rent, how much does he spend on food and other necessities. They only knew the rent and could not answer the other questions.

"My concern is if he pays me out of his earnings, he could find himself right back in a hole down the road. Elders, come over tonight with Hermano Juan and let's go over his budget."

That evening, we gathered around our dining room table with the two elders and Hermano Juan to see how best to help this good man.

Looking over the numbers, Bruce explained the situation to the American elder. "The loan as requested is a band aid. It's not enough to last. Does he have another job?"

No, there was no other job.

"Well, then, here's the situation. Let's say we loan him the requested amount. He works one day a week at our house, paying us back so much a time, plus paying the back rent he owes to his landlord. There's nothing left for food. He needs twice as much as what he wants to borrow. Otherwise, he will fall behind and find himself in the same situation. Unless he can work another job now and then."

Observing this wordy explanation in a language he did not understand, the slightly watery eyes of Juan Molina darted nervously from Bruce to the American elder, and then downcast at the table. He's afraid Bruce is turning him down, I thought. He is ashamed to be so poor and needing to ask for help. Oh, poor Juan Molina!

Bruce picked up the pencil to scribble numbers on his yellow pad of paper. The missionaries both looked peaceful and happy as these young men always do. Juan Molina looked nervous. I was expectant, wondering what Bruce would come up with. I knew his desire to help along with his wisdom regarding financial matters would combine on that sheet of yellow paper to resolve Hermano Juan's dilemma.

Finally, Bruce glanced up. "How's this? I loan him 2800 quetzales, twice what he asked for, and give him an extra day's work. This place needs two days a week anyway. He can pay me back out of the second day and still take home his full pay, or what he earns now. He can pay off his back rent with the 2800. This way he will have enough money for food and to keep up with his rent in the future. Once the loan is paid back, he can take home double what he earns now and perhaps save enough to get ahead a little."

The American elder listened carefully, took the yellow sheet and showed it to Hermano Juan, explaining the plan in fluent Spanish.

Hermano Juan closely examined the numbers, asked a few questions of the elder, and then nodded and smiled with relief. *"Sí, muy bien. Gracias, Hermano* Bruce."

This solution pleased everyone. Juan Molina came on Thursdays as well as Fridays and labored diligently on both days, stopping only when I called him for lunch. It gratified Bruce to see the property getting the care it needed, and I liked giving Juan Molina an additional solid meal each week.

At first, he felt shy coming into our house and eating with us in the dining room. As time went on, he grew more relaxed, talked more, ate freely at *"el restaurante de la hermana"* and shared a few stories in his quiet and timid way. He had been married once. Somewhere there was a son in school, doing well he proudly reported. Juan was vague about anything personal. I often wondered if he was one of those who had escaped to the hills during the war, a guerrilla fighter up against the government armies who had tried to wipe out the Maya. I wondered because of a few things he let slip now and then, about that war, about the violence—and then silence. He would have been the right age, in his prime back then.

Juan Molina knew the names and uses of every plant on our property, including the weeds, which apparently were not weeds at all. One of these grew copiously among the flowers. Hermano Juan called it chipilin. He showed me how to trim the leaves off the tall spindly stalk and said they go well in a salad or cooked in a bit of oil like any vegetable. I tried it a few times at our lunches together. It tasted fresh and good either raw or cooked but took a lot of preparation, especially to cut the tender leaves one by one off the tough stems.

I could imagine Juan Molina hiding in the jungles for months, perhaps years, with his fellow guerillas, living off the land as they fought the government armies and mercenaries. Entire villages were wiped out during this thirty-year civil war. Since the government considered the indigenous people guerilla sympathizers, the army murdered, mutilated, raped, burned, and otherwise tried to punish and eradicate the population.

Those hidden in the hills fought to protect the villagers. Perhaps Juan Molina was one of those young men in the jungle. Seeing his proficiency with a machete, he would have been a formidable fighter, although I couldn't imagine him enjoying it. Not like the German mercenary who bought our Barrio Norte house, who bragged about his history: "I was one of the bad guys."

For Juan Molina and every Guatemalan who worked the earth, the multipurpose machete was a knife, a shovel, a lawnmower, an edger, a plough. Tools common in any American household were expensive, scarce and if available, were shared among neighbors. But each man owned a machete, the one tool he made his own. It reminded me of the prophecy of Isaiah: "And they shall beat their swords into plowshares and their spears into pruning hooks." I used to think that verse prophesied the peaceful Millennium when the lamb would lie down with the lion. Until I saw its fulfillment in our own backyard whenever Juan Molina came to work with his machete.

The once weak and drastically pruned lime tree flourished. A couple times a month I couldn't resist making a big key lime pie with a cup of lime juice, a dozen eggs and two cans of sweetened condensed milk. Stir it together on top of the stove until it thickens and begins to boil then pour onto the graham cracker crust. While I stirred, Bruce squeezed the lime juice. He crushed the graham crackers to line the bottom of the handle-less frying pan that served as a pie plate. Add the filling and refrigerate overnight.

I gave away limes to people. I made limeade when Juan Molina worked. I considered making marmalade. There's orange marmalade, why not lime? I found a marmalade recipe online. It called for lots of sugar, but sugar was cheap and plentiful in Guatemala. I had a few glass jars and my large soup pot for boiling the jam.

At the dining room table, I cut fruit as the sun streamed in. The back door open, I listened to the many birds singing in the sunshine and fresh air.

Bruce wondered if there wasn't a faster, easier way to slice limes into thin strips. "This sure seems time consuming."

"I have plenty of time," I told him, feeling peaceful and happy. I delighted in the rare and wonderful luxury of spending a great deal of time doing very little. Knowing that marmalade was Bruce's favorite kind of jam added to my enjoyment of the task.

The end result turned out beautifully. The filled glass jars on the pantry shelf were so pretty. The jam was delicious on toast or spread on the big, thick oat grain cookies from the bakery.

When our banana trees grew several clusters of fruit, Juan Molina answered my frequent questions about picking them with a smile and a shake of his head.

Until the day finally came when he pulled the ladder up to the top of the trees and, with a deft swipe of his machete, cut down the sizable bunches packed tightly with green bananas. I asked him to bring them inside and lay them on the big square farm table in the pantry. Two magnificent bunches of ripening bananas on this rustic table under the window looked beautiful, a living work of art.

Each week, our yard and gardens grew lovelier under Hermano Juan's careful stewardship. The few times Helen came by, she exclaimed, "Oh, the gardens! They are beautiful!" And they were, thanks to Juan Molina.

19

If You Bake It, They Will Come?

I have seen servants upon horses,
and princes walking as servants upon the earth.
Ecclesiastes 10:7

RJ came back the end of February, much later than the original, "right after the holidays." The delay had given us time to find the perfect house on our own. It gave Bruce and Dago time to further refine their best practices while continuing to attract guests.

When he returned, RJ promptly took back control of operations, from cleaning to who gets hired and fired to what bills get paid or, more often, not paid. The stress of it showed in Bruce's blood pressure readings. I suggested he take an extra half hour after lunch each day to rest in bed before going back to work. He didn't like the idea.

"If I lay down, I'll fall asleep and won't wake up for hours."

"I'll watch the clock and not let you sleep more than an hour."

"I can't afford the time away, Karen. Dago and I worked too hard to let RJ ruin everything now."

"But you can't risk your health. Both my parents napped in the afternoons. My dad lived to his late eighties and my mom to ninety-two."

"I doubt I could rest anyway. There's too much to do. Sally and I came to an agreement. Between the two of us we'll handle management and financial decisions and leave RJ out of it. Sally wants him free to work on his boards, and I agree. He can stick to his precious paddleboards and let me run the hotel."

Bruce resisted my nap idea until one Saturday morning. While organizing shelves in his tool room next to the house, he blacked out. "One minute I'm digging through a box," he said, "and the next thing I'm on the ground. I don't remember passing out, but I must have."

That scared him enough to try the afternoon nap experiment, laying down in our cool, dark bedroom after lunch. He fell right to sleep and woke up within thirty or forty minutes.

After a week of this practice, his blood pressure stabilized and his energy increased. Initially, Dago or RJ came by asking for him. When RJ hollered his name at the back door, I hurried to tell him Bruce was resting for a few minutes after lunch. He looked surprised and told me why Bruce was needed.

I ignored the explanations. "He's asleep. He should be back over in twenty minutes or so." Eventually RJ realized this was a pattern he couldn't interrupt and let Bruce get his ninety-minute lunch breaks.

The afternoon naps were the beginning of an attitude shift where, in subtle ways, Bruce loosened his ties to RJ and the hotel. For example, I had hired Rosa to clean on Tuesdays and suggested to Bruce that we go out together while she works.

"Sure, why not?" he replied, surprising me. After his blackout in the tool shed, he began taking both Saturdays and Sundays off. I didn't expect him to agree to Tuesdays as well. "RJ doesn't need me there every day. Ricardo Juan is pushing me out of the way, and I'm done fighting him for position. It's his hotel to run or to ruin. I feel bad for Dago though. He did so well in front with guests and now RJ has him cleaning toilets again and on the floor scrubbing grout."

"What happened to your agreement with Sally? Letting RJ focus on his boards while you and she manage the business and financial decisions?"

"A great idea in theory but not in practice. Sally only knows what RJ tells her. He can't let go of control, especially with the money. Whether it's what she sends or what the hotel earns, he thinks it's his to spend however he likes."

"Sounds like nothing has changed. He might as well not have left."

"If anything, it's worse. At least before, he listened to what I had to say and seemed to respect my opinion. Not anymore. He wants to convert the laundry room, #9, to a rentable room. That might be a good idea except for the current cash demands. So far this year, four months in, we've only been sold out thirteen times. At the rate of 200 quetzales a room per night, we would only have made 2600 all year from that new room. Not even a return on the cost of building it, moving the laundry room, furnishing it with a bed, cutting out a window, and all the rest. It's a dumb idea, and so far, I haven't been able to talk him out of it. Despite showing him the numbers in black and white."

So much for the plan, where RJ works in LA while Bruce runs the hotel. There was a list of reasons why this was no longer possible.

"The state of California is broke and hospitals aren't hiring."

"We need to get the paddleboard business going first."

"The hotel isn't making enough money."

"The employees are taking too much income."

The respectful son-in-law turned into the pushy guy who wants what he wants and figures out how to get it. Bruce had been dealing with that guy at the hotel and, before long, the storm blew in my direction.

It began when Bruce commented one morning at breakfast, "RJ wants to use the palapas to finish the boards. Are you okay with that, Karen?"

It seemed churlish to say no. Our two palapas sat open and empty at the back end of the yard. Besides, it would get RJ out of the hotel and relieve pressure on Bruce.

"Only one, not both," I said. "The one farthest from the house. I don't want anything, not a single hammer, in the palapa close to my laundry area."

That very day, RJ moved his boards and tools to the designated location. "Thanks, Karen," he said. "Don't worry, I won't bother you. You won't know I'm here."

He needed someone to help finish his boards, to provide training for guests and take them on tours. He found a fourteen-year-old kid named Santiago who came every day to help him in the palapa. Whenever RJ took a board out on the lake, Santiago went too. Until one day the kid didn't show up. He went to the kid's house up in the hills to check on him. Santiago's dad, learning that RJ only paid him four quetzales an hour, wouldn't let him come anymore. The going rate for unskilled labor was ten an hour, or at least seven to start. The dad was upset about Santiago only getting fifteen for a full day's work when it should have been at least seventy-five. Unless RJ agreed to pay more, he would no longer allow his son to work for him.

RJ related the story at lunch when I invited him to eat with us and Juan Molina. "I'll find someone else," he concluded. "There's always some kid looking for a job." To him, "only a sucker pays the minimum wage." He couldn't believe we paid Juan Molina seventy-five a day. He thought we were fools, letting a simple gardener take advantage of us.

Wages were a recurring argument between Bruce and RJ, who said Bruce was "too soft" on the hotel employees. "They're taking advantage of you, Bruce. You're letting them get away with it."

RJ often paid Dago late or shorted him. He had to remind RJ for his pay then wait to get it handed out in part, RJ dragging it out for days as Dago continued to request it.

This infuriated Bruce. "It's insulting and demeaning! He's been like this since he came back."

We were on one of our Tuesdays out, having an early dinner at a favorite restaurant on a quiet side street off Santander.

Their sign out front said *The Last Resort,* a funny mistranslation and surely not what they meant to imply. They were rarely busy, despite the food being very good.

"Playing these kinds of games with Dago is childish," Bruce said. "What would they do if the hospital said Sally wasn't getting paid for three or four weeks but trust us, we're good for it? Why should we treat our employees any different than we expect to be treated?"

A little girl from the back had left a few minutes ago and now returned with a package of pasta and a stick of butter. "Here come the ingredients for your linguini, Bruce." That cheered him up for a minute.

"Good. I'm starving. I keep planning to order the meat, vegetables, and salad like you but then I always end up going with the linguini."

"They must not have many orders for it because the little girl always goes for butter, crema or pasta when we come in."

"It should be the most popular dish on the menu, as good as it is." With still no food in sight, Bruce continued his story. "When RJ arrived in February, he demanded Dago give him the payroll cash I had set aside. He used it for his taxi ride from the city and made Dago wait for his pay."

How RJ treated people he considered inferior, like Dago, Juan Molina, and Alicia, disgusted Bruce.

"He calls them Indians. He says, 'You don't have to pay the Indians what they ask, Bruce. They don't expect you to. They're glad to have a job.'"

These were the Maya, of an ancient culture that still defined them. They exhibited an innate spirituality and humility missing in us arrogant North Americans. Strip away the good jobs, the careers and education, the fine homes and fat bank accounts, and then take a closer look at who a person is, where it matters. Look in their hearts, their characters, see how they treat others. Look beyond the fancy trappings and discover what determines true success. These folks we lived among had little material worth, were small of stature, yet stood like giants around us. Perhaps RJ sensed their inner strength of character and felt inferior in comparison. Maybe that explained why he strutted about town like a big man. He needed to prove himself.

So many didn't have jobs. At church, since the members were clean and dressed nicely, I assumed that during the week they were busy at their employment. Jaime, our first prospective gardener, didn't have a regular job. Juan Molina didn't either; he was available to come work for us any day we asked. Dago's brother Walter's only job was on call as night guardian at the hotel.

The Jensens, an American expat family in our church, had begun their local farming project by teaching Juan Cosigua, the branch president, their techniques, until President Cosigua got a regular job.

When I asked what he did before then, Greg Jensen said, "Nothing." The skills he learned from Greg enabled him to qualify for a fulltime position elsewhere. "I was sorry to lose him, but glad for President Cosigua. It paid better and had more opportunities for advancement."

Lucy Jensen explained, "It's the middle class who have regular jobs and money to buy vegetables at the mercado. The everyday folks don't eat much besides tortillas, beans, and rice. Maybe a few vegetables in the rice, but nothing like the amount of fresh produce we eat in the States. They can't afford it." The Jensens taught square foot gardening, where families could grow their own vegetables in a raised box at home.

According to Juan Molina's rough budget, he spent twenty-five quetzales a week for food. Under five dollars. A liter of milk cost nine quetzales and a papaya ten. How does an active man get enough calories on twenty-five a week? Like many others, Juan Molina survived on tortillas and salt. Bruce and I ate more in a day than he did in a week. Except when he worked at our house. Then I made sure he had a morning snack, a solid lunch where he could eat as much as he wanted, and leftovers to take home.

⌒⟶

Before long, RJ showed up every morning with his cup of coffee to meet with Bruce. His blaring voice projected throughout
the house. I shut myself in the front bedroom, feeling trapped
and frustrated, trying to work on my new book. Some days he
hung around until noon, ate lunch with us and then had Bruce
walk with him somewhere. When that happened, it effectively
eliminated the power naps. Besides keeping the paddleboards in
our palapa, RJ occasionally brought people traipsing through our
yard to show off his work. Our Pana house, a family home meant
for family visits, had become an extension of his business.

In May, five months after we moved in, our daughter Liesel
and her husband Dale decided to celebrate their wedding anniversary in Guatemala. It was Dale's first time out of the U.S. He
had been nervously packing and unpacking for weeks, according
to Liesel. We did the usual touristy things: stopping in Antigua,
a day at the nature park and the butterfly preserve, shopping
for local crafts. One day, they went paddleboarding on the lake
accompanied by RJ's young assistant. Not Santiago, since neither
RJ nor the dad had given in.

Afterward Liesel said, "Mom, you should have gone with us. I
think you would have enjoyed it. The water was perfect, and we
had fun trying to stand and then falling off and swimming around."

"Did you go anywhere, like across the lake to another town?"

"Oh, no, we weren't interested in doing that. We only wanted
to play around on the boards and have fun in the deep water."

After Liesel and Dale left, I couldn't get back to writing.
Instead, I baked, missing our family back in the States.

"You're operating under the assumption that if you bake it,
they will come?" Bruce observed.

This made me chuckle. How silly to think making Texas cake,
a pan of brownies, or a key lime pie would fill the house with
family. The baking made no sense. RJ accused me of trying to

make him fat, and Juan Molina didn't eat rich desserts. "Too sweet," he said after one bite. Bruce and I certainly didn't need them. I gave up the baking and returned to my writing and editing projects.

The oranges came in plentiful and sweet but wormy. "The worms know which fruit is good," said Bruce. After cutting them in half, Bruce, less squeamish than me, took the wormy ones. He squeezed them dry using the crystal hand juicer I inherited from my mom, then he poured the juice through a strainer to catch the seeds and worms. The good oranges we set aside for eating and for marmalade. I didn't get as much orange marmalade as lime, but we did enjoy many pitchers of freshly squeezed juice.

The small lemon tree grew only four lemons, but they were a gorgeous yellow color and as large as a big grapefruit. My sister Julie was coming to visit, and I saved back one oversized lemon to make a pie. The rest of them we squeezed into lemonade.

Julie took a room at Casa Colonial, pretty and charming with its bright colors and outdoor balconies, and only half a block down the street from us. After checking in, she raved about Dago. "He is the nicest guy! He wouldn't let me touch my luggage and carried everything up all those stairs. He has such a wonderful smile and pleasant personality."

"I know. RJ is lucky to have him. He's the best, does everything with enthusiasm, and always seems happy."

Julie frowned. "Is his name really Dago? That seems odd."

"It's Dagoberto, which is what his wife and siblings call him. Dago is RJ's nickname and how he introduces him to everyone. We thought it was his name for the longest time."

"Well, I'm going to call him Dagoberto," she declared. "It seems more respectful."

Julie and I hiked around Pana, one morning following the road uphill that led to Santa Catarina. The little town that had consumed an entire day by paddleboard, she and I walked there and back in a couple hours.

Another town on the lake, San Juan, had the artist colony. Julie wanted to go there and buy a painting to commemorate her first trip to Guatemala. Since I still had not tried the boat taxis, I asked if she was willing to take one to San Juan.

"Sure! It will be a fun adventure!"

Our public boat was filled with people. Mothers with children and holding babies, vendors, tourists and backpackers. As we skimmed across the lake, with close-up views of the shoreline and the bordering volcanoes, I regretted not doing this with Travis, Jessica, and Emree. It was affordable and they would have loved it.

Arriving at San Juan, Julie and I disembarked with a cluster of other passengers. We climbed the hill to the artist shops, where we viewed their work until she found a painting she liked.

On the ride back, the lake was rougher than the way over. Julie joked about how Daddy must be entertained in Heaven by the sight of us bouncing around in this boat without life jackets. He and Mother had always been strict about us girls wearing life jackets the second we climbed in the boat, even in a simple rowboat to go fishing close to shore.

The boat taxis had lifejackets under the seats, but nobody used them.

Julie's short blond hair blew every which way. "Good thing I can't see us from the outside," she laughed. "This boat is probably really low in the water like it will sink any moment."

"That's how they look from the shore. You can see why I needed moral support before I tried one."

"I'm glad my visit is giving you a chance to do something new you wanted to try. That makes me happy."

That ride was the first of many I took, either alone or with Bruce or with visiting family. Boat taxis were the easiest, fastest way to get to another town on the lake. Like traveling on a chicken bus, it was part of the Guatemala experience, and that's what made it fun.

20

Renard Jaques, the Spanish Don

Blessed is the man unto whom the Lord imputeth not iniquity,
and in whose spirit there is no guile.
Psalm 32:2

When Liesel and Dale visited, RJ didn't come over, not to work on the boards or meet with Bruce. I wasn't sure why, but I liked the break.

Liesel understood my feelings about this triangle consisting of our home, our son-in-law, and his hotel. "You have every right to be upset, Mom. This is your home, and it's being taken over by a business. They need to have their meetings someplace else."

Later I told Bruce what she said. "I think Liesel's right, Bruce. He's here every morning to meet with you and in the afternoons to work on the boards. It's too much. I don't want those meetings here anymore."

"RJ doesn't want to meet at the hotel," he replied. "People can hear us. You know how he is about privacy."

"Then go someplace private, like you did before we moved here. You never met like this at Barrio Norte. Go wherever you used to go before we got this house."

"It was my idea to have them here, where I'm comfortable. RJ used to drag me all over town to talk business, walking up and down secluded streets in the heat of the sun. This is a big house. I should be able to use my office however I want."

He had a point. I certainly didn't want Bruce pushed into a forced march at RJ's whim. I let it drop.

Besides, soon after Liesel and Dale left, RJ left town as well. He gave no explanation why. If he had, I wouldn't have believed it. Like "looking for a job" or "not wanting Dago on his own while you guys are in Utah." Those kinds of fake reasons for why he came and went. He would of course return to Pana. His life plans had always centered around the hotel and the paddleboards. If he achieved the desired success, he would remain to carry on with it. Until he did, he would keep after it. Whether he liked it or not, RJ was trapped in Pana.

Bruce and I, back from our Tuesday afternoon out, relaxed in the living room to finish out the day. Rosa had come and gone, leaving the place sparkling clean with that fresh Fabuloso scent we liked. With RJ in California, our home was now our own. We soaked up the exhilarating atmosphere of freedom.

"Why is RJ so annoying?" I wondered out loud. "He says one thing then does another. He breaks promises and he takes advantage of people. Is he a sociopath?"

I didn't expect Bruce to respond, since he didn't like to judge or criticize people. He surprised me by saying, "I think he might have multiple personality disorder."

"Really?"

"It explains everything," he continued. "There's the Macho Guy, the Protector. He's the one who shows up a lot in Pana. When RJ is Macho Guy, he struts around in his wifebeater shirts and doesn't wear his glasses. He gets into fights."

"How well I know the Macho Guy. I can't stand that guy."

"Then there's the Family Man. It's the side of him who loves Sally and believes in God. When he's the Family Man, he's giving and generous."

"Yeah, he's not so bad as the Family Man," I admitted. "Although I don't think I've seen that one much in Guatemala."

"Because he's Macho Guy here. He thinks he has to protect his interests against the bad people in Pana."

I snorted. "What bad people in Pana? Maybe if he didn't hang around bars and drug dealers, he wouldn't see any bad people." I had no idea if RJ hung around bars or drug dealers, but he did have some sketchy associates.

"Then there's the Businessman," Bruce went on. "That's when he goes by Ricardo Juan, focuses on paperwork and makes people leave him alone so he can get things done. And there's the Kid, the vulnerable person who doesn't show up much. The Kid is quiet, studious, and the one who needs Sally the most."

"Probably it's the Kid when he's trying to learn something and asks Sally for help. She loves it when he's in school. It makes her feel needed and like she's important to him. She likes to help him learn and improve himself."

"Yeah, the Kid is kind of sweet," Bruce agreed. "The Spanish Don, on the other hand, acts superior and won't listen to anyone, because he thinks he's better than everybody. The Spanish Don is racist, talks about 'those people' and 'Indians' and thinks they should act subservient. To serve his needs. That's when he goes by Renard Jacques."

"Seriously? He calls himself Renard Jacques?"

"Yep. He has signed emails and letters as Renard Jacques Martín. I've heard him tell people that's his name."

"I like Family Man, when he is a nice, respectful, courteous son-in-law." Family Man was agreeable and pleasant. Fun, too. I wished RJ was always the Family Man. Our whole family loved that guy. "It's hard to know who he really is. You think you know and then he turns into something different."

"I think the last one is the Entrepreneur," Bruce said. "That one causes his Businessman persona all kinds of grief. Entrepreneur is full of ideas, false starts and abrupt endings. He's easily distracted and looking for the fast buck. The Entrepreneur puts Sally into debt while the Businessman tries to clean up the mess. The Businessman needs Sally's input and values her common sense."

"He has clothes to fit every personality, Bruce. I see him bike through the streets wearing jeans or cargo shorts, sunglasses and a partially buttoned shirt, and next thing you know he's business professional with his wire rim glasses and long pants."

"Businessman wears glasses and is very focused, tucks in his shirts and wears nicer pants. Goes by Ricardo Juan instead of RJ. Macho Guy likes the black wifebeater, struts around, uses patchouli cologne, gets into fights and flirts with women. The Spanish Don of course is Renard Jacques."

We rarely sat together like this in a quiet home, uninterrupted by RJ's demands on Bruce, whether in person or Skype. Even now, certain sounds I heard from outside made me jump, thinking RJ was coming around to interrupt our peace.

"The Entrepreneur, or maybe it's the Businessman, is the guy who spent the reserve I saved to get the hotel through the rainy season," Bruce said. "I come back from Utah, and he's used it to buy new curtains we didn't need. And the fancy furniture custom made for the rooms and the lobby."

"It is beautiful furniture though and really dresses up the place."

"Sure, but now instead of having a reserve to draw on, we rob Peter to pay Paul. We have to sell things to cover basic bills like first of the month expenses. There's Claro, SAT, INGUAT, the accountant, the electric, WiFi. Plus payroll."

"Before we came to Guatemala, I liked RJ. He seemed impulsive, sure, but generally reasonable and trustworthy."

"He pretty much stuck with Family Man when he was around us back in Utah," Bruce said. "That and the Businessman."

Family Man had disappeared, making brief appearances only when he wanted something, such as moving his paddleboard workshop to our property. Entrepreneur was the main guy these days.

"You know, Bruce, RJ would be a lot happier if he knew who he was; if he claimed his heritage, for example. He's half Mexican, half Guatemalan, yet he seems ashamed of it. Why? He should be proud of that instead of trying to fit into these other personas."

"I doubt he's capable of it. He wants to overcome his background and be this big success and make lots of money."

RJ called Bruce on Skype every morning and throughout the day, with instructions on where to cut hotel expenses and how to build up the paddleboard business.

Bruce kept telling him, "Let's get one business solvent before we focus on the other," and RJ kept ignoring him.

Early one morning Bruce got a Skype call from Sally, no RJ on this one. I heard her say, "RJ is going to China to buy boards where they cost less. He has his ticket. He goes next week."

The news stunned Bruce into silence. After claiming lack of funds, RJ buys a round trip ticket to China? He would stay for a month, buy two dozen boards and have them shipped to Guatemala. While there, he planned to buy other items available for less in China. Paddles, life preservers, mosquito netting, who knows what else.

"As long as there's room on the ship, why not?" Sally said. Exhausted after working her night shift, she signed off.

When the call ended, Bruce said, "It's the Entrepreneur who's going to China, Karen. RJ might pretend like it's the sensible Businessman but no, it's the gambling Entrepreneur. That trip will come to no good end. They'll go into debt for it and never make back a fraction of the cost."

The next morning at seven, once again I heard the annoyingly familiar, persistent ding of Skype. Bruce stepped into his office and opened his laptop. He left the door open since he liked for me to hear. That way if it was something to discuss later, I already had the information. Sometimes I paid attention, sometimes not.

RJ, upset with Bruce for not sufficiently cutting costs, got right down to business. "Quit paying Dago so much, fire everyone but Dago, don't pay those Inguat fees the accountant said to pay. Fire the accountant. You're too soft and you're letting these people take advantage of you."

Then came another bombshell, worse than the China trip. Sally's financial support for the hotel was being withdrawn, since "paddleboards are where the money is." From now on, Bruce must pay expenses solely from whatever guests came in.

"Fire employees, cut back Dago's pay, do whatever it takes to make ends meet," RJ told him.

It was everything Bruce had warned them against. Don't withdraw your financial support too soon. See one business through to solvency before starting another.

The call ended; Bruce's face was red and swollen. I tried to get him talking, to go for a walk with me. No, he needed to think and ponder, not walk and talk.

For a week he considered his options as he pored over the profit and loss spreadsheets. "I don't think it's doable," he muttered. "I keep trying to figure this out. Maybe if RJ hadn't spent the reserve on incidentals, we might have had a chance. They're throwing away everything they've worked for. My numbers clearly show the hotel could have been self-supporting by the end of this year. Or at the latest, *Semana Santa* of 2016, two years after opening. *If* they had followed the plan. *If* RJ hadn't dug into the hotel cash reserves instead of letting me pay the bills with it."

"I doubt if RJ reads those spreadsheets, Bruce," I said. "He's too caught up in his grandiose plans and thinks he knows everything."

Bruce did not easily get over this blow. He turned quiet and was often tired, despite continuing with his afternoon nap routine. To avoid worrying or pressuring him, I needed a distraction. I would let him stew and leave him to it.

I remembered Liesel's statement about paddleboarding. "You should have gone with us, Mom. You would have enjoyed it." She raved about how fun it was, how peaceful and tranquil, and how easy to stand up on the board. "Dale couldn't stand, tall as he is, but I did easily. I think if you worked at it, Mom, you could too."

With RJ in California, it removed the danger of him trying to control the situation. I mentioned the idea to Bruce, who liked it. "I'll have Dago take a board down to the lake and help you get set up. Say the word and we'll do it."

I got online and researched paddleboarding, especially how to stand up. Easy really—make sure you're in the center of the board with your feet equidistant, toes pointing forward. It's easier to get upright from a kneeling position, the article said, and having the paddle in the water helps to balance you on the board.

What basic, simple information, none of which RJ had provided. His training was "you can sit, or kneel or stand, whatever is comfortable." The article stated it's best to not go out when the water is choppy. *Another fail, RJ.* Five minutes of research and I knew more about it than he did.

The weekend came, and I decided to go on Monday morning despite being filled with anxiety. Scared half to death, really, but the more anxious I felt, the more determined I was to get back out there.

Eight a.m. Monday, Bruce stood ready to leave for work. "When do you want to go to the lake? I'll be here with Dago and the board." We settled on nine-fifteen. The sky should be clear, the morning coolness burned away. "See you in an hour," he said.

I wore my swimsuit with a wrap around my waist and a white linen shirt buttoned up partway. I pulled my hair into a high ponytail. I felt eighteen again until I looked in the mirror.

When Bruce came at nine-fifteen, he said Dago was already at the lake with the board. He and I walked on down, arriving at the

dock in five minutes. RJ's dog Bailey, who we always took care
of in his owner's absence, trotted along, excited about going to
the lake. RJ took her whenever he went paddleboarding, and she
jumped right on. He had designed a few boards with paw prints
on the front.

"I'm not taking Bailey," I said to Bruce.

"Why not? She loves it. She will be so disappointed."

"I couldn't care less what Bailey loves. I can't worry about her.
I'll have enough trouble worrying about myself. Maybe another
time but not today."

At the dock, Dago waited where trucks backed up for launching boats directly into the water. No trucks or boats were there,
giving us plenty of clear space. Dago stood in the water next to
the board. I took off my wrap and shirt and headed down the concrete ramp, still wearing my flip flops. The second I hit the water,
my feet slipped out from under me on the algae-covered rocks
and I landed on my butt.

Dago rushed to help me back up. I took off my flip flops, tossed
them ashore, and held onto the board. I managed much better
without them slipping around on my feet. I climbed onto the board
in a sitting position; Dago handed me the paddle and fastened the
ankle strap.

Bruce watched with a worried expression. "Karen, did you
hurt yourself?"

"I twisted my ankle a bit, but it should be okay." It hurt but
I wasn't about to give up now. I wanted to achieve a standing
position. If I did it with a sore ankle, then I could do it pain free.

Sitting felt comfortable and familiar, since it was how I had
navigated in rough waters for five hours. Worse than anything
bad that ever happened to me before that day. Today I put it
behind me. This time I would have a positive experience.

"When do you want us to come back?" Bruce asked as I settled
on the board. I was eager to get going, especially since private
boats came and went from this dock.

"Maybe an hour or so? I'm not sure. I have no idea."

"I'll watch for a while and then come back in an hour." He looked anxious, standing on the shore with Dago and Bailey—all of them watching me—while I set out by myself. Bruce didn't take pictures this time.

I paddled out and away from the docking area, going to the right toward a cove. The lake was smooth. Not glassy, but with a subtle movement that made the board gently rise and fall. Whenever a boat came near, the movement increased slightly in its wake.

Once in the secluded cove, I tried to stand. First, I went from sitting to kneeling, then paddled around until I felt secure in the higher position. The sandpaper surface hurt my knees. Standing had to feel better, if only I could do it. According to the online article, I center myself, feet equidistant, toes facing forward, and use the paddle in the water for balance.

This was indeed the secret formula. My legs were weak and wobbly, but I remained upright and able to paddle forward. It felt awkward, with my toes curled against the board and my knees shaking, but there I was. The first day's attempt was a victory.

Feeling shaky, I returned to the comfortable sitting position, paddled around the cove awhile and back to the dock before the hour. Bruce and Dago were there waiting. Dago held the board, while Bruce helped me climb on to the dock.

"How was it?" he asked.

"I liked it. I'm out of shape, I feel weak and pathetic, but I stood on the board!"

Bruce looked as pleased as if I had won an Olympic medal. "Just say the word when you want to go again."

"I'm thinking two or three times a week sounds about right, if I can manage it."

From then on, twice a week was my average. My new hobby took me away from everything that bothered me about walking in Pana. Too many people, noisy traffic, street dogs underfoot. On the lake, boats avoided me, and if I fell off, I got back on. An ankle strap connected me to the board, and both the board and the paddle floated. At first when I fell off, I kept hold of the paddle with a death grip like it was my raft or lifeboat. Until I realized the actual raft was the board, floating right there like a patient horse, waiting for me to climb back on.

On the lake I felt free and open. When the surface was glassy smooth, I stayed out longer and lost track of time. It was like sliding across the top of the earth on a hover board. Unfortunately, it was rarely smooth. Lake Atitlán is a strange body of water that can suddenly turn rough for no apparent reason. It can be a perfect day with the sun shining, no clouds and no wind, yet the waves will start churning wildly. They call this the Xocomil, based on ancient legends.

My favorite is the story of two young lovers from warring villages on opposite sides of the lake. They meet and fell in love, but their people refuse to let them marry or to see each other. They die of broken hearts, leaving their sorrow, anguish, and misery to come together in the wide expanse of the water that separates them. Xocomil is the turmoil that remains as witness to their unrequited love.

When the Xocomil starts to heave itself up from the deep, things can get dangerous quickly. Fear of it was what most often brought me in. It usually started around noon, but if I managed to get out before ten, I had plenty of time to enjoy the morning serenity of a smooth lake. Getting on and off the board became easy. Moving from sitting, kneeling, or standing and back again was second nature. I felt more comfortable on the paddleboard than when I rode that bike.

I never did take Bailey.

21

Ugly Brown Sludge

Be of good courage and he shall strengthen your heart,
all ye that hope in the Lord.
Psalm 31:24

RJ flew to China on a one-way ticket to buy paddleboards and anything else he thought might come in handy. He had an English-speaking contact in Shanghai to guide him through the process.

Bruce, who normally made it his business to know details of whatever concerned the hotel, was too irritated by this trip to ask questions. He knew there were cheap paddleboards to be had in China, and that RJ bought thirty. He knew the shipment would go out of Shanghai next month. It would take at least another month for the ship to arrive in Guatemala City. From there, RJ would load his purchases in the pickup truck and drive to Pana.

That gave me two months free of RJ coming around to run his business at our house. Two months for Bruce to redo his spreadsheets and figure out how to support the hotel solely from guest income, per Sally and RJ's latest instructions. Two months for me to enjoy freedom on the lake without RJ disrupting the pleasant routine.

On my paddleboarding mornings, Dago would meet me at the dock with the board. He then returned at the agreed hour and carried the board back to the hotel. Without Dago's willing assistance, I couldn't have pursued this activity I enjoyed so much.

By now, I stood easily and paddled my way from one cove to another. I stayed close to shore away from taxi boats and to avoid the sense of being alone in the middle of a wide expanse of water. One time a large houseboat passed by with party music blaring from the speakers. The people on board waved and cheered. With nobody else in sight, I assumed it had to be me they were cheering. I saluted them with my paddle, and they hoorayed even louder.

A few weeks before RJ's scheduled return, nature itself disrupted my outings. It had been a drier and hotter August than normal, a break in the rainy season, and the blue green algae began to bloom in the lake. I noticed strands here and there, especially in the cove near the Towers, a high-occupancy double tower hotel. I assumed it was due to polluted water and didn't go near that area. Lake Atitlán was never a pristine mountain lake on the best of days. The pollution was such that tourists were always advised not to swim in the water or eat fish caught from it. Locals did, but they were either used to it or had no other choice.

One morning as I approached the lake, I was astonished to see a thick blanket of brown sludge covering the surface. I stood at the dock wondering what the heck happened when Dago came with the board, Bailey trotting alongside. Bailey never gave up hope of getting invited on my board. She ran to me on the pier, observed what she saw as solid ground and jumped onto the greenish brown surface.

"Bailey, no!" She realized in a flash her danger. Light on her feet, she jumped back onto the pier where she licked her green paws.

As Bailey, Dago and I trudged back after that disappointing discovery, I asked him what happened to the lake. He confirmed it was algae, called it *algas* and said it happened sometimes when there isn't enough rain and when there is *mucho sol.*

"Will it go away?"

"*Síííí.*" The long drawn out yes.

Uh oh, I knew what that meant. Definitely not tomorrow.

Every day I went to check if the algae had dissipated enough for going out the next morning. Still there, like an ugly brown carpet. During the afternoons, when normally the Xocomil held sway over the water, instead it moved beneath the sludge like a great sea creature struggling to dislodge.

Then by sunset, nothing had changed. The Xocomil was quiet, and the lake slept on under its thick covering. That algae didn't look like it would ever go away.

Meanwhile, Sally instructed her dad to prepare for RJ's return. "Prepare the open space next to the lobby to make room for the shipment. Drive the truck to Guatemala City and leave it at the repair shop. They'll hold it until RJ arrives. Have Lucas go with his taxi to bring you back."

In measured words, Bruce expressed his concerns to Sally, and later to me. "I've always felt like a steward over Sally's investment. How can I walk away now and let RJ burn through everything with his big ideas?" He sat in the chair at his desk, looking worried after Sally's call.

I had heard the tail end of the conversation. Sally had not paid attention to her dad's counsel because it ran counter to her husband's desires. "It's the circle of life, Bruce. You find your mate and leave your parents. Even the Bible says so. I think you're fighting a losing battle."

He didn't want to hear it. "She's my daughter!"

"And RJ's wife. She chose him and she loves him. Let them run things the way they want, Bruce, and if it bothers you then walk away. Whatever the outcome, it's their choice to make."

He raised his voice. "Karen, she has earned six figures a year since they were married, and she stands to lose it all if this keeps up."

"Well, don't get mad at me. I'm just telling you how it is. A girl falls in love, leaves her parents, and joins her husband. I did it. Sally did it. For better or for worse, remember? Maybe you and

I got too personally involved. Maybe you should have stepped back well before this and let them make their own mistakes."

Bruce rubbed his face. He straightened papers on the desk. "RJ has a lot of ideas for making money, that's fine. Finish one before you start another. Ideas don't make money; correct implementation of ideas is what makes money."

"I know that, and you know that, but we're still back where we started. Our kids have to make their own choices, Bruce, solve their own problems and learn as they go. We're better off staying out of it."

"Maybe," he said, although I could tell he didn't quite believe it. Not when it involved his daughter and her hard-earned money and her future happiness.

Later that week at dinner, Bruce asked if I knew Rowan, the woman RJ hired to create a website and do social media marketing for the boards and the hotel.

"Pretty blond lady, about thirty-something? I met her a couple times when he brought her over to see the paddleboards. Why?"

"She came by the hotel today very upset, looking for RJ. She said she has put hundreds of hours into setting up the website, Facebook page, and Airbnb account and gotten nothing back. I don't know what he promised her besides a commission of some sort and a free hotel room when she comes to Pana, but she was furious."

"RJ and his promises. He loves getting people to work for nothing."

"Rowan told me, 'The biggest problem with your business is the trust factor. *There is none.*' That's what she said."

"Ouch."

"When Rowan left, I couldn't get over what she said. *Your business.* All my life, I've tried to be honest in my dealings. People trusted me in the mortgage business and referred their friends. When it ended, at least I knew I'd been upright and cheated nobody. Now here's Rowan, including me in her condemnation. People see me involved with operations. It's not only RJ. I'm a part of it. I have a role in the underhanded business dealings. Not paying fees, breaking promises, not paying employees. I endeavored to create a trustworthy and professional management process, but I've failed."

I didn't know what to say. Bruce had wanted so badly for Casa Colonial to be a success for Sally and RJ. He knew how to do it, had worked hours without pay to achieve it, and it was on the way. Until RJ stopped the progress and ended the plan. Nothing Bruce could say or do, no spreadsheets he could create made any difference. It was over, and he had failed.

We sat wordlessly as the late afternoon rays of the sun cast shadows over the dining room table.

Bruce stacked our plates and utensils in organized piles. Then he said, "We're done storing paddleboards on our property. They can go back to the hotel. Dago and Walter will move them tomorrow."

During these final weeks of September, Bruce composed a letter in preparation for RJ's return. "A word of warning, except it's turning into a book. I'm getting everything down before trimming it to the key points. Will you read it when I'm done, Karen, and tell me what you think?"

He had emailed many business letters to Sally and RJ, spreadsheet attached, for his monthly report. This was the first one he asked me to review. "Of course," I said.

Bruce was still working on the letter when RJ arrived in mid-October. When he saw his boards had been moved from our palapa back to the hotel, he exploded in fury. No more agreeable son-in-law. No more Family Man. No more of the humble Kid listening to another viewpoint. He was full on Macho Man, Entrepreneur, and Renard Jacques. He told Dago to bring back any tool or small piece of equipment left in our palapa.

"And Karen is no longer allowed in the hotel or to use my boards," he told both Bruce and Dago during one of his rants.

Bruce tried reasoning with him. "What's the problem? Since you're adding thirty new paddleboards, why not keep them together at the hotel where people can see them?"

I supposed RJ saw it as a betrayal, a lack of respect, to move his property while he was gone. To touch them or make any decision about them without his permission or direction.

Ricardo Juan was on the rampage. Bruce came home each evening with another example of his insane fuming. "He went over the cleaning today with Dago and me. He pointed out paint spots from the painting of Room 9 where some lines weren't exactly straight. Mold on the doors is an ongoing problem, and we've been cleaning doors weekly. Not good enough, says Ricardo Juan. He fires the help and expects Dago to do the maintenance and upkeep as well as housekeeping. He says to me, 'I can hire someone from the coast for thirty Q a day to do this.' Well, fine, I'd like to see it. I'd like to see someone work for four dollars a day and be as good and dependable as Dago's family has always been."

Nothing upset Bruce as much as how RJ treated Dago and others RJ saw as inferior.

"Because things apparently aren't up to standard, he threatens to cut off Dago's pay for several weeks, but still expects him to come in and work. Totally wrong to treat your employees that way. Lay them off if you want to punish them, but slave labor is illegal in Guatemala. How will that teach Dago anything? Being punitive and insulting is no way to build a work ethic of trust and loyalty. Dago has invested time and developed a vision for the hotel and its future, and he deserves to be treated like a valued employee. He threatened Dago with demotion or removal for not learning to use a computer we don't have. 'You could have taken classes,' he said. When is Dago going to take classes when he is working six days a week?"

The hotel had always been RJ's dream, but this second year of its operation, he had transferred focus to the paddleboards. Bruce with his "best business practices" was in the way. Karen, the interfering mother-in-law, was in the way. This was RJ's world, and we were intruders. Even Dago, whose passion was for the hotel over the paddleboards, was in the way.

There were no more friendly meetings at our house. Some days Bruce didn't go back to work after lunch. Instead, he hunkered down in his office composing The Letter.

Then came the day when Bruce stormed home at ten, his face a red rage.

I was shocked at his expression. "What's wrong?"

It took him awhile to get the words out. He blew through the house, tossed aside his backpack, took a drink in the kitchen. I hovered and waited.

"I can take anything Ricardo Juan wants to say against me. His accusations about how I don't know what I'm doing, I'm weak and ineffective, a pushover. That I have Alzheimer's. That I stole his stupid refrigerator. But when he talks against you, that's it!"

Oh, is that all. Nothing RJ said about me would be a shock. "What did he say?"

"I don't want to talk about it. It's going in The Letter." He retreated to his office. "I need to finish it and free myself from this entanglement once and for all."

The next morning, Bruce didn't go to work. He ate his usual breakfast of granola and yogurt then hunkered down in his office until lunch. "I should have a draft ready for you this afternoon, Karen. Will you be around?"

"I might go outside and pick flowers is all." I had not gone paddleboarding since September. The thick sludge was especially dense and ugly near the shoreline. The boat taxis still ran, although slowly, needing to stop frequently to clean off the motors.

Bruce cloistered himself until five, when he called out. "I'm done, Karen. You want to read it on my computer, or shall I email it to you?"

I came into his office. "Can I sit in your chair and read it on your laptop?"

"Be my guest." He pulled himself stiffly out of the chair. "It started out as a voice of warning, but it's turned into my resignation."

The seat was warm from his body heat. I adjusted the screen and read. Bruce paced the room, went to the kitchen, to the bathroom, came back and paced some more.

The letter summarized his counsel, emails and spreadsheets of the eighteen months since Casa Colonial opened for business in Easter of 2014. Filled with wisdom and warnings, it reflected his business ethics, management style and belief system.

> *There were a lot of little things that never got finished when we opened. Next year there will be more painting and things to be fixed including replacing some of the beds, and we can afford them if we follow the plan for the hotel.* ***Cutting off your financial support a year early was not in the plan. Not paying our employees on time was not in the plan. Diverting funds to other opportunities was not in the plan.***
>
> *The hotel is open, proven and has generated income despite cash flow challenges. We are reaching a critical time when we will need significant increase in guests, or assistance with capital to keep the doors open.*

I read through several more paragraphs about profit and loss and ethical business practices, the gist of which echoed Bruce's ongoing advice about making sure one enterprise is profitable before starting another or you risk losing them both.

RJ, if, as you say this hotel can be run by you and Sally alone, I am glad to back out and let you guys have at it. But the Gowen family has invested much support and finances into this project, and they deserve credit for their help. Those who have invested their hard-earned money deserve the expected return of the principle as promised. You also made some serious allegations last Friday that I will address just this once.

You accused our family of not supporting this hotel. *That is patently false. Travis brought his family down here to work for six months. Karen and I moved here based on certain assurances of compensation, which never materialized, and I've given thousands of hours working to make this a profitable business. Others of our children have loaned literally thousands of dollars to you for the completion of this hotel, and now you treat that financial support as though it never happened. Karen has promoted both the hotel and paddleboard business on her blog that has a wide following. We have invited family members to visit and stay at the hotel and many have come and spread the word.*

Then Bruce outlined where RJ crossed the last line, his final unforgivable affront.

You told me my wife is not a loving person. *If not for her, what do you think these ten children would be like? How many large families are as close as ours? The love she has given to our children has been the glue that built this family into the powerful unified group that we are. This summer Karen went out on the paddleboard from one to two times a week, not only to improve her skills but to increase visibility for the boards. People would stop and ask me about the boards because of seeing her continued presence on the lake.*

You implied that I stole the hotel refrigerator. *RJ, you smilingly commented that "someone" had stolen the hotel refrigerator. Coming on top of your accusations and assertions about* *our family, I didn't take it as a joke. We have given the hotel three refrigerators, two ladders, an air compressor, airless paint sprayer, battery powered car jump starter, and numerous other hand tools and items. Tools belonging to me that I collected through the years and valued highly. None of which I asked compensation for. What were you thinking implying that I "stole" your refrigerator?*

When I read that, I laughed out loud. "I can't believe he accuses us of stealing his refrigerator. It wasn't used except for a dozen eggs here and there that easily fit in a mini fridge costing less to run. If he wanted it, he could have come and gotten it at any time. He knew it was in our kitchen, all the lunches he ate here, why didn't he say anything then if it bothered him?"

"I left out a lot, believe me. It was twice as long as it is now."

In closing, Bruce reiterated the family's contributions.

If it weren't for the money loaned for this hotel by our family, I'd walk away right now with relief. But I feel I owe it to those of Sally's siblings who have contributed to this project with their financial support. They are investors and their contribution is cast off like it doesn't matter. This is the only reason why I'm writing this letter, as one last effort to make you see sense. Otherwise, I'd send the reports and say goodbye and be done with it and let you two deal with the mess you've created.

"It's an excellent letter, Bruce. Professional and well written, certainly clear."

"You don't think it goes too over the top?"

"No. Actually, you barely touch the surface with the many issues you've had to deal with. The trust issues especially, not only with you and Dago, but Rowan too. Not paying her as agreed. Cheating people, essentially."

"When Rowan came to me with her complaints and mentioned the betrayals of trust, it really sunk in how, as far as others are concerned, I am no better than RJ. I represent the hotel as much as he does. When he doesn't pay bills or honor commitments, it's on me too. I can't be part of a business ethic like that. I can't represent it. As much as I have stayed to support Sally and protect her interests, I can't get into these shady areas. Lack of integrity is a whole lot worse than no business sense."

Together, we went over the final paragraphs.

*Consider this my resignation **unless** the two of you are willing to seriously address these concerns. Sally, I will wait to hear from you. RJ, I have nothing more to say to you until you make a full and complete apology for the things you said about my family **and** a personal apology to my wife for the things you said about her.*

Bruce still couldn't let go. He couldn't quite walk away, "unless the two of you are willing to seriously address these concerns." Well, that wasn't going to happen.

The letter concluded with a summary of his key points, along with a few additional issues, to make sure his position was clear. He signed it Regards, Bruce Gowen. No Love, Dad on this email.

"When are you sending it?"

"Tomorrow, after letting it sit overnight. Then I'll review it again and hit send."

Bruce and I wandered around the house a bit, eventually ending up together on the sofa, staring at the cold, empty fireplace. Weeks and weeks Bruce had worked on this letter, wavering between what to say and where to draw the battle line. All the while, business at the hotel deteriorated along with his relationship to RJ. Still, Bruce could not bring himself to outright quit. The letter was his last attempt to get RJ to see sense and make changes.

"What possessed him to travel to China and buy thirty more boards?" I threw out there.

"Who knows what motivates him? I'm done trying to figure it out."

"I can't believe he thinks Lake Atitlán is a paddleboarding paradise," I said. "It's too choppy, with not enough coves or secluded areas. I couldn't stay out more than a couple hours before the Xocomil came on and ruined it for me."

"No, it's not a recreational lake," Bruce agreed. "It's a deep bowl of water that people cross to go from one town to another."

RJ had made a dozen excellent paddleboards, handcrafted works of art that functioned beautifully on the water. He could have opened a paddleboard shop in LA and sold them at premium prices. In Pana the boards held little interest; three, in fact, were plenty. Between the seasonal algae blooms and the daily Xocomil, not to mention the numerous taxi boats, Lake Atitlán wasn't well suited for sport.

A fire would be nice and comforting right now, I thought. But we'd have to bring in firewood, and I didn't want to move. I wondered about dinner. It was five p.m. I mentally composed available ingredients into an easy meal. Vegetable soup and grilled cheese sandwiches.

"I can't help Sally any longer," Bruce said. "Not at the risk of my own integrity. Besides, she's a grown woman and makes her own decisions."

Decisions that always favor her husband, I thought. Like mine always favor Bruce. But then my husband is wise and good while hers is . . . RJ. Was he anything at all like her patient, giving, kind father? Could he *ever* be? It never made sense to me how, with a father like this, Sally had chosen that husband.

Still, over time, RJ might overcome his demons and become the person our daughter sees when she looks at him. One could always hope.

22

Toxic Gas

Turn us again, O Lord God of hosts, cause they face to shine;
and we shall be saved.
Psalm 80:19

B ruce slept late the next day. At nine, Dago knocked at the back
door. "Is Mr. Bruce okay?" he asked with concern. "Not sick?"

"He's fine, Dago, just tired and sleeping late."

"I was worried. He didn't come to the hotel yesterday."

"He was busy writing a letter. It took him the whole day."

"He got mad at Mr. RJ. I never saw Mr. Bruce like that before.
I thought he was going to hit Mr. RJ." Dago maintained his usual
smile and laughed a little to lighten the message, but his uneasi-
ness showed through the words. "They yelled at each other. I was
afraid they were going to fight."

This must have been the day RJ spoke against me, when Bruce
stormed in with his angry red face. I smiled back at Dago, thankful to him for this brief description of what happened. Bruce had
told me very little about their argument.

"Yes, there are some problems right now. But don't worry
about Mr. Bruce. He is fine."

"Okay, then good. I will see him later at the hotel."

You probably won't, I thought, but didn't say anything more
to worry Dago.

Shortly after, Bruce woke up and went to his home office. An
hour later, he hollered, "I am clicking send!"

"Okay!" I yelled back. Yelling through the house felt good for some reason.

Bruce found me in the kitchen peeling and slicing a papaya into a bowl.

"It's done, Karen," he declared. "Let's get the heck out of here. Where shall we go for lunch?"

"Let's have papaya while we think about it."

We sat at the table and ate the entire fruit. Hermano Juan wasn't scheduled for today, leaving us free agents.

"Where should we go?" Bruce repeated.

"You're not going to the hotel?"

"Nope. I'm done there. I brought home my laptop and note-books yesterday. RJ can keep whatever else I left."

I told him about Dago coming by earlier.

"I will email Dago. Let's get out of here."

We washed up the dishes then grabbed our trusty Guatemala bags. Bruce put on his backpack. We locked up and went around the block to catch the bus to Sololá, as though it were any other afternoon off.

We got off at the mercado, bought some fruit and nuts: mac-adamia, cashews, almonds, and peanuts. Our bags and Bruce's backpack were full, signifying the end of shopping.

We sauntered over to the park where we rested on a bench. In Guatemala, people lived outdoors. Rain or shine, the neighbor-hoods, streets and parks are busy with human activity. Today was overcast and slightly misty but so far, no rain. We watched the people and didn't talk about the hotel or the letter or Sally and RJ.

We ate lunch at our favorite hamburger place. A young couple with two small children came in but didn't stay long. After lin-gering an hour, we went next door to the pastry shop and shared a dessert at one of their fancy little tables. Finally ready to head home, we traversed the four blocks downhill to the park. Sololá, the county seat, is higher and farther from the lake. Bruce always needed to stop and rest halfway up to the hamburger café, but not on the way back.

At the park we caught the five o'clock bus to Pana. As soon as we arrived home, Bruce rushed to check his email while I put away the fruit and nuts.

"Nothing yet," he reported.

"Good. You need a break from the drama. Let's go to bed early and watch a cozy mystery on Netflix, then have a good night's sleep."

The next morning, Dago came by again to see if Mr. Bruce was okay, having missed another day at the hotel. Once again, Bruce was unavailable, this time in the shower.

"Yesterday, Doña Sally was on Skype crying. Mr. RJ got violent, yelling, throwing things," Dago reported. "Is Mr. Bruce coming to work today?"

This must have been after they got the letter. "Probably not," I responded. I figured RJ would fill Dago in later with whatever he wanted Dago to know about the situation.

We didn't hear anything more until the following morning, when Sally rang her dad on Skype. In a monotone voice as though reading a script, she delivered RJ's message. The call went on for a while and I left the room. Seeing my daughter hurt by what happened made me want to cry.

The gist of it was, "Tell your dad this. Tell your dad that. Tell your mom I'm through with her. I know she wrote that letter. She put your dad up to it. He wouldn't have done it on his own, it was all her. If your dad wants to come and talk to me, he still has a chance but not your mom. I'm through with her. She's done. Tell her that. Your family doesn't respect or support me. They never have. I'm done with your family."

With all RJ's emphasis on respect, how ironic for him to show so little respect to Bruce. He thought Bruce was weak and soft, too easily fooled, and he couldn't have possibly written such a letter. It had to be me putting him up to it, writing it myself and forcing my husband to send it in his name. RJ could not even credit Bruce with this much.

Afterward, Bruce said, "In my head I added 'my sociopath husband' to each of Sally's statements. It was the only way to stay calm. I don't want to get upset with her."

"How can we be upset with Sally? None of this is her fault, and I imagine she suffers the most, feeling torn between her husband and her parents."

"Here's how her report went in my head—'My sociopath husband doesn't understand forgiveness. If he feels someone slights him, he can never let go of it. My sociopath husband didn't mean to say the rest of the family doesn't support him. He meant Mom doesn't support him. My sociopath husband will give you one more chance, but if you say or do anything out of line that will be it for you, too. My sociopath husband won't ever go to Utah again. And he won't ever set foot in your house.'"

What a relief, I thought, RJ never setting foot in our house.

Later, probably after her sociopath husband left for the gym, Sally called her dad in tears. "RJ says it's me or my family. He wants me to break off with my family or I can't be with him. How can I do that? Why is he making me choose? Why does it have to be one or the other? He says I have to give up the church, too. I can't pay tithing or give any more money to the church."

Sally was hurting, which hurt us, too. But we knew she would be okay despite RJ's ultimatum. She would keep her own counsel while allowing him to rant and rave. She was like a professional lion tamer who can get in the cage with the beasts because she doesn't lose control or show weakness, fear, or aggression. Sally knew how to handle RJ, and it was always with love and patience. Eventually he would back down on forcing her to reject us and to leave the church.

RJ—flawed, wild and unpredictable—hated us now, especially me. If he saw us go by the hotel or passed us in town, he got a hard, angry look and turned his back. This toxic atmosphere spread down the street to our property. By now, we had lived a year in our dream house, much of that time disturbed by RJ. Working on his boards in our backyard, popping over for meetings with Bruce; RJ acting like he owned the place. Those first months without him around had been bliss in our Pana house, until he came back to disturb its peace and tranquility.

Earlier, Bruce had taken a bag of dog food over for Bailey, left from when we had kept her while RJ was in China.

Dago brought it back to us, saying, "Mr. RJ doesn't want this at the hotel. He told me to bring it back."

I thanked him and asked if he minded dropping it in the garbage on his way out.

We had to get away. RJ wasn't leaving, so we had to.

As much as we loved our home, how could we continue like this? How can anyone feel at peace with such animosity directed their way?

American expats live all over the world, anywhere they can enjoy a good life for less. Retirees can't survive on Social Security alone. It also takes a healthy retirement fund. Or lacking that, a side career, and then you're working well past retirement age. No wonder so many like us were leaving the country for Mexico, Central and South America, Asia, and elsewhere. Being debt free, having a modest savings, and an open, adventuresome nature was all it took. WiFi was everywhere, air travel relatively inexpensive.

We had options. We didn't have to stay in Pana, or in Guatemala for that matter.

On the Facebook Lake Atitlán group, a comment caught my attention: "I'm done with this place. Things are too expensive here. I am leaving the land of the Maya and going back to the land of the Azteca. The exchange rate is better and so is the food."

I looked up the exchange rate: 18 to 1 in Mexico compared to 7 to 1 in Guatemala. I came across a blog by a retired couple traveling through Mexico and Central America. They crossed the border between the state of Chiapas, Mexico, and La Mesilla, Guatemala, then bussed from La Mesilla up to the Lake Atitlán region. They gave step by step directions, along with a charming photo of musicians in the central park of a pretty town called Comitán. I bookmarked their blog post and transcribed the instructions into my journal.

If this couple could travel so easily from Comitán to Pana, then why couldn't we do the same from Pana to Comitán?

Bruce showed little interest in my research, apparently not yet ready to think about a move. He spent hours at his desk, studying conference talks and printing out inspirational quotes to tape on the wall of his study. He read books on the Kindle, ate his three meals a day, took an afternoon nap, and was ready for bed soon after dinner. RJ and his hotel were no longer a topic of discussion. Bruce had written his letter, and now it was over.

He did submit to a day trip to Chichicastenango, despite having to get there on the chicken bus. We visited the famous mercado and enjoyed lunch under a large tent. At the mercado, Bruce found a leather-tooled belt that fit him. This made him happy, since he had looked throughout Pana and Sololá for such a belt.

We decided to try a day trip to Guatemala City on the chicken bus, too, just to say we had done it. Nothing bad happened, despite RJ's early warnings. Our own silly little victory.

A town near the Mexican border called Huehuecastanango came next on my travel wish list. For that trip, we found a hotel and spent the night, then visited some nearby ruins before returning home the next day.

Although Bruce enjoyed these excursions, he didn't want to go as far as Tikal in the north, or to cross the border into Mexico or Belize. Glad to at least get him out as much as I did, I left him alone to rest and to read. He deserved a break after everything he'd been through this past year.

The Pana house was too close to the hotel for me to concentrate on my book. I took to working in a place near Pollo Campero, a nice indoor plaza with adjoining cafés and offices. The lounge area had comfortable seating, tables, decent WiFi and a view to the street. I always faced out in case RJ entered. I could focus on my laptop and ignore him. He never did come in, at least not while I was there. It may not have been somewhere he frequented.

One afternoon a chunky woman with spiky blond hair and dark roots introduced herself to me. "I'm Jenny Black. I've seen you working here in the afternoons. Are you a writer?"

"Yes, I actually am. I'm finishing up a book."

We exchanged the usual get-to-know-you expat information. Where are you from, what brought you to Pana, where are you staying, do you like it and how long are you here for.

Jenny was easy to talk to, friendly and interesting, and asked questions about Bruce and me. She was renting property for a hotel across the lake in San Pedro and needed a retired couple to manage it. She and two of her children were in San Pedro; her husband remained behind in Arizona with their other three kids. Once Jenny got the hotel negotiations underway, she was going back to finalize business in Arizona and the whole family would then move to Guatemala.

"The hotel is in San Pedro, but we want to live in Pana," she said.

"It's a lovely little town," I agreed. "Bruce and I recently got out of the hotel business. We came here to help our daughter and her husband run their hotel, Casa Colonial. Do you know it?"

She didn't but said she would look for it. "I would sure love to hear more about your hotel experience," she said.

"It was really my husband. I have my own work that keeps me busy." My eyes strayed to the laptop.

Jenny stood up. "Well, I should let you get back to it. But I'd like to talk to the two of you."

We exchanged phone numbers. Bruce had recently installed a landline in his office that could receive both local and U.S. calls. That landline, more intimate and personal than Skype, had stayed busy recently with Sally's calls to her dad seeking comfort and reassurance. I gave the number to Jenny.

"Be sure and call. Bruce will be interested in talking to you." She assured me she would.

When I told Bruce about Jenny Black, he was intrigued. His weeks of rest and reflection had refreshed him, perhaps bored him. He had no further interest in travel but wanted a project, a job to do. "See, I knew it was important to put that phone in," he crowed.

Bruce was convinced a landline would bring what he needed to feel useful again. A phone on his desk brought him business, helped him make money, strengthened friendships, and forged new relationships. He was never happier than when leaning back in his chair with the phone to his ear, his rich deep voice bantering with someone on the other end, his infectious, drawn-out chuckle responding warmly to the dialogue. He never took much to the cell phone.

"Tiny little slippery things. Like trying to talk with a cold flat fish in your hand. What's the appeal? And the connection is never as good as with a landline."

PART FOUR

San Pedro

I, the Lord, am not displeased with your coming this journey,
notwithstanding your follies.
Doctrine & Covenants 111:1

23
The Whirlwind

Thou rulest the raging of the sea;
when the waves thereof arise, thou stillest them.
Psalm 89:9

Greg and Lucy Jensen who had four boys, had searched for a house like ours, a family home in Pana with a garden instead of their isolated place on the other side of the mountain. Greg couldn't believe the deal we got and often said, "If you ever leave, let me know."

That gave me a brilliant idea. "Bruce, we could sublet to the Jensens short-term! That way if things don't work out in San Pedro, we can come back."

Bruce moved papers on his desk, made a new pile and straightened another one. "I still haven't heard from Jenny. None of this may pan out, Karen."

"We should get prepared just in case. We should get our ducks in a row. Call Greg and run it past him. Believe me, Jenny was very interested in us."

Bruce lifted the receiver and dialed Greg, who liked the idea. He and Lucy would discuss it.

Jenny did call as I knew she would. We met with her twice at our house and again in San Pedro. She had rented a grand, spreading place on the lake. Gardens sloped down toward the shore where there was a dock, a rowboat, and several kayaks, all part of the property. She met us at the San Pedro city dock, took us to view the property, then for lunch at a nearby café.

Many of the San Pedro eateries were throwbacks to the psychedelic hippie culture of the Sixties and Seventies, catering to the youngish generation of expats. The sights and smells of their drug culture permeated the town. Barefoot, dreadlocked 21st-century hippies clustered about, lingering in the coffee shops where they ate their sprouts and tofu, smoked their pot.

This café was no different, but "the food is excellent," said Jenny. After we ate, she offered Bruce the position to live in and manage the hotel for free rent and a small stipend, perhaps a percentage of profits.

Bruce countered with an actual salary, saying, "I already did that once. It's a tough situation and not worth doing for no pay."

After some hesitation and bargaining where Bruce didn't budge, Jenny said, "Let me think about it, and I will let you know."

As he and I crossed the lake back to Pana, I realized the disgusting brown algae had disappeared. Must be the cooler weather, I thought. Since the blow up with RJ, I had given little thought to the lake and its moods.

We trudged up the road back to our house. It had been a long day, leaving home at ten and now it was close to four. "Do you think Jenny will meet your price?"

"I don't know. It's high for Guatemala. That place was incredible though, wasn't it? She's getting a strong staff on board, including a local man like Dago. A type of supervisor or assistant manager who reports to me."

"It's beautiful, more like a ranch than a house or a hotel. I half expected to see a corral to the side with a couple horses."

"I hope she goes for it. I'm tired of doing nothing. I'm ready to get back to work."

"Hopefully they have the money for it," I mused.

"They must have. They're paying $3000 a month just for rent. That was the advantage to Casa Colonial. RJ owns it free and clear."

"We could sure use a change of scene. As much as I love our house, I'm feeling trapped lately. Pana has lost its glow, Bruce."

We reached our gate, unlocked it and let ourselves in. Bruce had asked for Dago's key as well as RJ's. I liked knowing no one had come in our absence. Still, the place felt different, as though it were slipping away. The month's events had been a powerful whirlwind, an irresistible force swooping us up and away. I knew God was in charge, I trusted Him, but I had my concerns about Jenny.

"You know what, Bruce, I'm not entirely convinced Jenny is legitimate. I don't mean dishonest or anything like that, but that she's overzealous. She has these big plans and how do we know there's money to back them up?"

Bruce looked surprised. Apparently, the thought had never entered his mind. "Why would she run such a risk? Why agree to the rent, offer to hire me and the other staff if she doesn't have the funds? That's plain crazy."

In the office, he unloaded his backpack and plopped down in his chair.

I stood in the doorway. What a lovely room this was, with the window opening to the lime tree, now lush with its round, green fruit. "I could be wrong about Jenny, but it's a gut feeling. That she's one of those people who think they can jump off a cliff and not get hurt, thinking something will save her if only she has the nerve to take the plunge."

"Well, if she doesn't agree to my terms, I'll know she can't afford me. End of story."

"What if she agrees and wants us over there right away? We have kids coming for Christmas, remember?" Sean and Erin were coming along with Forrest and Tommy, one of the neighbor boys who grew up with our younger kids. This would be Tommy's and Forrest's first trip out of the country.

"I could start work, and you and the kids can stay here. I can commute on the boats like everyone else does."

"Bruce, that sounds awful. It wouldn't be fun at all. Your boys want to spend time with you, not just say goodnight at the end of the day." Putting work over family and at Christmas, too! Upset, I turned to go.

"I guess we cross that bridge when we come to it," he said. "Let's see what develops."

The phone rang, and Bruce picked up. *It's Sally*, he mouthed to me. Then, "Oh no!" he exclaimed with a stricken look.

"What happened?" I shouted. "Is she okay? Did something bad happen?"

He shook his head. "Sally's okay. Paul died."

"Paul? Paul *died*?"

They finished their brief conversation, while I waited to hear the full story.

Not feeling well, Paul was recently hospitalized in Sololá and had died shortly after. "RJ says nobody ever comes out alive from that Sololá hospital," Sally told her dad. "If you or mom get sick, don't go there. Have Lucas or Pedro take you to Quetzaltenango. Never to Sololá."

Paul gone. Our first real friend in Pana, and we never got to say goodbye. His apartment had been our first home in Guatemala. It truly did feel like the end of an era.

"I wish I'd known he was in the hospital," Bruce lamented. "I could have gone to visit him."

RJ knew. He could have told us.

A few days later, Jenny called to say she would meet Bruce's salary. However, she needed him right away as there was a large group of guests scheduled next week. A family of twelve had reserved four rooms for a reunion. Bruce congratulated her on getting business so soon, and said he'd talk to me and call her back about timing. He had not told her about our kids coming. Funny how Bruce tended to forget he had a family when he got focused on work.

"Ask Jenny if the four of them can stay at the hotel with us. Otherwise, I don't know what we'll do, and our Christmas is ruined."

"I'll ask her about Juan Molina too. She doesn't have a gardener yet, and she needs a good one considering the size of those grounds."

"If Jenny is okay letting our kids stay there, then I'm okay moving right away," I said.

He called her back, and she was fine with them taking rooms. "They don't need to pay," she offered. "It's good advertising for people to see the place busy with guests."

The whirlwind blew and the deal was done.

Greg and Lucy liked the idea of renting our house. He dropped by to look it over. "What if this situation doesn't work out for you guys. Will you want your house back?"

We stood in the bright and sunny dining room. Bruce shook his head no. "We are done with Pana."

"What will you do then? Go back to Utah?"

"No," he said. "We burned our boats."

"Where would you go?"

I blurted, "Mexico!" But really, we had no idea. The whirlwind was blowing us to San Pedro, and it was up to us to make the best of it. "Come what may and love it," as my grandmother used to say.

Greg said he would help us move. "The best way is by boat. There's a guy we used once. I'll get a quote from him and let you know, Bruce. My boys and I will haul your things to the dock in my truck."

Since our Pana house came furnished as did most home rentals in the area, our only furniture were the two beds we bought from

Morris, brand new when we moved to that house. Our destination was one hotel room and an office, already furnished. We would leave the beds behind for the Jensens, along with a few other items like a trunk, a couple bookshelves, and Bruce's office chair.

The trunk, a family antique handed down from my mother's side, sat at the end of the bed in my writing room. Bruce and RJ had brought it in the truck on their trip to Guatemala before Bruce's knee surgery. I sat on the bed and rested my hand on the trunk's rough surface. It had traveled from Norway to Nebraska in 1890 with my homesteading great-grandparents.

The wood was warm under my hand, like old, stiff flesh. I could almost hear it saying, "I am old. I am tired. I crossed the ocean, and I don't want to cross the lake. Let me stay in the Pana house. Leave me in peace." The Norway trunk would stay.

Bruce boxed up an electric saw and drill, electric paint sprayer, a leather tool belt stocked with basics, and a fully equipped metal tool kit—part of the equipment brought on that early trip with RJ, when they had shared such hope and enthusiasm for the work they would do together on Casa Colonial.

"RJ has enough of my things," Bruce declared. "These are going with me. Besides, they'll come in handy at the new hotel. When Jenny showed us around, I didn't see anything in the shed by way of tools."

In the blink of an eye, the whirlwind brought our moving day. Greg, his sons, and the boat driver loaded our things onto the boat. We climbed in and skimmed across the lake to San Pedro. Greg and his boys helped us carry everything up to four tuk tuks, then said goodbye and good luck in our new endeavor. At our final destination, the tuk tuk drivers took our stuff down the long steps to the front door. They charged us double, but we still added a big tip; we were just so glad to be done with this.

Bruce and I carried our things to the back bedroom, thankfully on the first floor. It had a bath and adjoining office, our private space at the sprawling hotel. Jenny's two boys, ages ten and twelve, watched as they climbed around the inside ceiling beams like monkeys. I asked where their mom was, and one of them pointed upstairs.

Jenny, her assistant Maria, and several local women were cleaning and arranging the second and third floor rooms. Two other women were down at the shore washing the sheets and blankets in the lake, then bringing them up in a wheelbarrow to hang on the clothesline at the side of the house. It was early December and cooler weather but still plenty of sunshine.

Bruce and I chatted awhile upstairs with Jenny. She was busy, said not to worry about helping and just get ourselves settled in. That sounded good to me, since we were tired and hungry. We left to go find someplace to eat and came across a cheerful-looking hamburger place. As we paused to read the large print menu posted on the front window, a smiling, pudgy man about the age of one of our sons, came out to greet us, speaking some English mixed with the Spanish.

"We recently opened our rooftop seating. It's very pretty. Welcome to Big Burger, come in, *bienvenidos!*" Drawn in by his friendliness, we followed him up the stairs to the balcony. He showed us to a table set with a brightly colored Maya cloth and handed us plasticized menus with appetizing photos of burger platters.

He was so pleased to have us and so attentive and excited to take our orders that we felt quite happy to be there. He requested a picture of us at the table, "for Facebook." Later, I found his page, Big Burger owned by Manu Roche.

"I'm not sure this guy's new burger joint will do well in San Pedro," I reflected. "There's nothing here for vegans except this avocado, sprout, mushroom burger. And only one kind of tea."

Bruce scanned the menu. "We should come every day to keep him in business!"

Our food came on platters with generous servings and too much for one person. Next time we'd do better to share an order. I thought of Hermano Juan and his tiny food budget. Jenny had agreed to hire him as gardener at ten quetzales an hour plus boat fare both ways.

"I'm glad our move didn't put Hermano Juan out of a job," I said.

"Me, too. Jenny is all right," Bruce said. "A little abrasive at times, but that doesn't bother me. They are putting a lot of cash into this place. She wants to add a restaurant in that large empty building by the street."

"She gets things done, that's for sure. I can't believe how quickly she hired people and already has guests scheduled. When you consider how long RJ has been at it yet still putters around with a near empty hotel."

We let the conversation drift to manage our big, messy burgers. Thankfully, there was a full napkin dispenser on the table. Most places provided one tiny thin napkin per person. If you asked for another, they brought you one more.

Bruce dug into his cheese jalapeño fries. "This food is incredible. Let's bring the kids here when they come next week, Karen."

"Oh, for sure! I can't wait to see them. Family here for Christmas is my dream come true."

After our meal, Bruce reluctantly agreed to walk the five or six blocks back to the hotel. "I know it's good for me, but I don't like these steep hills. I get too out of breath."

San Pedro was laid out on a higher incline than Pana. My legs hurt after only fifteen minutes uphill. Bruce, in between deep breaths, complained about the heat, the traffic, the steep hills, and the hippies everywhere.

San Pedro would take some adjustment.

24
Messy Mortality

We spend our years as a tale that is told.
Psalm 90:9

The reunion group confirmed their reservation for one week in December. Jenny would be gone by then with Bruce in charge. Those two met for hours in his office, often with the supervisor and the head housekeeper, discussing management and staff. It reminded me of the early days at Casa Colonial when everyone was unified and excited for occupancy.

The head housekeeper, a local woman who Jenny called "my Maria," did not like me, perhaps since I wasn't involved. Jenny knew I worked online running my own company plus writing a novel, but perhaps Maria thought I was just lazy. She rebuffed my friendly overtures and scowled when I used the kitchen. She did all the cooking for Jenny and her boys. "My Maria takes such good care of me," Jenny liked to say.

Maria or no Maria, I planned on making special meals for Christmas Eve and Christmas dinner. My kids were coming. I would cook, ignore Maria's dirty looks, and she could stay out of my way.

Jenny, like RJ, was not clear on timelines. "My husband and I have to stay in Arizona for a few weeks and manage our accounts. After that, we're going to live in Pana." She vaguely referred to property management or real estate or some such arena. I suspected they had been in the home mortgage business like Bruce, in which case there might have been money at some point but no longer.

It was 2015, five-plus years after the crash, and the real estate and mortgage businesses had yet to fully recover. There was still blame to cast, undeserving lenders for the government to bail out, home loans left to figure out which company held the property note. There were short sales and lost payments. When I heard Jenny use the familiar mortgage business terminology, I wondered how this story would end.

When I mentioned my concerns to Bruce, he said, "I guess we will find out next month when it's time to pay the bills."

"What if it's another RJ situation?"

"Then I'm gone. Nobody here is married to my daughter."

Since they wanted to live in Pana rather than San Pedro, Jenny asked about renting our house. Running it past Greg, he said go ahead and give her the first option, since he and Lucy were still undecided.

"I'll Paypal you the first month's rent as soon as I get back in the States," Jenny told me, "and you can fix it with the owner."

We had not yet spoken to Helen about our plans and didn't intend to until we had someone lined up to take our place. She had been so nice to us, we didn't want to walk out on her. First, we wanted to find another family for her beautiful house.

I wondered what we'd do if our plans collapsed and left us stranded. I researched expat destinations, with Mexico rising to the top. It bordered Guatemala, had the best exchange rate, and I had step-by-step instructions on crossing the border to the Mexican state of Chiapas. I liked the look of Comitán, the pretty little city pictured on that lady's travel blog.

My backup plans held no interest for Bruce. He focused on the here and now instead of the what ifs. When I touched on Mexico, he said, "We'll cross that bridge when we come to it."

Jenny and her Maria found an artificial Christmas tree with boxes of ornaments and lights in a storage closet. Jenny said she and her boys wanted to decorate it before they left, but those two wild monkeys wanted nothing to do with that idea. The two women got as far as setting it up and adding a few lights. After Jenny left, Maria didn't touch it. I added a decoration here and there, but then went back to getting out our end of the year titles.

The large family group arrived. They swam and took the kayak on the lake; the men and boys played soccer in the street; the women chattered and laughed. They shopped in San Pedro and brought food back to eat in the dining room. Kids ran everywhere over the grounds while Juan Molina toiled, smiling at their antics.

Bruce, energized, was at his jovial, fatherly best. He made friends with the other dads, many of whom spoke some English to go with his little Spanish. He stood ready to make sure the group had whatever they needed for their stay. The final day, they handed Bruce their cameras to shoot photos of the various family groupings.

When the guests left, Maria and her girls cleaned the upstairs rooms and stripped the beds. She rearranged the refrigerator one last time, moving our things to the back like she always did. Then she and the rest of the staff left for their Christmas holiday.

Feeling a joyous surge of festive spirit with everyone gone, I finished decorating the tree. It stood in sweet splendor waiting for our Gowen Family Christmas.

The kids were due to arrive on the eleven a.m. Delta flight from Salt Lake City. Since Pedro and his van did not come to San Pedro, Jenny had earlier arranged transport with a driver named Chema, who she said was excellent.

He picked up Bruce and me at five that morning. Chema didn't seem as friendly or helpful as Pedro. In fact, he came across as somewhat sullen, rather like Jenny's Maria. What was it about Bruce and me that Jenny's people did not care for us, treating us like inconvenient interlopers? Or perhaps it was the difference between San Pedro and Panajachel. We were paying Chema; this was a job. Why the attitude?

We arrived at the airport an hour ahead of time. Chema dropped us off and said to text him when we were ready. He had to go somewhere.

"Wait. Their plane arrives at eleven, can you come back at eleven?"

He ignored me, wrote down his number on a scrap of paper and said, "Message me here." Then he left.

Bruce and I wandered over to the adjoining café. He ordered a breakfast sandwich; I had a muffin and a can of Diet Pepsi. It was a pleasant interlude, knowing our kids were in the air—the two of us waiting expectantly—no Jenny or Maria or sullen van driver.

When the welcome crowd gathered in the allotted area, I was impatient to join them. Bruce said, "Standing too long hurts my back." I left him to go find a spot with a good view. He found me later, in plenty of time.

Finally, our group came through the doors! Seeing them safely arrive in Guatemala, greeting everyone with hugs and happiness—this was my heaven.

Unfortunately, it didn't last. The van was nowhere in sight. Chema did not respond to our texts or calls, which he most likely didn't receive since U.S. phones never worked in Guatemala outside of WiFi. Exactly why I asked him to please come back at eleven. Pedro would not have left in the first place. Pedro would have parked his van in airport parking and then driven over to the adjacent waiting area well before eleven.

We waited two hours, standing there by the pickup lane. We hesitated to linger in the café in case Chema drove by and didn't see us and decided to leave again to visit his girlfriend or whatever. Or worse, drive back to San Pedro without us.

Bruce was miserable and nearly ill with the standing. A few times he went back to the café to sit and rest. The kids had been up all night, getting to the Salt Lake airport at midnight for a two a.m. flight with a layover in Houston. They took turns sitting with their dad or staying to wait with me.

And so, we passed the time, until finally Chema showed up close to one, two hours after I asked him to arrive, three hours since he dropped us off.

Nobody wanted to stop for anything, not that Chema asked like Pedro always did. We had water bottles from the café along with a few sandwiches; we were anxious to get on the road.

Normally, when guests arrived on the early flight after being up all night, they slept in the van on the way to Pana. However, the road to San Pedro was rough and bumpy, with hairpin turns and rutted roads in disrepair. Nobody could sleep through that. Forrest was dizzy and nauseated. I handed him a plastic bag in case he got sick.

It was dusk when we got to the hotel. The kids jumped right out, grabbed their luggage and strode down the many sloping steps to the front door. I followed with the key to let them in. Bruce stayed behind to pay Chema, hopefully not to tip him.

"Do you guys want fruit? I have papaya and pineapple cut up in the fridge."

"That sounds perfectly lovely!" said the beautiful Erin. Dark hair, green eyes, slender and graceful, Erin spread light and joy wherever she went. No sleep, a miserable airport pickup, and still she was cheerful. She followed me into the kitchen.

I pulled the big bowl out of the fridge, where it had chilled since last night when I cut up two pineapples and two papayas. I sliced several bananas into the mix.

"Forks and plates?" Erin asked. "Napkins? Or paper towels?"

Sean came in and helped carry things to the table, where the others had followed Bruce's example and collapsed in exhaustion. They made short work of the large bowl of fruit.

"This is incredible," said Sean. "I've missed the Guatemala tropical fruit. I'm going to eat nothing but fresh pineapple while I'm here."

"And street food," said Forrest. "And whatever good stuff Mom cooks for us."

"And choco-bananas and tacos and pupusas," Sean added.

"I can't wait to eat authentic tacos," said Tommy.

When the fruit was gone, the boys washed up the dishes while I showed Erin their rooms. The others soon followed. They seemed pleased with the layout. Erin and Sean had a room of their own with a queen bed and gorgeous view of the lake. Forrest and Tommy took a dorm room with five beds and a game table, in case the four of them wanted to have a sleep over on Christmas Eve and stay up late playing board games.

I left them to settle in and went downstairs to find Bruce stretched out on the bed. "It's been a long day," he groaned. "I am way more tired than I should be."

"I'm gonna put some ice on these mosquito bites and then join you."

While I sat at the dining room table holding an ice pack on my bites, I heard banging and clattering upstairs and figured it was our kids. Then Jenny came down the stairs. "Hi!" she greeted, taking a seat at the table.

"Hi! You guys back already? I didn't think you were coming 'til after Christmas."

"We got in right before you did. Funny, huh? We're staying in Rooms 4 and 5, on the floor below your kids."

"Oh, that's so funny! I had no idea. I heard a lot of racket upstairs, but I thought it was our boys."

"No, it's ours. They're full of beans. Your kids are quiet. I think they've already gone to bed."

"They were exhausted, up the whole night and then waiting two hours for Chema to pick us up." I explained what had happened.

She was surprised to hear about the problem with Chema. "I've never known him to be anything but responsible. How strange."

We chatted a little longer until I excused myself to go to bed. "It's been a big day and Bruce and I are pretty worn out." I wondered again why she had chosen a couple of tired old folks like us for her hotel.

"See you tomorrow," Jenny said.

I broke the news to Bruce. "Interesting," he said. "Did she say anything about paying rent on the Pana House? It's due January fifth." He removed his glasses and rubbed his eyes.

"Not a word." I kicked off my shoes and flopped down on the bed. "I *hate* this! We didn't have a single day of just us and the kids!"

"No. They rushed right back."

"I'm upset about it, Bruce. I was so looking forward to having the whole place to ourselves."

"Well, it's a big hotel, way bigger than Casa Colonial. It's practically a resort." He set his glasses on the bedside table and folded his arms behind his head in resting position. "There's plenty of room for two families to stay at the same time. I'm sure it will be fine. They'll do their thing, and we'll do ours."

As usual, Bruce's perspective calmed me down. "You're right. It's not like we have to share meals or activities. Tomorrow we can show the kids around town and take them out to dinner."

"I won't be able to go since Jenny's back. She and her husband will probably want to meet with me, to see how things went with that family group."

"Tomorrow is Christmas Eve!"

He put his glasses back on then sat up to unbutton his shirt. "Yeah, but I haven't met Aaron yet. I'm thinking we'll meet together a couple hours in the morning. I'll give them a report and have the rest of the day free."

What a workaholic. We finished getting ready for bed, both too tired to talk, especially to argue. Choosing work over family was the source of too many conflicts. We needed money to live, and he felt the pressure to earn it, a fact I understood. Except when it was unreasonable.

As Bruce drifted off, I stayed awake thinking about food. I'd get up early before anyone else, namely before Jenny's crowd, and start pancake batter for breakfast. Cut up more fruit to blend with Greek yogurt. Make homemade salsa and guacamole for later in the day. Maybe I'll bake a cake. I'll cook until it's time to stop. We'll eat dinner out. Hopefully a few restaurants will be open on Christmas Eve.

Christmas Dinner would be meatless lasagna and lemon bars for dessert. My last batch of yogurt came out as ricotta cheese instead of Greek yogurt. When I saw it, I thought, *lasagna!* How serendipitous, a little Christmas miracle! I could always make more yogurt, but I had no idea how to force it into ricotta. It either happened or it didn't.

I fell asleep thinking how funny life is with its blend of good and bad, sometimes in the same moment. Take Bruce, for example. He was responsible and committed and worked hard at whatever he did, but often failed to set proper boundaries, putting his job ahead of me and the family.

Picking up our kids was wonderful, but Chema was awful. Having them here under the same roof was a dream come true, but Jenny waltzing downstairs an hour later shattered my dream. Leaving Pana and RJ was a huge relief, but the village of San

Pedro lacks Pana's charm. The yogurt fails, but instead turns into ricotta cheese for Christmas lasagna.

Pleasure and pain, fortune and misfortune, joy and sorrow, everything mixed up together in one eternal round of messy mortality. When disappointment comes, a person can't stay upset for long, since something better is sure to follow.

25

La Frontera

I am forgotten as a dead man out of mind:
I am like a broken vessel.
Psalm 31:12

After a breakfast of pancakes and tropical fruit, the kids and I went out to explore the town. Stopping at a tourism vendor, they signed up to climb the San Pedro volcano.

"Come here at six in the morning the day of the hike," the man instructed. "Eat a good breakfast and bring water. The price includes transportation to and from the park, the entry fee and a guide. Dinner is available after the hike but costs extra."

I translated for them and added, "Never mind dinner. Dad and I will take you to Big Burger."

"You going to come, Mom?" asked Forrest.

Climbing the San Pedro is *not* an easy hike. As much as I wanted every second with my kids, I would slow them down and dampen their enjoyment. "No, Dad and I will meet you afterward for dinner."

They scheduled the hike for the day after Christmas and paid the fees. From there, we wandered down to the dock, going in and out of shops along the way. Forrest wanted a full-size Guatemala quilt and locally made shoes. Tommy looked at the woven shoulder bags. Erin helped the two boys find what they wanted, and Sean kept his eye out for appealing places to eat, meanwhile buying a collection of fireworks to set off for Christmas.

At four we returned to drop off purchases and pick up Bruce. When I asked how it went with Jenny and Aaron, he replied, "They stayed busy with their kids. She said to enjoy Christmas with my family and don't worry about work right now."

Good! Bruce had permission to be normal.

We went to eat at a place Sean picked out earlier. The kids ordered plate-sized burritos and nachos, I chose curry vegetables and rice, Bruce got a medium burrito. Sean and Tommy suggested we top it off with ramen at a small Korean café nearby. The Korean waiter took a picture of us happily crowded around a little table.

Christmas Day was nice despite the weirdness of two families trying to avoid each other. Not from animosity, but simple courtesy of allowing each other space to celebrate in their own ways.

In the afternoon when the lake was smooth, Forrest and I paddled a far distance in the kayak. Several hours out, it remained placid with no sign of the Xocomil. Forrest wanted to stop along the shore at a spot with huge boulders and a pathway going up the hillside. I stayed in the kayak, enjoying the stillness while he hiked. Leaving my youngest behind when we moved to Guatemala was at the time my greatest loss. I would not be there for his post-mission, young adult life, miss meeting the girls he might bring to family events. It still hurt, knowing what I was missing. I felt like we had abandoned him.

"It's fine, Mom," Forrest reassured me whenever I brought it up, probably more often than he wanted to hear. "I'm living my dream. Going to college and living downtown, biking everywhere."

He was twenty-three, grown up, and I could not let go. To me, he was still the skinny little boy who used to lie on the floor next to our bed, holding either my or his dad's hand until he fell asleep. Then Bruce would carry him into his own room and tuck him into bed.

Forrest returned to the kayak, and I asked him what he had seen. Not much. A kind of maintenance shed but nobody around. Lots of trees.

As we paddled on the still lake, I ventured a few subtle questions about the girl he was dating. He had grown into a pleasant but quiet young man, keeping his own counsel and not inclined to disclose personal feelings to his mom. I knew he was interested in a girl at school, enough to call her a few times while alone on the lake, but I didn't want to pry. Well, I *wanted* to, but I resisted the temptation.

A few days after Christmas, Jenny and Aaron pulled Bruce into the office for a lengthy private meeting. They shut the door, not even Maria invited. When it ended, Bruce came out looking cross and red in the face. He asked about our lunch plans and suggested we head out now.

On the road to town, safely out of hearing, he said, "You were right, Karen. They don't have any money. Things didn't work out as hoped back home. They're going to stay at the hotel and run it themselves."

Whoa, this happened faster than I expected.

"They won't need me, of course," Bruce continued, "and in fact can't pay me for the three weeks I've worked."

"Oh, good grief," I said. "They better pay Juan Molina."

"I'm sure they will. At least while there's enough business to keep the place open. They asked if we could call it even since we had room and board over December, and I agreed. They said we can stay on as long as we need."

"Good, because we need time to implement our backup plan."

Later, Bruce and I discussed it and agreed on the next step. We didn't want to go backward and return to our Pana house. We were done. Already burned our boats, even there at the home we had loved.

Bruce called Greg to see if he and Lucy were still interested in renting it. They were, and he arranged a meeting with Helen, who agreed to their family taking over the house.

That settled the business of our Pana house. We were free. Time to move on.

Our family's visit was a whirlwind of activities. Some days in San Pedro, some in Pana, a boat trip to San Juan for buying artwork, one morning on the chicken bus to Chichicastenango for their famous market day.

Nobody loved the chicken bus like I did, and I didn't understand why. Settling into one of these colorfully decorated buses to go off somewhere made me giddy. I was the only one who enjoyed the ride to Chichi. The others judged our excursion by how long it took to get there, despite the gorgeous views en route. Layers upon layers of high green hills framed by soft misty sky; it felt like we were in a movie about a faraway place in a time long ago. To me it was magical, but for everyone else, riding two hours each way brought the Chichi market down considerably in their estimation.

The kids left the morning of New Year's Eve, walking briskly down the road pulling their carry-ons. The four of them tall, strong and lean, Sean and Erin just turned thirty, Forrest six years younger, and Tommy somewhere in the middle. They didn't want to bother renting another van, Chema or no Chema. The bus to the city was a fraction of the cost, and the road out of San Pedro was rough and bumpy either way.

Bruce and I followed them with our backpacks and Maya shoulder bags. We were going along as far as Santa Lucia and then on to the Guatemala/Mexico border. It was time to pursue research for our Primary Backup Plan: move to Comitán in the Mexican state of Chiapas. Our backpacks were stuffed for an overnight stay, maybe two.

As we boarded the bus, Sean handed me a thick wad of quetzales. "What's this?" I asked.

"I meant to talk to you yesterday about exchanging them for me, but I forgot."

"Okay, I'll PayPal you whatever the exchange rate adds up to."

"There's no hurry. This can help you and Dad with moving expenses. It's not money we needed or expected, just a lot of cash RJ kept throwing at us when we went to see him the other day." Sean chuckled at the scene. "We only went to say hi, not ask for money. But he said take it, take it. Money was flying everywhere."

I laughed out loud at the image of RJ throwing quetzales at Sean and Erin. Needing to prove he didn't owe anyone in our family anything.

"What was he wearing?" I asked.

Sean looked confused. "What was he wearing? I don't know. Shorts, I think. He was sanding the boards."

RJ the Surfer Dude, I thought. Casa Colonial is doomed.

After a short bus ride past Sololá, we got off at the busy Santa Lucia intersection. Among the lines of buses pulling in and out, crowds of people with packages, bags and crates rushed to board their buses. We said goodbye to our kids and waved as they got on a bus to Guatemala City.

Once it pulled away, Bruce and I looked for one to Quetzaltenango or Huehuetenango, commonly known as Xela and Huehue. To get to the border town of La Mesilla, our idea was to start with a bus to Xela. On the way, we get off at Cuatro Caminos to catch a bus to Huehue, which is closer to the Mexico border. We had visited Huehue earlier and enjoyed it. If things didn't work out for connecting to the La Mesilla route, we could go on to Huehue. It had a nice hotel we liked, only twenty dollars a night. It also had an extensive bus station with many going to La Mesilla.

Today we'd be all day on a chicken bus, taking us past quaint villages and into the jungles. It was my Disneyland. That fake place where people paid hundreds of dollars for silly rides taking them into fake jungles, and in Guatemala you had the real thing for a fraction of the cost.

At the Cuatro Caminos stop, we found a bus for Huehue and settled into our seats. I noticed a couple men get on right after us. One sat a few rows ahead of me. Bruce was in the seat directly behind me. The other man stood at the front looking in our direction. It felt uncomfortable and strange, because the Maya don't seem to notice anyone else on the bus. They do not in fact look directly at people unless in conversation.

When the bus pulled out, the man up front still didn't take a seat, despite there being a few empty ones. I felt like he was staring at me. My discomfort increased as we continued the four-hour journey to Huehue.

It was New Year's Eve, probably not the safest day to travel around the country on a chicken bus.

Two hours passed. Bruce slept in his seat, and the man next to him was also asleep. The two people sitting next to me dozed off as well. I felt alone in my fears. I worried about arriving at the Huehue station. It was a huge, crowded lot filled with numberless people and buses traversing the country. Would these men also get off to follow and rob us? I prayed to know what to do. I prayed for safety.

I took my backpack off the shelf above, used it to block the view of my stalker, and removed the cash to place inside my shoes. RJ always said that was the safest place to keep your valuables. I cuddled my backpack on my lap like a round puppy and felt somewhat better.

Never before had I felt anxious or afraid during our two years in Guatemala. Not when Bruce and I took a chicken bus to the city, although RJ had said we should never go without him. Everyone was as nice and helpful to us there as anywhere. Friendly Bruce in his cowboy hat, plaid shirt and jeans, towering over these short folks, attracted attention and goodwill. They called him *caballero* and smiled warmly and laughed at his awkward Spanish.

But this time felt different. I sensed we were prey. Was it my imagination? I didn't think so, especially since I couldn't shake it off.

Finally, after another hour or so, the bus pulled into a minor connecting stop, an intersection, before the turn to Huehue. Bruce said something to me about La Mesilla. The man in my seat roused and said to get off at this stop. The fellow next to Bruce woke up and said the same thing. "Get off here for La Mesilla. *Aquí, aquí!*"

Then things happened so fast, like we were celebrities in protective custody with bodyguards hurrying us along while the bus crept forward. The two *ayudantes*—those young guys who pack everything on top of the bus and take fares—pushed us toward the back, assisting with our high jump down from the back doors. One ran to a bus whose electric sign above the windshield flashed *La Mesilla*.

We hurried after him but before reaching it, he said, "No, not this one," and led us to the next. "*Rápido, rápido,*" he said.

The moment we set foot on that bus, also flashing *La Mesilla,* the driver, who had waited for us, took off. We quickly found seats together. No one else boarded.

Back on the road, I said to Bruce, "Once I calm down, I need to tell you what just happened there."

"Yeah, that was really something, wasn't it? How we got swooped up and, in a flash, basically carried from one bus to another."

"Angels watching over us, I'm sure of it. Wait until I tell you the whole story. It's too noisy on the bus to explain now."

"Okay. Looks like we are going direct to La Mesilla instead of Huehue."

If those men were stalking us, we were safe now. We had disappeared before anyone could realize it. Our two seatmates waking up as one and saying, "La Mesilla? *Aquí! Vaya vaya!*" And the two *ayudantes* who whisked us from one bus to another and on to the next so suddenly no one could have followed or tracked us. I kept playing it out in my mind, how events occurred as though a finely orchestrated scene in an action film. Now headed to La Mesilla, the border town, I relaxed and enjoyed the ride.

Having told the *ayudante* we wanted "la frontera," he signaled to us when it was our stop, some hours later. It was the town park, I assumed in La Mesilla. Anyone still left on board gathered their things and disembarked.

Bruce and I wandered up the street for a half block until we came to a hotel—La Sarita—the same name as the ice cream we liked. We checked in, figured we'd go to the border to see what that was like, and then return to the hotel for the night.

First, we found a little restaurant and ate tacos at their outdoor tables.

After confused discussions with taxi drivers, who told us it was too late for "la frontera," we finally learned that this town was Comija, pronounced like Omaha, and not La Mesilla. At the park, people could catch a van or a taxi to drive them the forty minutes to the border town, where they could then cross over from Guatemala to Mexico.

The taxi driver who helped us realize our error said, "If you want to go tomorrow, come to the park at eight in the morning. I will drive you to La Mesilla."

I had neglected to bring my passport and so could not enter Mexico. Next trip, we'd cross over and go to Comitán, the town pictured in the travel blog.

We had set off that morning with no clear destination, escaped potential danger, ended up in the right town despite our ignorance, found a nice hotel, ate delicious tacos. We made a new friend in the taxi driver, who watched for us in the morning and drove us to La Mesilla. There, we walked among the crowds of travelers and shoppers. We stopped at an outdoor grill for carne asada before catching a cab back to Comija.

We would come this way again, next time crossing the border to Mexico.

26
Finding Comitán

He shall not be afraid of evil tidings:
his heart is fixed, trusting in the Lord.
Psalm 111:7

Traveling back to San Pedro from La Mesilla, Bruce paid close attention to the transfers. "Pretty sure we can streamline this border trip to go further in less time," he said, commenting on towns and stops as we went.

Bruce had a built-in map and GPS in his head. If there were a way to shorten the route, he would figure it out.

We planned to leave San Pedro again in four days, after the weekend. This time we'd travel equipped with passports and pesos for crossing into Mexico and on to Comitán, ninety minutes from the border.

I let Jenny know we were researching housing options in Mexico, so that she understood our clear intentions.

Ever since the Christmas bombshell, the four of us had maintained a friendly though awkward relationship. Bruce and I ate most of our meals out. I rarely went into Maria's kitchen and had already packed up our things there. I no longer used the washer and drier, instead taking our laundry to a nearby lavanderia. We found several cafés with good WiFi where we carried our laptops, bought food, and settled in to work or communicate with our kids.

Despite the prospect of hours on a chicken bus, Bruce looked forward to this next trip as much as I did. At least we would be in motion with a goal in mind.

After a long weekend in San Pedro, we were eager to go.

We took the bus to Los Encuentros, then to Four Corners and on toward Huehue, with the stops and transfers going smoothly. On the Huehue bus, the *ayudante,* knowing our destination was *la frontera,* directed us to get off at a place along the road. It didn't look anything like where we had caught the La Mesilla bus, back when we avoided the suspicious men.

Worried at the emptiness of the intersection, I asked both the *ayudante* and the driver, Is this right? This is where we wait? They assured me this is it. The bus to La Mesilla will come soon and stop. Don't worry, it arrives soon, *no se preocupa. Llega pronto.*

There on the corner, Bruce and I stood with our luggage, feeling deserted and vulnerable, waiting as instructed for the La Mesilla bus. Sure enough, it arrived within ten or fifteen minutes. Never yet had the bus drivers or their helpers steered us wrong.

Oh, how friendly and welcome is a big, comfortable chicken bus who sees you, stops and takes care of you! With its *ayudante* jumping out to check on your destination, to signal you onboard as he takes your heavy suitcases to the top and straps them down, often as the bus takes off. While the driver picks up speed and you settle into your seat, the kid crawls about on top securing the loads, and then scrambles down to swing through the open back door like a gymnast on the parallel bars. He goes up and down the aisle, collecting fares and making change as needed. Such small fares. Such a small amount for so much value! Oh, how wonderful are the Guatemala buses!

Many hours later, in Comija, we disembarked and again stayed at the Hotel Sarita.

The next morning, we found the same helpful taxi driver at the park. Recognizing us, he asked if we wanted to go to La

Mesilla again. Yes, we did! Vans and cabs lined up at the curb to take people to the border, but we already had a friend. He loaded our luggage in the trunk, and we set off. It was twenty minutes from Comija to La Mesilla, along a paved road. Cars, vans and cabs drove back and forth on the road. No buses.

Driving slowly through the crowds and shops of the border town, I asked the taxi driver if we could catch a bus from here for San Pedro.

He pointed back to a side street. "The bus stop is there," he explained. "You take a bus going to Huehue, get off at Cuatro Caminos, then take one to Los Encuentros and then San Pedro."

In other words, we go the same way we came, only backwards, with the added convenience of catching the return bus in La Mesilla and bypassing Comija.

Our cab driver drove us as far down the main street as he was allowed to go. He dropped us off near the border crossing and wished us well.

I had exchanged quetzales for pesos back in San Pedro, allowing us to bypass the guys holding out pesos for sale. We entered the Guatemala immigration building to show our passports and have them stamped for exit. Then we walked the short distance to the Mexican side, where taxis waited to take you to Mexican immigration a few miles away, a ten-minute ride. They parked, dropped you off, and pointed to the low brown building across the street. "*Immigración por allá.*"

Like bus drivers, taxi drivers are valuable sources of information, a trusted web of support as you travel the country. If you need food or a bathroom, they tell you where to find it. If you need a way to get to Comitán they tell you, pointing to where a few vans are parked. Throughout Guatemala, we found them always willing to assist with luggage, give directions, and provide information of any kind. I couldn't imagine doing such a trip the American way: renting a car and, with stubborn independence, navigating on one's own.

At Mexico Immigration, the stern, unsmiling man behind the counter did not respond to my greeting and stared back wordlessly when asked a question. Nonetheless, we managed to fill out the appropriate paperwork and receive our six-month traveling visas. We exited the small building with relief. Just like that, we were in Mexico with travel visas.

A man appeared out of nowhere and asked where we wanted to go. "San Cristobal?"

"Comitán," I replied.

He led us to the group of minivans and loaded our things on one of them, telling the driver we wanted Comitán. He pointed me toward a ticket window to purchase our fare.

"Get us two seats together," I told Bruce, who stared blankly at the van with our luggage. He seemed to have gone numb. So much happening so quickly and all of it in Spanish. I gestured toward the minivan. "Climb in and get us two seats, my love. I'll buy the tickets."

I paid our fare and returned to my dear overwhelmed husband now waiting in the van. At least he could relax in a roomy upholstered seat. I squeezed his hand, and he put his arm through mine.

The drive was a comfortable, air-conditioned ride on smooth, straight roads. No cramming oneself in child size seats on a crowded chicken bus.

"It's sure different from Guatemala," I whispered. There was no road noise or air rushing past through open windows to drown us out.

"It's nice. I could get used to this."

Instead of hilly, lush jungles, we traversed flat brown fields where sparse settlements of adobe houses clustered together under a bit of shrubbery and a few trees. Now and then, riders asked to be let out along the dusty road or someone at the roadside flagged the driver for pick up.

About two hours later, I saw the outskirts of a town up ahead. Comitán, according to the road signs. Our vehicle entered an immigration checkpoint. Everyone stayed seated as an official came on board. He checked papers on one or two folks and asked them a few questions before waving us on.

Soon we passed a small airport, then a Walmart and Sam's Club on the edge of town, where the driver stopped to let people off. I suggested to Bruce we get off more toward the center of town where the main park must be. That's where we'd find the hotels and restaurants.

The road was long and straight, lined with various businesses, like a few car dealerships and nice gas stations. Landscaped intersections led to side streets and residential areas. Our van kept stopping to let off passengers as the town thinned out a few blocks in the distance.

"You see anything that looks like a park?" Bruce asked. "The edge of town is up ahead."

I stepped toward the driver. "Where is the central park? That's what we want."

He nodded and a couple minutes later pulled over to the side. "*Aquí.*" He pointed to the right.

We disembarked with our bags, not seeing a park anywhere but trusting his instructions. We pulled our suitcases down the sidewalk to the right, going several blocks along residential streets without a sign of a downtown or even a Catholic church. We turned here and there, until our load felt heavier, and we got thirstier and still no sign of a central area.

There weren't many people around and we saw no corner tienda to buy water bottles. The sidewalks were lined with brightly painted narrow homes connected one to another, behind locked doors or enclosed patios—a well-maintained residential district showing pride of ownership.

Bruce tried to flag a cab, and finally one stopped. I told him we needed a hotel near *el centro*. He nodded and we climbed in.

The first place he stopped looked more like a hostel than a hotel, and I saw no park nearby. The second hotel, however, was adjacent to the park and looked promising. I asked him to wait while I checked for rooms. Bruce stayed with the cab.

The hotel had a luxurious lobby with a vaulted area around a staircase that wound up three floors. Greenery accented the stairway. A tree and a fountain added glamor. The clerk showed me a nice second floor room for thirty dollars a night. I asked her to wait while I went to check *"con mi esposo."*

"It's a lovely hotel, Bruce, and close to the park and the restaurants. I'm thinking two nights. What do you think?"

Bruce, who did not make decisions quickly, surprised me by saying, "Only one night. Because tomorrow we will find our house."

"Are you sure? It's so cheap, we could do two nights."

"Why pay for an extra night? Tomorrow we will pay our rent and stay in our own place."

He sounded so sure I couldn't help but believe him. "One night it is then."

The driver unloaded our things. I paid him and said, "We are looking for a house or apartment. Do you know of anything?"

He nodded and replied, *"Sí,"* drawing out the vowel sound in the way that means *we-e-ll-ll, perhaps I do.* "I can come by tomorrow and take you around, if you want."

Bruce and I settled on ten in the morning, giving us time to shower and have breakfast.

We finished checking in and were shown to our room, where we relaxed and discussed what kind of home we hoped to find. After two days of travel, it felt luxurious to stretch out on the bed. "Something small and inexpensive but private and charming," I said. "Good WiFi is essential, and a decent kitchen. An oven and full-sized fridge like what's normal back home would sure be nice."

"I'm thinking rent of one hundred fifty dollars a month. In Pana, we had the big house and garden, but it cost us, and we don't need that much space. One bedroom is fine."

"I like how close Comitán is to the border, and our visas are for six months instead of three. Border runs will be easy."

"It's just as well things didn't work out in San Pedro," Bruce said. "This gives us a nice change."

"Getting out of the hotel business is the best thing that's happened since we left Utah, don't you think so, Bruce?"

"We needed it though or we wouldn't have come to Guatemala. And Jenny's deal got us out of Pana."

I thought about Jenny and RJ and how each of them took advantage of Bruce's willingness to help them succeed. It had upset me at the time, but not now. "In church the other day, Bruce, I prayed for any lingering ill will over the events of this past year to go away and get replaced with gratitude."

"That's a good prayer," said Bruce.

"I think it was answered, because I can look back and feel thankful instead of irritated at any injustice. Without RJ and Sally, we would still be stuck in Utah doing the cookie business and wondering how to manage retirement when everything is so expensive. Instead, here we are having adventures together."

"I'm excited about what's coming next." Bruce lifted himself from the bed and peeled off his socks. He pulled his flip flops out of his backpack. "Let's go check out the park."

Outside our hotel, we followed a wide paved boulevard with greenery in the middle and shops on either side. It opened onto a raised avenue that circled the park, showcasing more shops and terraced restaurants. Intermittent steps led to the green area with its inviting landscaped walkways and benches. Christmas lights decorated the trees. Groups of people strolled about enjoying the mild late afternoon.

"Let's eat first, Karen," Bruce suggested. "I need a solid meal."

We chose a restaurant set back along the raised avenue. Its quiet, peaceful atmosphere attracted me, and Bruce was always fine with wherever we ate. We ordered meat, tortillas, rice and beans—typically Mexican and quite good. I remembered the woman on Facebook saying how she could live cheaper in the land of the Aztecs than in the land of the Maya. And the food was better, she said.

We lingered, no need to hurry or go anywhere, until their dinner crowd came in and noisily filled up tables.

We meandered through the park as the Christmas lights turned on. The tall, impressive Catholic church at one end lit up, along with other official buildings of a stately architecture that beautifully set off their many strings of twinkling white lights.

"What a gorgeous, magical place is Comitán!" I exclaimed.

There was a slight chill in the air as the sun went down. I pulled my denim jacket out of Bruce's backpack, and he put on his warm vest. He had bought it from a little old lady in the park one day at Sololá. His vest—but only in cold weather—cowboy hat, plaid shirt and jeans was his mode of dress on every day but Sunday, when he wore dress slacks and a white shirt and tie to church.

Musicians in traditional regalia set up their instruments in the center pavilion. Chairs had been placed five or six rows deep for the audience. We took seats, anticipating a concert. As the band played and the seats filled, couples drifted toward the pavilion and danced to the live music.

We were enchanted with this park still decorated and lit for Christmas, enchanted with the music and the dancing. I rested my head on Bruce's shoulder. He put his arm around me and said, "Tomorrow we will find our new home in Comitán."

Salsa, rumba, samba, cha cha cha, couples of many ages and skill levels danced late into the night, long after Bruce and I left for our hotel. We still heard the music faintly play as we drifted into sleep.

27

In Motion

Weeping may endure for a night,
but joy cometh in the morning.
Psalms 30:5

We slept well, showered, and gathered our things to check out and meet the cab at ten. My choice would have been to leave our bags, go house hunting, and return for another night. However, through the years I learned that when Bruce has one of those rare strong feelings, it pays to listen because then he is always proved right.

The cab driver arrived on time. Bruce carried out the black suitcase, his backpack and Guatemala bag, and a medium size gym bag. I had my Guatemala bag, backpack and the large, lightweight purple suitcase. The driver loaded our luggage as I climbed into the back seat. Bruce took the front because of more leg room.

We drove to the edge of town, to what looked like a motel. "Are those apartments?" I asked.

"Yes, some of them are."

"No, thanks." We drove on.

The second place was behind a high private gate. Our driver got out to knock and ring the bell but was unable to raise anyone. We might try again later.

The third was an orange building of two or three stories on a quiet residential street. Across the way I saw a Catholic church and a pretty, shaded park. Our man parked and approached an attached tienda. An older woman, trim and efficient looking with short dark hair, came right out with a set of keys in her hand.

Bruce and I stepped onto the sidewalk. Finally, a place to see!

The driver stayed with his cab while the woman unlocked the building and led us through a spacious lobby devoid of furnishings. Its shiny, white floor tiles gleamed. In the back was a small kitchen and *pila*. I saw a girl filling a bucket as the aromatic scent of Fabuloso permeated the air. The woman spoke shortly to her in such fast Spanish I caught little of it, but the gist was to not do the floor or stairway until we left.

Upstairs she showed us two apartments. One had a main room followed by two or three bedrooms strung together with doors passing through from one to the other. I saw no kitchen.

The other apartment opened into a bright square kitchen, most of which was taken up by a table and chairs too large for the area. There was a sink and counter space but no stove or refrigerator. The kitchen had a window pass-through to the next room along with a wide doorway and a step down. That room held two double beds side by side and a heavy, double dresser. It opened onto the living room with seating arranged around a coffee table and a cabinet with a TV.

Off the living room was a sparkling clean bathroom and shower. The second bedroom was adjacent to the living room. Another fine, grand dresser stood as a wall between the bedroom and living room.

The furniture was solid and high quality, the beds firm and equipped with excellent bedding and thick blankets. Except for the living room rug, which was of a thick weave but worn at the edges, everything else looked expensive and new. And such light! A wall of windows framed with drapes let in the sunshine. The window over the kitchen sink opened to the sunny hallway. In the hallway, stairs led up to the flat roof where white sheets billowed from a clothesline. The hall and stairways were open to the sky and brightened the interior of the whole building.

Rent was 6500 pesos a month, electric, propane, and WiFi included. If we agreed to stay six months, she would take 6000, or about 300 USD. Double Bruce's desired price, but this was a lovely clean building in an attractive location.

Neither of us liked the first apartment with its string of bedrooms. We decided if she provided a stove and fridge and changed out the kitchen table for a smaller one, we would take the second apartment.

"Shall we finalize things today, before we make sure there's a stove and fridge?" I asked Bruce. "I think she will want rent down before she invests in it further."

"We came to find our home, and this is a nice place. What do you think, Karen? Do you want to live here?"

"Yes, I do."

"Me, too," he responded. "Tell her what we want and if she agrees, we'll take it."

The lady agreed to our terms, and the three of us came downstairs pleased with our negotiations. The cab driver would drive us to an available ATM and then bring us back to sign papers. The landlady slipped him some folded bills on his way out. They did it surreptitiously with quick covered hands, but I don't miss much.

We concluded our business across the counter in the lady's little tienda, as she carefully counted out the 6000 pesos. She asked us to sign our names to a hand-written sheet of paper with today's date and the agreement to stay six months. Before doing so, I reiterated that we expected a fridge and stove installed before we came back next week. She agreed to have everything ready, and we signed.

She handed Bruce a set of apartment keys with the WiFi code and then returned to her tienda. We escaped upstairs. The taxi driver had carried up our bags before he left and set them inside the front bedroom.

First, we tried out the Internet, which worked fine. Then we lay on the three beds, trying first one then the other like Goldilocks. We chose the back bedroom as ours, leaving the front one as "my study," since I always wrote leaning against pillows on a bed. Bruce claimed the kitchen table as his office, with the pass-through window between the two rooms allowing us to chat back and forth if we wanted.

The neighborhood was charming with its park across the corner. A lavanderia and a bakery as well as a Catholic church stood on cross streets facing the park.

Bruce and I, flushed with success, decided to explore the area. First, to the Walmart we had seen on our way in. We walked three blocks to the main street and watched for a bus marked with Sam's Club and Walmart on its front window. Flagging it down, we boarded and arrived in ten minutes.

Outside the shopping center, taxis lined up next to the curb, waiting for shoppers heading home with their purchases.

"That will be us next time we come to Comitán," Bruce said. "The border van can drop us off here and we'll take a cab direct to our apartment."

We ordered hot dogs at the Sam's Club patio food court. "Time to trade in our Costco cards for a Sam's Club membership," I said. "Let's go through the mall and see what's there besides Walmart." Since the kitchen came unfurnished, I'd have to buy the basics. Not today, but once we settled in.

Later, back in our apartment, we went over logistics for moving. Bruce wondered about his tools. "There's no point in hauling them to an apartment in Mexico. If I can sell them, that's cash to help with expenses."

I opened my laptop for listing his tools on the Lake Atitlán Facebook group. That job done, he checked it off his yellow pad and turned to transportation. "We can rent a van in San Pedro and move in one trip. I'll get a quote when we get back." He penciled in a couple notes on his paper.

"Wouldn't moving via chicken bus be cheaper?" I suggested. "We know the system now. Even with multiple trips, it should cost less overall than a private van rental. Plus, it's going to take time for your tools to sell. We can move our things while we wait."

Bruce shook his head. "One van ride compared to three or four bus rides may end up costing the same, and a heck of a lot easier and more comfortable."

"If it's possible to hire a private van driver from San Pedro to Comitán, crossing the border and all that. The buses can't. They don't go past La Mesilla."

He added a few lines to the list on his yellow pad. "We don't have to decide now. The tools are for sale. I'll check about the van, get a quote, and we'll see how things work out."

In the morning, after kneeling together for morning prayer, a sense of peace descended on me. "Bruce, I got this thought during our prayer that we're on the right track. God will help us through whatever difficulties lay ahead. I'm sure of it."

"That makes me feel better. This has happened so fast with barely time to think it through to the next step."

I opened the living room drapes to let in the morning sun. Bruce turned on the laptop to check bank accounts.

"Selling my tools will make up for the extra expenses of January and December," he said. "All those boat fees added up, not to mention eating out so much. Then not getting the expected payment from Jenny."

This brought on a series of lamentations over what we had recently endured, things that felt like such total failures. Along with concerns for the future.

Finally Bruce said, "Never mind. We will resolve our future problems same as we did the past ones. And then there will be new problems to get answers to, and we will grow in the process and become better people."

We sat planning and daydreaming until past ten-thirty. To return, we had to flag a cab to Main Street, to the small station where the *colectivos* came and went to *la frontera*. Cross the border from Mexico to Guatemala, get on the Xela chicken bus in La Mesilla, get off at Cuatro Caminos, find the bus to Los Encuentros and San Pedro. Flag a tuk tuk from the drop off point back to the hotel. We'd get back around eight or nine, perhaps later, depending on stops and waits for our connecting busses.

"We better not hang any pictures here, Bruce," I said as we gathered our empty bags. "The landlady seems stern and probably won't like anything on the walls."

"Not a problem. There's four dressers to display photos on."

We paused at the kitchen door to look back. "If this kitchen had appliances, I wouldn't want to leave," Bruce said. "This feels like home now."

"Except everything we own is in San Pedro."

"And I want to say goodbye to Juan Molina, Dago, and our friends at church. And sell those tools. Let's get on our way. We have a lot to do."

We exited our little home and locked the door until next time.

What a letdown to wake up the next day in San Pedro, in the hotel run by Jenny, Aaron, and Maria. Bruce and I, in the way, felt awkward and unhappy. In our apartment, we had been at peace and things made sense. Here we felt turmoil and confusion and impatience to leave. We had the weekend and then on Tuesday we'd go back to Comitán. Meanwhile, we would streamline our things down to the minimum.

Bruce went out early to get breakfast and find where to rent a private van shuttle.

Through a window, I saw Juan Molina beginning his work in back. I walked down the pathway to say hello and ask how things were.

"*Hay mucho que hacer,*" he said, looking around. "But now they only want me coming two, three days a week."

"They are making changes. Did Bruce tell you he is no longer in charge?"

"Yes, he told me that. I am sorry."

"We are going to move soon, Hermano Juan. We are leaving Guatemala."

"Back to the United States?"

"No. To Mexico."

He looked surprised at that and then smiled at me with teary eyes. "I will miss you and Hermano Bruce. You are very good people." He noticed Jenny coming down the path and turned back to his work.

"*Hasta luego,*" I said and left him. If she wanted to talk to Juan Molina, it was better if I weren't around.

Jenny and I met on the path. "Bruce mentioned he was going to check on renting a shuttle for your move. It's great you found a place already."

"Yes, we're happy about it. We're considering making several trips and going by chicken bus."

Jenny lost her smile. "Oh, you don't want to do that. It makes way more sense to rent the shuttle and do it at once."

"Maybe." She can't wait to get rid of us, I thought.

"There's plenty of good shuttle places here in town. I can recommend a couple to you."

I'll bet you can. Like you recommended Chema. "I'm letting Bruce handle that end of things. My job is to organize and get rid of what we don't need."

I moved to go, but she had more to add. "I can't imagine moving by chicken bus. You're limited in what you can take because of so many transfers. You'd have to haul your things from one bus to another, sometimes quite a distance. You can only take what you each can carry."

"Difficult but not impossible. Doable actually. And cheaper, I think, than renting a shuttle despite the extra trips. We're running low on funds right now and need to economize." Take that, Miss Know It All with your spiky black and yellow hair.

Jenny shook her spiky head in disagreement. "I think Bruce will find out the shuttle makes more sense." Like she knew what Bruce would think and do.

"Maybe." I gave her a friendly smile. "Well, I better let you get to it." I returned to the hotel and surveyed our roomful of possessions.

Let's say we each take our backpacks, Guatemala shoulder bags and two suitcases on every trip. Take them full and bring them pack empty, then do it again a few days later until we finish. Three trips, I figured, four at the most. We stay in our apartment a few nights, return to San Pedro, take a few days rest then go again. We could do it. As I gazed at our stack of luggage, the whole scenario unfolded in my mind's eye.

Bruce returned and found me sorting and figuring. "I found a shuttle place!" he announced. "Two hundred fifty dollars and ten hours to move us to Comitán." He sat on the bed and waited for my enthusiastic response.

"Two or three trips on the chicken bus won't cost that much if we go straight through."

"No, but it's a lot more trouble, and it will keep us stuck here that much longer."

"Jenny told me you would say that."

"She did?"

"Yep. That it was impossible to do this move on chicken buses. She recommends the shuttle and said you would agree."

The pleased expression left his face. He rubbed his cheek, took off his glasses, rubbed his eyes. Cleaned his glasses with his shirt.

"She wants us out of here," I added. "I told her we needed to economize and that's why we have to consider the cheapest transportation."

Bruce chuckled. "I bet she didn't like being reminded of how they didn't pay me anything." He put his glasses back on and stood up.

"Using the bus system will be our final Guatemala adventure. I know we can do it, Bruce, despite what Jenny says."

He sat back down and massaged his chin. "I can reduce our connections and eliminate that overnight stay at Comija. That saves us a bundle."

"I can streamline our stuff."

"Funny that I haven't heard anything back about the tools I listed. We could use the money."

"Well, this will give you more time to sell them. What do you think? Chicken bus?"

"Sure, why not?" He grinned. "Jenny is in the office. I'll pop in and let her know we will be around a little bit longer."

⌒⌒

Tuesday morning as we prepared to leave, Jenny came down and asked for our keys to the front door. I told her we would arrive late, and wouldn't it be easier to let ourselves in?

"No," she said. "Ring the bell and someone will let you in."

"Can we keep the keys to our room?"

"Yes, I only want the ones to the front door." We handed them over and she marched back upstairs.

We had two suitcases each to pull behind us. We wore our backpacks and Guatemala bags. The Pullman didn't leave the park until eight-thirty. At seven-thirty we went out to flag a couple tuk tuks. Bruce was getting a cold, suffering with congestion and a cough, and his voice sounded rough.

The numerous transfers went well despite the extra baggage. Not easy, but we managed. We arrived at our favorite hotel in Comija before four that afternoon, two hours earlier than before.

"Next trip," Bruce said, "we skip the hotel, go straight to the border and on to Comitán in one day."

We might have done it then, except his cold was worse and he needed to lay down and not push through. In the morning after a hot shower and breakfast, he felt better.

The border crossing and van ride to Comitán was now familiar to us. We got off at Walmart and flagged a cab to take us home.

Entering our apartment, we saw a welcome surprise. Against one wall stood a shiny new, six-burner stove with a griddle and gas oven. It only lacked the big red bow. On the other wall, a fridge sat proud and ready for service on top of a small cabinet. It practically saluted me in its eagerness to be useful. It wasn't full size, but roomy enough for my yogurt maker and big soup pot with room to spare. The rectangular table and six chairs had been replaced by a round table with four chairs. They fit perfectly in the center space, leaving room to work around.

It felt like Christmas morning. Oh, to begin meal planning and prep in that kitchen. I'd cook granola in the large oven. I could bake bread!

28
Bruce Finds a New Job

Unto the upright there ariseth light in the darkness;
he is gracious, and full of compassion, and righteous.
Psalm 112:4

It was the morning of our final trip, the culmination of our move to Comitán. I ceased my usual restless bustle and went to sit on the balcony. There, I watched Lake Atitlán awake to the dawn. The placid surface reflected the pink glow of the early morning sky. The volcanoes loomed as high, rounded shadows in the distance.

We never dreamed our Guatemala adventure would last only two years. We had arrived in Pana the first week of February 2014 and thought we'd stay forever.

After the blow up with RJ, Bruce hoped we might continue as before, minus the hotel. Except that he missed having a job, and I couldn't bear the toxic gas from down the street. Jenny's offer took us to San Pedro and when that fell through, we knew our time was over in Guatemala. How things can change in two short years.

It surprised me how much Bruce liked Comitán. A compact, second-floor apartment in a hotel? Traffic noise outside our windows? People dressing up to go shopping? Comitán was a blend of the historic with the modern. We took cabs instead of tuk tuks, and regular buses or *colectivos* instead of refurbished American school buses. Of course, you still couldn't drink the water or flush the toilet paper, but we were used to that.

Hippy town and the Jenny fiasco drove us away in the end. Otherwise, how could we have so easily forsaken our Pana house. To undergo tortuous bus rides. To say goodbye to beloved friends in our Pana church. To say goodbye to the beautiful Guatemala highlands and its people. We had fully embraced this land with no plans to leave and then in a flash we are gone.

Bruce never did sell his tools. Instead, he gave the lot of them to Juan Molina, who Jenny had let go. "Those tools at least will keep him in food and rent for a while," Bruce figured. "I'm glad they never sold. I'd rather Hermano Juan have them. He needs the money more than I do."

The lake was coming alive. A few fishermen in their flat boats drifted out to find a spot to drop their lines. The loon-like, slender black ducks swooped down to land on the surface and dive for food. It was a picture of peace and quiet stillness. Pale clouds stretched over the peaks of the volcanoes, lit blue by the rising sun.

I heard Bruce hauling the bags out and went to help. Neither Jenny nor anyone else was in sight, sparing us the awkward goodbyes. We left our room unlocked and the keys on the dresser.

Instead of waiting around for the 8:30 Pullman bus—which was supposedly more comfortable but really was not—we caught the seven a.m. Guatemala City bus. It stopped at Cuatro Caminos, where we got off for the first transfer. Due to this and other of Bruce's shortcuts, the latest trips back and forth had taken us considerably less time.

The previous one, we had arrived at Cuatro Caminos well before the connecting bus back to San Pedro. Bruce went to get fried chicken while we waited. His order was delayed, our bus arrived and parked in its usual spot to wait the scheduled fifteen minutes for people to load. The order still wasn't ready. *Muy pronto, muy pronto,* they said. A shame to leave it now, since he'd already paid.

The bus *ayudante* saw the familiar tall gringo with the cowboy hat and waved a "come on" signal. By now they recognized us and knew we always took this afternoon bus to San Pedro. The next one didn't come for another four hours. They waited a few minutes longer, waved again, Bruce waved back with a signal of We're coming! I headed over as the fried chicken came out hot and steaming and packaged to go, Bruce and his luggage right behind me. The bus still waited, the *ayudante* watching us traverse the parking lot then cross the street. As we arrived with our load of luggage, he carried it in ahead of us. The driver watched until we were securely up the steps, then he pulled out while the kid hauled our suitcases up to the roof. They had waited an extra ten minutes for us.

This and countless other vivid remembrances filled my heart as we drove through the highlands on our final trip out of Guatemala.

We arrived at the border around two that afternoon, at our apartment by three-thirty. What a difference from a few weeks ago on our initial voyage to *la frontera.* Back when we had no idea what we were doing and took two days getting to La Mesilla.

Even our border crossings were easy now. We skipped checking out at Guatemala immigration and instead joined the locals on the side lane going back and forth for trade. No one noticed except the random helpful tuk tuk or taxi driver asking if we went through immigration. We already did it, I told them. *Ya lo hacemos.*

Still, we barely held it together on that final ride, exhausted as we were after three weeks of moving by chicken bus. What an ordeal. Bruce's original idea to rent a van and take everything in one trip would have been easier by far. We paid a steep price for saving a few dollars. Bruce had developed a sore neck and shoulders due to what he supposed was muscle strain from the uncomfortable rides. Whatever he had, I soon caught as well. No fevers, only cold symptoms, fatigue, and aching neck and shoulders.

In Comitán, we unlocked the apartment, dropped our bags and collapsed into bed. We slept for three hours.

Bruce got up to unpack and to wonder about dinner, but I had too little energy to care. Headache, backache, legs hurting—how could one hurt so much yet have no fever? No wonder Bruce had thought it was muscle strain. Watching him neatly place clothes in the big dresser, I felt encouraged and got out of bed. We were home at last. No more traveling back to San Pedro.

We found a small café nearby and took an outside table. Their specialty was miniature tacos with pork or beef and horchata to drink. There were no menus, just tell the waiter pork or beef, horchata or soda, and how many tacos.

When we saw how small they were, we realized we didn't order enough. No matter. I wasn't that hungry.

Bruce tried the horchata. "What is in this drink?" he exclaimed, gulping it down. "I swear it has healing powers. I feel better than I have in weeks."

"It's a rice drink. Rice water, cinnamon, and sugar. Maybe some milk in it, I'm not sure."

He insisted I taste it, but it didn't do anything for me. I still felt sick and weak. Bruce ordered three more glasses and filled up on horchata instead of tacos.

Before long, we reclaimed our former health and energy. We found the LDS chapel and attended church as soon as we felt well enough. Afterward, people gathered around to find out who we were, are we members, are we senior missionaries, are we visiting Comitán? When they heard we moved here, they asked where, they would come visit.

Such overt friendliness rather overwhelmed me, while my gregarious husband delighted in it. He could not stop talking about church, identifying members, who was married to whom, who was in the branch presidency. He hoped our records arrived quickly, because he wanted officially to be part of such a wonderful group. He wondered what kind of calling he could do with his limited Spanish.

"I doubt language concerns will hold them back," I said. "They were so friendly and interested, they didn't seem to care how poorly we spoke Spanish."

"Mexicans sure are more outgoing that Guatemalans," he observed. "Funny how Chiapas is quite close to the border, yet everything is so different."

The people around Lake Atitlán were such quiet, shy folks. The Mexicans, on the other hand, seemed always ready for a party, to dance, to eat, to talk and laugh. Perhaps yet another difference between the land of the Maya and the land of the Azteca?

Our records arrived by the next Sunday, and we were interviewed and extended callings that very day. I was asked to serve as a counselor in the district Primary presidency, and Bruce called to be executive secretary to the branch president. Neither of us had the Spanish skills to feel like we could be any help in these significant positions. But they wanted us, apparently needed us, and we said yes, we would do what we could.

One Sunday, a slender fellow we had not met before approached us after the meeting. He wore a fancy blue suit and greeted us like he knew us. Finally, I caught enough of the rapid-fire Spanish where it dawned on me. This brother was the unsmiling, unhelpful Mexican immigration officer at the border! He explained he hadn't been to church recently due to his work schedule, but he recognized us the second he saw us.

"*El caballero*," he laughed, pointing to his bare head. Yes, Bruce had always worn his cowboy hat on our many border crossings.

"*Pero iglesia no*," Bruce said, patting his head and laughing at himself as he always did when he made a joke in Spanish. People loved it, and they loved him as much in Comitán as they had in Pana.

Our new friend, the immigration officer, explained how he couldn't talk or smile at work because cameras were always on him, and they watched for corruption. "I have to be careful," he said. "Since I was a boy, I wanted to be an immigration officer. It is my dream, and I don't want to lose my job."

He was as nice as could be, as was his wife, who served as the branch Primary president. A dentist, she had an office in town that we visited several times to have work done at a fraction of U.S. prices.

Our life in Comitán developed into a satisfying routine. After breakfast, Bruce went out for a walk to explore the town and make friends while I finished my latest book and planned the next one. In the afternoons, after my walk and Bruce's nap, we worked together on our publishing business.

Happily, we filled the hours. We saw *Finding Dory* in Spanish at the mall. We visited the fair when it came to town and ate the best churros ever made. We attended meetings and activities for our church callings. True to their promise, members visited us regularly. The sister missionaries came over for lunch on Wednesdays.

The weeks and months flew by in a lovely dream, with no sense of time passing as events rolled on. We took local transportation to see the ruins of Tenam Puente and another time to El Chiflon waterfalls, both a short distance from town. A young couple in our branch invited us to go with them to Lagunas de Montebello, a series of beautiful turquoise lakes set in an extensive natural reserve.

In August, seven months in Comitán, we celebrated our anniversary with a day trip to San Cristobal, a historical city two hours away. We ate sushi; not very good, but we didn't care. We climbed the hundreds of steps to the top of the famous hill and looked over the city. Such a contrast from the previous August when we lived at Casa Colonial, went nowhere, and had a silly argument to mark forty-five years.

Once as we ambled along a wide sidewalk, Bruce said, "I'm tired, Karen. Let's sit for a while at this bus stop."

After a few minutes watching the traffic fly by, he said, "Lately, every so often, I see myself back when we were young. I had boundless energy, always in a hurry, and I remember striding ahead of you and the kids, totally oblivious. I remember doing that once in an airport. Rushing ahead while you fell behind trying to keep all the kids together."

I remembered, too.

"What a fool I was. What an arrogant fool. Now you are the one who can easily outpace me, but you never do."

Often in that distant past I had asked him to stay with me, don't push ahead, let's go side by side. He would pause for a bit but never for long. It was not from meanness—more thoughtlessness than anything—and a need to stay active, a resistance to slowing down.

"I am trying to change," Bruce said. "I'm working on considering you more. I want to be a better companion."

Bruce had never expressed a sentiment like this. He had apologized for random thoughtlessness now and then, but never said he needed to fundamentally change anything about himself. This was important, and I paused to consider an appropriate response.

"I'm glad for it," I said. "I've noticed, and it makes me happy. It makes me feel loved."

"I think about the mortgage business, and how hard I worked, how much family time I sacrificed, and for what? It ended overnight, and I had nothing to show for it. Same with the hotel. Two years of labor and sacrifice, and in the end, nothing."

At meals now, Bruce offered to refill my water glass without being asked. If I happened to say, "Oh, darn, I forgot the saltshaker," he got up to put it on the table next to me. If I said, "I should have brought more napkins," he went to get them. Who was this new and improved husband?

I was almost afraid to remark on it, for fear he might stop. The few times I did comment, he simply repeated, "I am trying to be more companionable."

Occasionally he mentioned our married sons and how he learned from their example. "They are much better husbands and fathers than I was."

"They do a great job, don't they?"

"I see them with their wives, and I wonder what the heck was wrong with me. Why was I so selfish?"

Perhaps without a job to distract him, with no workplace or boss or coworkers, with only his wife, Bruce had come to realize a need to improve at home. In Comitán, becoming a better husband turned into his new job.

One Sunday he brought back a pamphlet from the branch president. It was about serving a senior mission without leaving home. "Look at this, Karen. We could serve a mission and wouldn't have to leave Comitán," he said excitedly.

"But Bruce, this is for locals, native Spanish speakers. We don't fit this program."

"The branch president must think we do, or he wouldn't have given it to me and asked us to consider it."

"This branch has always been in denial about how awful our Spanish is and how poorly we do our callings. They think we are superheroes. They fell in love with you because everyone does. Since I'm with you, they like me, too."

Bruce picked up the pamphlet and examined it. "I always dreamed about us serving a mission together."

"Well, I never did because I knew what it would be like. You rushing off to talk to somebody and I'm left standing alone in a field or something. Missionary companions are supposed to stay together."

"Yeah, that guy. I've been trying to change. I don't want to be that guy. I want to be a better companion to you."

"I appreciate it more than I can say. But we would do better with English-speaking. Or Spanish with some language training, not thrown in with native speakers. How about India? Or Africa? I've always wanted to go there, and they're English-speaking missions."

We had no big savings to cover a mission. The monthly budget for an American senior missionary couple in Mexico was three times what we spent living here as ordinary folks. We set aside the idea, putting it in the "maybe one day" file.

Nonetheless, Bruce continued his thoughtful attentions. Never had I felt as settled and happy with my husband as I did in our tiny home in Comitán. The efforts to improve went both ways. I worked on being less critical and bossy. Once I said I wished I had been a better wife.

He responded, "You would have been a better wife if you'd had a better husband."

Burning our boats had, in the end, left us with nothing else worth clinging to. We were what remained. It was enough, and we were happy.

Epilogue

Bruce continued to feel the pull of serving a mission, the desire to prepare. Despite having no idea how to make it work, he couldn't let it go.

Around our eighth month in Comitán, Liesel called on Google Chat to say she was pregnant, due next April. She was nearly forty and never imagined having a child was in her future. My daughter pregnant! How could I not be there for that?

Her news in addition to our thoughts about a mission worked on us. We discussed moving back to Utah and wondered where to live. Bruce said, "I'd have to get a job. I have no idea where though."

Liesel suggested we live with them. They had an extra bedroom. "Dad can work at my call center. Every time I go to work, I think, 'My dad would *love* this job.' You could live cheaply with us and save everything for your mission."

Bruce and I talked and prayed and fasted. The answer came. Time to leave our paradise and go back into the lone and dreary world.

Our friends at church were sad to see us go, but the women especially understood about my daughter. Once again, we streamlined possessions, selling or giving away whatever didn't fit in our luggage.

Bruce sold his laptop to a lady who was originally from Veracruz, a city in the state of Veracruz, Mexico.

"Do you know Veracruz?" she asked excitedly. "Have you been to Veracruz?" No, I told her, we've only been in Chiapas. "Oh, you must go to Veracruz. It is so beautiful!" She described Christmas in Veracruz. The lights, the concerts, the dancing! Everyone so happy!

I wrote down her name and phone number. "When we come back to Mexico, we will go to Veracruz," I told her.

We boarded the plane in Tuxtla Gutierrez with heavy hearts. We were leaving behind memories and friends in two beautiful countries that had touched and changed us deeply.

As the plane readied for takeoff, I noticed an unusual event on the tarmac. The workers in their yellow vests lined up facing the side of the plane, smiling and waving goodbye to the passengers.

"Bruce, look at this!" I nudged him.

In the middle seat, he leaned over me to get a better view. "Oh, my," he said. "Oh, my."

"Isn't that the sweetest thing you ever saw?"

We hoped they could see us waving back. My soft-hearted husband had tears in his eyes. It was a sublime farewell.

About the Author

———

Born and raised in central Illinois, Karen attended Northern Illinois University in DeKalb and the University of Illinois in Champaign-Urbana. She transferred to Brigham Young University, where she met her husband Bruce Gowen, and there graduated with a degree in English and American literature.

Karen and Bruce have lived in California, Illinois, and Utah, with three years in Guatemala and Mexico. They are the parents of ten children and have twice that many grandchildren. Not surprisingly, family relationships are a recurring theme in Karen's writing. Learn more at karenjonesgowen.com.

www.ingramcontent.com/pod-product-compliance
Lightning Source LLC
Chambersburg PA
CBHW060250100426
42742CB00011B/1699